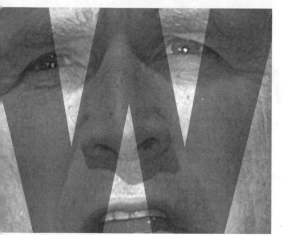

STANDS

wwwwwwww

Edited by
Michaele L. Ferguson
and Lori Jo Marso

wwwwwwwwwwwwwwwww

FOR WOMEN

wwwwwwwwwwwwwwwwwwwwwwwwwwwwwwwwww

How the George W. Bush Presidency

Shaped a New Politics of Gender

wwwwwwwwwwwwwwwwwwwwwwwwwwwwwwwwwwwwwwwwww

Duke University Press   Durham and London   2007

© 2007 Duke University Press
All rights reserved
Printed in the United States of America on acid-free paper ∞
Designed by Heather Hensley
Typeset in Quadraat by Tseng Information Systems, Inc.
Library of Congress Cataloging-in-Publication Data appear on the last
printed page of this book.

An earlier version of Timothy Kaufman-Osborn, "Gender Trouble at Abu Ghraib"
appeared in Politics and Gender 1, no. 4 (2005), 597–619. Reprinted with permission of
Cambridge University Press.
An earlier version of Michaele Ferguson's article appeared as "W Stands for Women:
Feminism and Security Rhetoric in the Post 9/11 Bush Administration," Politics and
Gender 1, no. 1 (2005): 9–38. Reprinted with permission of Cambridge University Press.
An earlier version of Iris Marion Young, "The Logic of Masculinist Protection:
Reflections on the Current Security State" appeared in Signs 29, no. 1 (2003): 1–27.
Reprinted with permission of University of Chicago Press.
Portions of R. Claire Snyder's chapter previously appeared in Gay Marriage and
Democracy (Lanham, Md.: Rowman and Littlefield, 2006). Reprinted with permission.

wwwwwww
Contents
wwwwwww

Acknowledgments

At the American Political Science Association meetings in Fall 2004, the two of us discovered that we were both working on feminist critiques of the Bush administration with the title "W Stands for Women." Our subtitles and subjects were different, though, so we joked about how we could coedit a series of essays each beginning with the same title. Of course, at the time we hoped that the results of the 2004 elections would make such a volume unnecessary.

On November 3, 2004, the day after George W. Bush was elected to a second term as president, we decided to transform our despair into action by making the book a reality. As we say in the introduction, there is a pressing need to understand the reshaping of gender politics in the Bush Presidency in order to have any hope of being able to respond and redirect rhetoric and policy in a feminist direction that truly takes women's lives and situations seriously, in the United States and around the globe.

We are gratified by the enthusiasm and support that our project has received over the past two years. A number of people deserve special mention here. Jane Bayes encouraged us to organize a panel for the Women and Politics Pre-Conference at the 2005 American Political Science Association meetings, hosted by Howard University. This panel gave many of us in the volume the opportunity to present and discuss our work on this project. We are also grateful to Iris Marion Young for generously agreeing to contribute her essay "The Logic of Masculinist Protection," which originally had appeared in *Signs*. This essay, among the first critical feminist analyses of the gendered changes wrought by the Bush presidency, significantly influenced many of the other pieces collected here. Iris died in July 2006 as we were completing work on the volume. We mourn her passing and thank her for her inspirational and important work in feminist theory, particularly on the questions that concern us in this volume. Jill Locke and Elizabeth Duquette gave us thoughtful feedback as we were composing the book prospectus. We also thank Peter Wissoker for his intelligent attention to this volume in its early stages.

It has been wonderful to work with Courtney Berger, our editor at Duke University Press, who has been engaged and supportive throughout the process. We are so glad that Jason Frank introduced us to her! We also thank the anonymous reviewers contacted by Duke, who gave us detailed and insightful comments on each essay as well as on the overall project.

Michaele's work on the book was supported in 2005–6 by a Visiting Research Fellowship at the Tanner Humanities Center at the University of Utah and a Junior Faculty Development Award from the Graduate Council on Research and Creative Work at the University of Colorado at Boulder. The Dean of Arts and Sciences Office at Union College supported Lori with funds for production of the book. We are also much indebted to Jason Beyersdorff for his help compiling the bibliography and the index.

Finally, Michaele would like to thank Jo, Ginger, and Francis; and Lori would like to thank Tom, Lucas, and Luci. Both of us thank our contributors for their wonderful chapters, good humor, and flexibility with tight deadlines. The two of us have greatly enjoyed working—and working together—on this project and we are thrilled to see it in print.

November 8, 2006
Boulder, Colorado, and Schenectady, New York

wwwwwwwwwwwwwwwwwwwwwwwwwwwwwwww
Michaele L. Ferguson and Lori J. Marso
wwwwwwwwwwwwwwwwwwwwwwwwwwwwwwww

Introduction: Feminism, Gender, and Security in the Bush Presidency

In 2004, the Bush–Cheney campaign organized a series of events under the slogan "W Stands for Women." These events targeted women voters and "security moms" in particular. The headliners were female members of the Bush and Cheney families such as Laura Bush, Lynne Cheney, and Barbara Bush. They praised President George W. Bush's record on women's issues specifically by highlighting gains for women in Afghanistan and Iraq as a result of U.S. military intervention. The main message of these events was that the pursuit of national security is not only compatible with addressing women's issues, but that security itself is a women's issue, since women, like men, care about their own safety and that of their children. Bush was portrayed as the ideal leader in a security crisis—publicly tough, masculine, and willing to protect his country, yet privately kind, considerate, loving, and, most of all, open to listening to the strong women in his life.

In fact, throughout his tenure in the White House, Bush has surrounded himself with professional and accomplished women. According to G. Calvin Mackenzie at the Brookings Institution, these women are more likely than those in any previous administration to be in central advisory roles (Tessier 2002). Condoleezza Rice, first National Security Adviser and now Secretary of State, and Karen Hughes, a longtime Bush adviser and now Undersecretary of State for Public Diplomacy and Public Affairs, are among the highest-profile women in the Bush administration. His first-term Cabinet included three women, with another two in Cabinet-level positions; in his second term, women serve as the Secretaries of Education, Interior, Labor, and State.

His commitment to women is further expressed in an active campaign for women's rights around the world. The best-publicized aspect of this campaign is the administration's effort to support women's rights and freedoms in Afghanistan and Iraq; indeed, this was a central justification for our military interventions in both countries. The administration has hosted conferences for women's activists in Iraq and Afghanistan, as well as in the United States. It has supported and pressed for constitutional protections for women's equal treatment and the rights to vote and run for office, and it has encouraged the careers of specific individual women in the new Afghan and Iraqi governments through appointments, networking, and mentoring. The administration has also provided funding targeted specifically at the training of female political candidates and journalists. In addition, the Bush administration has spoken in support of women's rights in countries beyond Afghanistan and Iraq—especially in Muslim countries in the Middle East.[1] Laura Bush, Condoleezza Rice, and Karen Hughes have made well-publicized diplomatic trips to Afghanistan, Egypt, Israel, Saudi Arabia, and Sudan. Laura Bush made very controversial calls for greater attention to women's rights in the Middle East during her tour there. Rice met with women who claimed to have been raped in the conflict in Darfur and pressured the Sudanese government to take action to protect refugee women from further sexual violence (Kessler 2005). Hughes met with professional women in Saudi Arabia about expanding their freedoms.

Feminists have responded to the Bush administration by pointing out the many ways in which "W" stands *against* women. For example, according to *Women's ENews*, an online feminist news organization, the number of women appointed to sub-Cabinet positions in the administration is significantly lower than under President Bill Clinton, who had by far the greatest number of women appointees of any U.S. president (Tessier 2002). Furthermore, many feminists have questioned whether Bush's policies really demonstrate a commitment to women's rights. The National Women's Law Center (2004) produced a seventy-seven-page report in April 2004 detailing the various anti-woman policies pursued explicitly and implicitly by the administration. The National Organization of Women sponsors a website that claims to reveal "The Truth About George W. Bush," further documenting these anti-woman policies.[2] The dominant feminist response has been to argue that the Bush administration cynically deploys rhetoric supporting women's rights to appeal to women voters, but that Bush is not really committed to women's rights (Flanders 2004a, 2004b). Richard Goldstein (2003) has called the Bush administration's strategy "stealth misogyny."

While it is important for feminists to draw attention to the administration's many lapses when it comes to women's issues, Bush's presidency invites a deeper exploration of feminism, gender, and security at the beginning of the twenty-first century. Consider the "W Stands for Women" campaign events. Bush's commitment to women's rights was presented at these events as consistent with a conservative model of the family. Indeed, these events reenacted particular traditional gender roles: Bush was presented as a strong and chivalrous man willing to use violence, if necessary, to protect the vulnerable women and children of the United States. The framing of national security as a women's issue at these events is therefore not (or, at least, not only) evidence of an insincere campaign strategy to appeal to women voters. Rather, it is deeply connected to the performance of gendered, hetero-normative family by the Bushes and Cheneys, which is itself portrayed as compatible with support for independent career women like Rice and with support for women's political and economic rights around the world. The "W Stands for Women" campaign reveals a complicated nexus of feminist rhetoric, conservative gender ideology, and neoconservative national security policy.

The essays in this volume take a critical look at the interconnections between feminism, gender, and security in the Bush presidency. We go beyond the question "Does 'W' stand for women?" to ask "How does 'W' stand for women?" How do we analyze Bush's stance on women's issues when considered in relationship to feminist politics; gender, racial, and class inequity; and broader and critical definitions of security? How do Bush's words and deeds reproduce hierarchies—between "us" and "them," between the compassionate and the needy? Who are the real beneficiaries and who are the real victims of Bush's policies on women, gender, and security? How are these policies gendered, sexualized, raced, and classed? How does Bush's political philosophy relate to and transform conservative, and especially conservative religious, ideology? How has the Bush presidency reshaped popular understandings of feminism, gender, and security? And finally, how should feminists respond?

These questions concerning *how* Bush stands for women provide a starting point for the essays that follow. This book brings together nine essays from a variety of feminist scholars addressing issues of interest to legal studies, American politics, security studies, political theory, communications, and, of course, feminist theory and politics. Together they provide a nuanced feminist analysis of the Bush presidency that takes Bush's rhetoric of feminism seriously rather than dismissing it cynically as mere rhetoric. Clearly, this rhetoric and its centrality to the administration have significant consequences for his policies. Collectively the book's essays argue that Bush's use of feminist rhetoric is deeply and problematically connected to a conservative gender ideology that in turn supports a variety of domestic and foreign policies. While we might expect conservative views about gender to motivate Bush's stance on so-called women's issues like abortion, the essays reveal that these views also underlie a whole range of policies that on the surface do not appear to bear any relationship to gender—most notably, policies that undergird the development of the post–September 11 security state. Our gendered lens of analysis reveals the complicated interconnections between Bush's stances on feminism, gender, and security.

How do we reconcile his willingness to take some women and some women's issues seriously with a political record that is far from feminist? Without an understanding of how Bush redefines feminism and the goals of the women's movement, it is difficult to comprehend his appointment of women like Rice and Hughes and his support of certain female politicians in places such as Afghanistan and Iraq. In her contribution to this volume, Michaele Ferguson argues that we can understand Bush's "feminism" as having a kind of self-consistency if we look at how he and others in his administration understand the women's movement. They define the goals of the women's movement in very limited terms: as restricted to the achievement of political (and some economic) rights. Bush thus can position himself as a champion of women's rights—and, indeed, as a kind of liberal feminist—at the same time as he works to curtail reproductive freedoms and to eviscerate policies like the Violence Against Women Act.

This redefinition of the goals of the women's movement facilitates the alignment of women's rights with a conservative gender ideology. Once feminism is restricted to political and economic rights, it can be compatible with the advocacy of conservative and inegalitarian gender roles. This explains how Bush can be equally comfortable with Condoleezza Rice, a woman who has never been married and has never had children and who has devoted her life to pursuing an ambitious career in a male-dominated field, and with Laura Bush, a woman who quit the pink-collar job of librarian to raise her family and support her husband's political aspirations. Both are praised as role models for women: supporting women's equality, the message seems to be, means allowing women to choose whether they want to be traditional.

Bush's support of a limited schedule of women's rights, his appreciation of the contributions of working women, and his concern about promoting traditional families are all grounded in a conservative gender ideology. This ideology, which is described further in R. Claire Snyder's and Iris Young's essays, characterizes men as dominant, masculine protectors, and women as submissive, vulnerable, and therefore deserving of and in need of men's respect. The ideal self-sufficing unit of private life is therefore the heterosexual nuclear family held together by marriage. This ideology finds expression in many Bush family policies, from the promotion of marriage to Laura Bush's campaign to teach inner-city boys to respect women. It is also manifested in President Bush's performances of masculinity (as David Gutterman, Danielle Regan, and Andrew Feffer show in their contributions to this volume), in which he attempts to portray himself as a macho leader prepared to use violence to protect his people. What is less expected, however, is how this conservative gender ideology finds expression in a range of policies that do not appear on the surface to have anything to do with gender. Karen Zivi's essay shows, for example, how it is manifest in the notion of "compassionate conservatism" and in Bush's AIDS policy.

Perhaps most disconcertingly, this conservative gender ideology finds expression in the development of the post–September 11 security state. As Young points out, the security state operates as a kind of gendered protection racket in which a masculinized state extorts obedience from a feminized populace in exchange for protection against a purported threat. The hyper-masculinization of diplomacy under Bush ("You're either with us or against us") promotes an uncompromising and militaristic foreign policy. The result is an understanding of security in neoconservative, stat-ist, and gendered terms that feminists have long argued diverts attention from and undermines the status of women—even as it claims to protect them. Timothy Kaufman-Osborn and Mary Hawkesworth extend Young's analysis by showing how similar gendered logics are at work in military culture more generally and in neoliberal free-market economic policy. Lori Marso warns against the extension of this logic into the relationship that Western feminists have with non-Western women. Feminist support for Bush's campaign to free the women of Afghanistan and Iraq risks impli-cating feminists in this gendered security logic. Marso draws on Simone de Beauvoir's conception of freedom for the conceptual resources to argue that the kind of "liberation" the Bush administration has promised Iraqis and Afghanis has resulted not in greater freedom, but in increasing inse-curity for many women.

Thus, a feminist analysis of the Bush presidency reveals the connections between Bush's feminism, gender ideology, and security strategy. To study Bush's use of feminist rhetoric means thinking about its relationship to a foreign policy that aims at the liberation of women in the name of national security. To think about security is to reflect on the feminization of "vul-nerable" populations vis-à-vis the masculinized state that promises to pro-tect us. To reflect on Bush's performance of masculinity is to think about its relationship to both women's issues and national security policy. The essays in this volume show how policies and rhetoric that we might not ordinarily recognize as gendered are deeply and problematically so.

Feminist analysis can also be a valuable resource for thinking about how to respond to Bush's rhetoric and policies. Many of the essays in this volume, in addition to analyzing the Bush administration, offer possible strategies for resisting a conservative gendering of feminism and security. We aim, therefore, not only to diagnose the role of a conservative gender ideology in Bush's presidency, but also to suggest conceptual and practical strategies for resisting it.

But why focus on Bush's presidency in particular? After all, as we write this introduction in fall 2006, Bush is in the midst of his second and final term of office and experiencing a sustained drop in his approval rating. Even before the midterm elections, many pundits are calling him a lame-duck president and declaring the impotence of his second term. His ideas and policies are increasingly criticized from the left and the right. Why, at such a moment, would we want to subject his presidency to an analysis that presumes Bush's ideas and policies have had and will continue to have a tremendous impact on the politics of gender?

We contend that the constellation of an eviscerated liberal feminism, a hierarchical gender ideology, and a neoconservative security strategy articulated by the Bush presidency represents a new configuration of gender politics whose significance and impact will extend far beyond Bush's two terms in office. While Bush's ideas and policies have been and will continue to be contested, we can nonetheless expect them to have substantial effects on American politics beyond January 2009 for a number of reasons.

First, as a two-term president in a time of national crisis and war, Bush has exercised substantial influence over how Americans view their world. The authority of the office of the president combined with the White House's access to the media has made it possible for Bush to set a political agenda and frame the terms of public debate on issues ranging from education and national security to women's rights. While Bush has never had complete control over the shape of public debate—his agenda has always had its critics (although they have been more numerous and more vocal in recent years)—we nonetheless expect he has been able to exercise significant influence on how many Americans think about the political issues of the day. Even if he should be unsuccessful at pursuing his political agenda during the remainder of his second term, as some predict he will be, we cannot overlook how the influence of his ideas has been reinforced by major institutional changes. The pursuit of women's rights has been undercut by the elimination of the White House Office for Women's Initiatives and Outreach and the appointment of antifeminist conservatives to crucial positions on the Food and Drug Administration's Reproductive Health Advisory Committee and the National Advisory Committee on Violence Against Women. Neoconservative national security and neoliberal economic views have been bolstered by shifting funding priorities from domestic social-welfare programs to defense and tax breaks. Bush's presidency, furthermore, has set a precedent of expanded executive powers in wartime, giving institutional expression to the role of masculine protector that he has assumed on behalf of the American people. Even as his popularity wanes, these changes magnify Bush's ability to shape our political worldviews by controlling access to the agenda via a combination of appointments, funding, and consolidation of power in the office of the president.

Moreover, support for many of Bush's ideas and policies will outlive his presidency because they resonate with significant groups of Americans. Most important, as Snyder shows, his gender ideology draws on both religious conservative and neoconservative traditions to solidify a larger conservative movement. This religious right and neoconservative coalition was able to attract many moderate voters in 2004. The voters, politicians, and strategists who made this possible will not simply disappear by the 2008 presidential elections: we can expect them to continue to exercise a voice within the Republican Party, as well as within American politics, for years to come. Understanding the convergence of conservative gender ideology with security policy is essential to understanding this movement and to learning how to best contest it to appeal to those same moderate voters in the future.

The institutionalization of many of Bush's ideas combined with their appeal to members of a politically engaged and successful conservative movement means that it will be difficult, if not impossible, to reverse the effects of what his presidency has already accomplished. Of greatest concern for many feminist organizations has been his appointment of two conservative judges with antifeminist records to the Supreme Court; these are lifetime appointments whose consequences will be felt well beyond 2009. We also need to consider the long-term effects of the changes in government funding priorities and of significant new policies, like the new National Security Strategy authorizing preemptive war and the USA PATRIOT Act (renewed in 2006 after contentious debate with only minor changes). It will take time to identify all the changes and effects his policies and rhetoric have had, and then it will take even more time to reverse the policies. In the meantime, they will have effects that will themselves be irreversible.

The difficulty of this task is compounded by the fact that we do not yet fully understand the gendering of these policies and so cannot fully comprehend their impact on gender politics in particular. For example, consider that while the justification for the war in Iraq has long been challenged, in the broader public discourse the connection between Bush's national security policy and his conservative gender ideology is never made. Without understanding how these two are intertwined, we risk making essentially superficial changes in policy without engaging in the more difficult task of interrogating the assumptions about gender and feminism at the heart of Bush's agenda. One of the most important contributions of this volume of essays is to begin the difficult task of identifying the gendered dimensions of Bush's presidency.

We can expect, therefore, to be contending with the legacy of Bush's peculiar constellation of ideas about feminism, gender, and security well into the future. So while the goal of this book is to understand Bush's ideas and their manifestation in his actions, we do so with the larger project in mind of making sense of the terrain for feminist politics over the years to come. At the same time that we stress the lasting effect of these policies, then, we also stress the importance of these essays as engagements in the critical thinking needed to open up alternative futures. Collectively, these essays, read as critical theory on the gendered politics of the Bush presidency, help us understand the underlying ideologies and accompanying sets of behaviors that have been set in motion. Without this critical understanding, we cannot hope to open up possibilities for the future within our present.

We will turn now to the essays themselves to introduce the range of issues they address. Though the essays are all interconnected, we have organized them into specific parts that explore "Compassionate Patriarchy," "Bush's Masculinities," "Gendered War Logics," and "Feminist Responses."

In Part I, the essays by R. Claire Snyder and Karen Zivi examine how Bush's policies are grounded in the perpetuation of gendered inequality and hierarchy. Snyder explores the roots of Bush's views on gender in both the Christian right and neoconservative ideology. She reveals that both traditions embrace the reconsolidation of patriarchy in the family. They conceptualize men and women as complementary opposites to be united in a heterosexual marriage, led by the compassionate, benevolent, and disciplinary husband/father. Drawing on feminist analysis of justice in the family, Snyder concludes that this patriarchal family, which entrenches inequality along a model of male domination and female submission, undermines democratic beliefs and institutions.

Zivi reveals that this gender ideology pervades Bush's political worldview by showing how it undergirds the concept of "compassionate conservatism." Compassion, like the patriarchal family, is grounded in inequality: here, it is the inequality between the subject who suffers and the person who feels compassion for her. Our capacity to feel compassion, therefore, depends on the perpetuation of suffering. Furthermore, for Bush compassion is figured as an instinctive reaction to the suffering of others. Zivi reminds us via a reading of Jean-Jacques Rousseau that the exemplar of this natural feeling is maternal instinct, the selfless concern for one's child that good mothers are supposed to embody. In the context of AIDS policy, then, the discourse of compassion obscures concerns about what is the best course of treatment for HIV-positive pregnant women in favor of concerns about what is best for their children's health. Zivi argues that compassionate conservatism risks entrenching gendered assumptions in AIDS policy that compromise women's health and status as rights-bearing citizens.

In Part II, David Gutterman, Danielle Regan, and Andrew Feffer analyze how, within this conservative gender logic, Bush performs and conceptualizes masculinity. Gutterman's and Regan's essay focuses on how Bush has sought to portray himself as a masculine leader in a time of war. They argue that Bush's hyperbolic performances of masculinity are symptomatic of the fact that masculinity is an impossible ideal that he can never reach. While heterosexual masculine identity is always manifest in an imperfect performance, its performance has become more and more uncertain in recent years as a result of changing gender roles that have made it more difficult for men to inhabit the role of patriarchal breadwinner. These societal changes have led to a widespread performance anxiety, expressed most familiarly in the explosive demand for erectile dysfunction drugs like Viagra, but also in concerns about the preparedness of the masculine state to address the threat of terrorism. Bush, they argue, exploits this anxiety by championing the "lost cause" of masculinity, exaggeratedly portraying himself as a macho defender of a mythical past of gender security that he knows he will fail to re-create.

Feffer takes up another aspect of Bush's masculinity, manifest in the dual figures of the suicide bomber and the patriotic soldier willing to die for his country. Bush aims to distinguish these two masculine characters by insisting that the latter endorses a "culture of life." Feffer shows how this distinction between "good" men who sacrifice themselves for the nation and "bad" men who senselessly waste their lives in acts of pathological violence is echoed in terrorism studies, as well as in American cinema and popular culture. These parallels reveal the hetero-normativity of the culture of life: the patriotic soldier hails from a patriarchal family, whereas the suicide bomber is portrayed (despite sociological evidence to the contrary) as the product of a dysfunctional, fatherless household. In such families, mothers are presumed to have excessive power and therefore to disrupt the proper development of boys' masculinity, resulting in a misdirection of male violence. However, as Feffer notes, the distinction between the suicide bomber and the patriotic soldier is tenuous at best: both engage in self-destructive acts of violence in the name of an all-important cause. Just as for Gutterman and Regan the performance of masculinity is unstable, for Feffer the distinction between good and bad sacrifice at the heart of Bush's militarism continually must be shored up.

Part III analyzes how the conservative gender ideology of the Bush presidency manifests itself in the logics of national security and war. Iris Young's chapter shows that an exposition of the gendered logic of the masculine role of protector in relation to women and children illuminates the meaning and effective appeal of a security state that wages war abroad and expects obedience and loyalty at home. In this patriarchal logic, the role of the masculine protector puts those protected, paradigmatically women and children, in a subordinate position of dependence and obedience. Resonating with Snyder's essay on the patriarchal family in Part I, Young's essay demonstrates that to the extent that citizens of a democratic state allow their leaders to adopt the role of their protector, these citizens come to occupy a subordinate status like that of women in the patriarchal house-hold. Furthermore, the masculinized state presumes the authority to dis-tinguish good citizens (those who are obedient and subservient) from bad citizens (those who are considered a threat to the society and, by simply being objects of suspicion, forfeit their right to protection). Young argues for a conception of democratic citizenship as active and critical and that therefore can resist this undemocratic subordination of the people to the state.

Timothy Kaufman-Osborn's essay connects the gendering of the Bush security state to a larger military culture. He does this via a reading of the photos coming out of Abu Ghraib of prisoner abuse, specifically the fa-mous and well-publicized photos of Private First Class Lynndie England. Whereas commentators on the left and the right have focused on the fact that England is a woman—for example, to make arguments about the un-suitability of women for the military or to suggest that she represents a kind of gender-bending sadomasochistic monster—Kaufman-Osborn suggests that we can read these pictures instead as evidence of how the performance of gender can simultaneously reinforce gender norms and subvert them. He argues that England was not a sadistic aberration within the military but was (together with her colleagues) enacting practices of gender con-sistent with military culture. The methods of torture used on prisoners are similar to gendered practices used in basic training that oppose milita-rized masculinity with the sexual violability of femininity and homosexu-ality. England's sexualized torture of prisoners both repeated these norms and (insofar as she is embodied female) subverted them. Kaufman-Osborn thus draws attention to the multiple ways in which specifically gendered practices, which can be detached from the sorts of bodies they conven-tionally regulate, are deployed as elements within a more comprehensive network of technologies aimed at disciplining prisoners or, more bluntly, at confirming their status as abject subjects of U.S. military power.

Mary Hawkesworth shows that this gender logic extends even further, into neoliberalism and globalization. She argues that there are conti-nuities between the Bush administration's economic policy and foreign policy that have gone largely unnoticed. Both enact modes of "feminiza-tion," scripted practices of subordination that reinscribe traditional gen-der symbolisms to naturalize hierarchy and legitimate racist, neocolonial relations. Furthermore, this logic of neoliberal feminization works to obscure and de-legitimize feminist politics. She suggests that a successful feminist response should be modeled on the engaged transnational feminist praxis of the Women's Caucus to the Copenhagen Declaration and Program of Action in 1995. The Women's Caucus resisted attempts to pursue poverty eradication via neoliberal free-market policies and, instead, focused on concrete proposals to reduce the inequality and social instability produced by markets.

Hawkesworth's essay provides a transition to Part IV, which considers potential feminist responses to Bush's policies. Michaele Ferguson and Lori Marso examine Bush's presidency to ask how feminists might respond in ways that further the feminist agenda both at home and abroad. Ferguson points out that the Bush administration draws on existing feminist rhetoric but transforms it by combining it with two other kinds of discourse: a rhetoric of chivalrous respect and a rhetoric of democratic peace. In both rhetorical frames, the Bush administration bases its concern with women's rights abroad on the presumption that the women's movement in the United States successfully achieved its goals long ago. Ferguson's analysis of how current security rhetoric frames women's rights can help us to understand both how the Bush administration is able to use feminist ideas in new and non-feminist ways and how we, in turn, might redeploy the Bush rhetoric to challenge the presumption that women at home already enjoy their full rights.

Marso's essay complements this analysis by exploring the complications of the language and practices of freedom. Arguably more than any administration before, the Bush presidency employs the language of freedom to justify its policies at home and abroad. Marso analyzes varying understandings and uses of the language of freedom, focusing specifically on Bush's claim that the bombing of Afghanistan and the invasion of Iraq have freed the women of these two countries. Marso shows the limits of liberal accounts of freedom that obscure the larger context in which that freedom may or may not be realizable while pointing to the complexities of the use of freedom in and for feminist politics. She concludes that acknowledging plurality, particularly in terms of individual and collective desires, while positing and actively encouraging solidarity for women across cultures enables us to speak of freedom in more realistic, as well as more responsible and liberating, ways.

Collectively, these essays provide a sharp and focused lens through which to view the gendered politics of the Bush administration. Bush's use of the campaign slogan "W Stands for Women" has proved to be far more than a clever ploy. Indeed, as these essays show, his understanding of gender relations is central to his policies, whether directly addressed to women or not. We cannot understand the lasting impact of the Bush presidency without unpacking the gender conservatism at its core.

NOTES

1. This was made most explicit in Laura Bush's recent trip to the Middle East. See MSNBC 2005.
2. See especially www.thetruthaboutgeorge.com/women/index.html. The main webpage is available at www.thetruthaboutgeorge.com.

PART I

Compassionate Patriarchy

R. Claire Snyder

The Allure of Authoritarianism: Bush Administration Ideology and the Reconsolidation of Patriarchy

Marriage cannot be severed from its cultural, religious and natural roots without weakening the good influence of society.
—PRESIDENT GEORGE W. BUSH (2004B)

Have you ever wondered what it would be like to be placed in submission to another human being on a twenty-four-hour basis, 365 days a year—for life? That is exactly what God demands of your wife.
—REVEREND DR. TIM LAHAYE (1996)

A community that allows a large number of young men to grow up in broken families, dominated by women, never acquiring any stable relationship to male authority . . . asks for and gets chaos.
—DANIEL PATRICK MOYNIHAN (1965)

Over the past decade, rhetoric about the benefits of heterosexual marriage and the importance of fatherhood has become increasingly prominent as the battle against gay marriage has accelerated. The heterosexual aspect of traditional marriage is important to conservatives, partly because it means the presence of a father in the household, which they see as a remedy to a wide range of dysfunctions. Not surprisingly, President Bush has made heterosexual marriage and father-hood priorities of his Department of Health and Human Services with his "Healthy Marriage Initiative" and has come out in support of the "Federal Marriage Amendment," which would prohibit states from legalizing same-sex marriage.[1] Bush's socially conservative agenda finds support in two different yet overlapping constituencies within the American right—the Christian right and neoconservatives.

This essay examines arguments for the gendered hetero-normative family proffered by these two groups, arguments they have made for over thirty years, that have influenced Bush administration domestic policy and that will no doubt continue to have influence long after Bush leaves the White House. While the Christian right's vehement opposition to same-sex marriage has been widely covered in the media, less attention has been given to its positive vision of heterosexual marriage, which *explicitly* includes male dominance and female submission and plays a central role in its larger agenda of reconsolidating patriarchy. Similarly, while a lot of attention has been paid to the current neoconservative foreign-policy agenda, neoconservatives' advocacy of the traditional family has received less coverage. Yet the traditional family is central for neoconservatives because they view it as the "seedbed of virtue" that undergirds democratic self-government. But how can patriarchal marriage, which reinforces male dominance, provide the foundation for democracy, since democracy requires equality for all citizens, including women?

This essay makes an argument that should be obvious yet is increasingly obscured: the patriarchal family undermines rather than undergirds democracy by directly contributing to the inequality of women, which by definition erodes democracy as we know it today, which is premised on the principle of equality for all citizens. It also argues that while consenting adults have the freedom to engage in consensual practices of dominance and submission in their personal relationships, such freedom needs to be accompanied by a set of public policies designed to protect women from unwanted subordination and ensure that all children learn the values that undergird democratic society, including the principle of gender equality, despite whatever other lessons their parents teach.

THE CHRISTIAN RIGHT

The Christian right is a political and social movement that seeks to impose its interpretation of Christian morality on society at large. For example, the Family Research Council "promotes the Judeo-Christian worldview as the basis for a just, free, and stable society" because it believes "that God is the author of life, liberty, and the family."[2] Concerned Women for America (CWA) seeks to "bring Biblical principles into all levels of public policy."[3] Although "Focus on the Family's primary reason for existence is to spread the Gospel of Jesus Christ through a practical outreach to homes," the organization takes an active role in politics because it views government as one of the three basic institutions ordained by God.[4] The organization's Government and Public Policy outreach ministry focuses specifically on political change.

The Christian right seeks to reverse the progress of feminism—to reestablish traditional gender roles and restore the patriarchal family as the hegemonic family form in America. For example, CWA describes itself as "the nation's largest public policy women's organization";[5] it "was founded to provide an alternative to radical feminists—who claim to speak for all women—and who seek to impose policies that do not respect unborn babies, family or God" (CWA 2005). The organization condemns even liberal feminists like Betty Friedan:

> She was the impetus behind the devaluing of women as wives and mothers. . . . By devaluing home and hearth, far too many women have found their window of opportunity for marriage and family closed. . . . By eschewing marriage, single mothers have ended up both rocking the baby and paying the rent. The children of single mothers are paying an even higher price—one-third of U.S. children are born out-of-wedlock, the majority of whom will grow up in poverty and at-risk in every outcome category. . . . Divorce-on-demand has left 35 million kids bereft. And, finally, tragically, more than 43 million babies have been aborted, leaving untold pain for the women who would have been their mothers.

While "utopian" feminist principles—"women's rights, sexual equality and the fulfillment of women's potential—are high-sounding and noble," the reality is actually quite dystopic (Crouse 2006).

Christian right politics has a strong strand of authoritarianism within it, and this authoritarianism apparently appeals to a lot of people, women as well as men.[6] As Chip Berlet and Margaret Quigley have argued, the Christian right leadership "envisions a religiously-based authoritarian society" in which "Christian men interpret God's will as law. Women are helpmates, and children are the property of their parents. Earth must submit to the dominion of those to whom God has granted power. People are basically sinful, and must be restrained by harsh punitive laws" (Berlet and Quigley 1995, 17). Berlet and Quigley call the movement "theocratic" because it supports "a form of government where the actions of leaders are seen as sanctioned by God—where the leaders claim they are carrying out God's will" (Berlet and Quigley 1995, 16). For example, James Dobson, president of Focus on the Family (FOF), conveys the message that as long as a political leader is a conservative Christian, he can be trusted to do God's will, and all citizens should do is obey and pray for him (Apostolidis 2000, 156).

"THE DESIRES OF A WOMAN'S HEART":
DOMINANCE AND SUBMISSION IN CHRISTIAN RIGHT MARRIAGE

The Christian right valorizes the traditional patriarchal view of marriage, which it sees as natural and God-given. Beverly LaHaye, president of the CWA, explicitly links masculinity and femininity with dominance and submission, respectively. LaHaye sees male dominance and female submission as a loving form of natural complementarity that should not be confused with tyranny and slavishness. Rather, according to her vision, when husbands and wives embrace their true natures and enact their God-given roles with love and respect, both flourish. She quotes from *Recovering Biblical Manhood and Womanhood* by John Piper and Wayne Grudem (1991): "At the heart of mature masculinity is a sense of benevolent responsibility to lead, provide for and protect women in ways appropriate to a man's differing relationships" (LaHaye 1993, 66). In contrast, "At the heart of mature femininity is a freeing disposition to affirm, receive, and nurture strength and leadership from worthy men in ways appropriate to a woman's differing relationships" (LaHaye 1993, 66–67). According to LaHaye, "A man's role as leader is threatened when the woman refuses to give him the support he needs in the challenging task of undertaking godly leadership. We continue to see women usurp men's roles in the home and in the church, which squelches men's ability to lead, protect, care for, and provide for their families, churches, and communities" (LaHaye 1993, 117). Luckily, "women have an inborn desire to affirm and nurture others" (LaHaye 1993, 67). When they accept male leadership, everybody wins.

This theory of gender-based dominance and submission also underlies the Christian men's group Promise Keepers (PK), founded by Bill McCartney in 1990. The organization played a key role during the "culture wars" of the 1990s that helped discredit progressives and empower conservatives. While the organization has "declined in size, resources, and influence since the peak of its stature in 1997–98, it remains an active and vibrant organization" (Gutterman 2005: 96); its ideology illustrates the vision of patriarchal authoritarianism that has long animated and continues to animate the Christian right.

Promise Keepers utilizes a hierarchical, authoritarian model to organize participants. Men are expected "to submit to a cell group that in turn is closely controlled by a national hierarchy" (Bellant 1995, 81). McCartney's idea for Promise Keepers grew out of his involvement with the Word of God community, "which required total submission to a person called the 'head.' Members were required to submit their schedules in advance and account for every hour of every day. Marriage partner, movie choices, jobs, and other decisions also had to be approved by this leader" (Bellant 1995, 82). PK cells operated similarly (Bellant 1995, 84). And since September 11, 2001, Promise Keepers has increased its usage of militaristic language as a way of appealing to and organizing its members (Gutterman 2005, 109).

Defining itself in opposition to feminism (Gutterman 2005, 99), Promise Keepers wants to restore fathers to their rightful place at the head of the family, and it wants women "to submit absolutely to their husbands or fathers" (Bellant 1995, 81). The PK member Tony Evans advises husbands: "Sit down with your wife and say something like this: 'Honey, I've made a terrible mistake. I've given you my role. I gave up leading this family, and I forced you to take my place. Now I must reclaim that role.'" Brown continues: "'Don't misunderstand what I'm saying here. I'm not suggesting that you ask for your role back, I'm urging you to *take it back*.'" The man stresses that there can be "'no compromise' on his authority." Women should "submit for the 'survival of our culture'" (Bellant 1995, 82).

Promise Keepers presents male dominance as in the interests of women, who are called "Promise Reapers." As far as woman's role goes, the PK website advises the following: "Be grateful for the spiritual hunger your man is showing. Acknowledge the little steps he is making to lead you and your family well. Be affirming in public. Practice patience. Paul wrote in Ephesians chapter five that respect is one of the important things we can give our husbands." (PK website). Being a submissive wife is the biblically correct thing to do.

According to Christian right ideology, family leadership cannot be shared between husband and wife. LaHaye disagrees with "most feminists" who "say that marriage should have two heads" (LaHaye 1993, 128). She also denies the contention that while there must be one head, it could be the wife rather than the husband. On this point she quotes Elisabeth Elliot: "The role of the husband is the gift of initiation. This is a gift, not earned, not achieved, not dependent on superior intelligence, virtue nor physical prowess, but *assigned* by God" (LaHaye 1993, 134). Moreover, she says,

> The wife's role is a complementary one. To adapt herself to his needs, to respond to his initiation, to submit, to receive. To submit doesn't mean to become a zero. The idea is to acknowledge your head. . . . [W]hen the wife acknowledges that her husband is her head, she acknowledges that he is her source, her leader, her authority, and she voluntarily accepts the authority. She does it gladly, not in rebellion nor resignation, but in obedience to God. Her respect for her husband will not necessarily require that she keeps her mouth shut, . . . but the buck stops with the husband. . . . [T]he scriptural idea of submission is not servility. It's glad and voluntary obedience, each respecting the other, each sacrificing himself for the other. (LaHaye 1993, 134)

Despite their natural submission, however, many women today refuse to follow their God-given path. This is also part of women's nature, according to LaHaye. Like Eve in the Garden, women today "are more emotionally responsive to misdirection" and more "easily deceived" than men. In fact, that is why God put women under the leadership of their husbands (LaHaye 1993, 113). "As Christ loved the church, husbands are to love their wives and actively pursue their wives' spiritual maturity and purity of character in the sight of the Lord" (LaHaye 1993, 123). Because "women desire security, protection, and peace," when they do not get it from their husbands, they turn to the government. "Women favor bigger government because they see that they can no longer count on men to provide their needs with regard to money, home, and child care" (LaHaye 1993, 121).

Beverly LaHaye's husband, Tim, the co-author of the apocalyptic Left Behind book series, totally concurs.[7] He argues that "man is the key to a happy family life because a woman by nature is a responding creature. . . . That is one of the secondary meanings of the word *submission* in the Bible. God would not have commanded a woman to submit unless he had instilled in her a psychic mechanism that would find it comfortable to do so. The key to feminine response has two main parts—love and leadership" (LaHaye 1996, 226). He asks, "Have you ever imagined what it would be like to be placed in submission to another human being on a twenty-four-hour basis, 365 days a year—for life? That is exactly what God demands of your wife" (LaHaye 1996, 229). While a good Christian man should try to think about things from his wife's position, recognize that she has valid views, and consider her voice in decision making, he remains the God-given head.

The view of patriarchal marriage espoused by the LaHayes parallels the official Southern Baptist view of marriage. In 1998, the Southern Baptist Convention, the largest Protestant denomination in the country, voted unanimously to change its essential statement of beliefs for the first time in thirty-five years by adding a section on the family that includes the following vision of patriarchal marriage:

> Marriage is the uniting of one man and one woman in covenant commitment for a lifetime. . . . A husband . . . has the God-given responsibility to provide for, to protect, and to lead his family. *A wife is to submit herself graciously to the servant leadership of her husband.* . . . She, being in the image of God as is her husband and thus equal to him, has the God-given responsibility to respect her husband and to *serve as his helper* in managing the household and nurturing the next generation. (Southern Baptist Convention 2000; emphasis added).

The decision to emphasize the submission of wives as opposed to mutual submission of husband and wife to each other "represents a triumph for the denomination's conservative leadership" over Christianity's more moderate voices (Niebuhr 1998).

THE FEARS OF A WOMAN'S HEART

In making the argument about male leadership in the family, Christian right leaders seek to appeal to the fears and anxieties of women who live in the wake of a partially completed feminist transformation. For example, Beverly LaHaye argues that the feminist movement

> is clearest about what it is rejecting from the past. But the movement is not clear about what norms will replace those which have been rejected; new norms are hard to imagine. . . . In other words, feminists don't like where we've been, but they have no idea where we're headed! That is a frightening thought. They are bent on destroying traditional morality and restructuring our society, but they aren't sure if their new order will work. (LaHaye 1993, 72)

She asks, "Did women really want to be treated like men? Did we want to lose the respect and honor once shown to us? Did we want to lose romance?" (LaHaye 1993, 73)

Opposed to government-sponsored family support, Christian right women favor laws that force individual men to take responsibility for the children they father and for the mothers who bear those children. The '70s generation of conservative women feared that the changes inaugurated by feminism—the Equal Rights Amendment (ERA), reproductive freedom, no-fault divorce, and the loosening of sexual mores—would make it easier for men to get out of their marital obligations and familial commitments. As opposed to liberal feminists who wanted the right to compete equally with men, many antifeminist women did not have the educational level or job skills that would allow them to pursue satisfying careers if forced to work outside the home (Mansbridge 1986, 105–107). They feared that the ERA would eliminate the traditional legal requirement for husbands to support their wives financially (Mansbridge 1986, 108).

At the same time, the rise of "no-fault" divorce laws during this period further threatened the economic security of traditional "housewives" (Mansbridge 1986, 108). To this day, women on the Christian right condemn no-fault divorce, which "allows one person to decide when a relationship can be severed," often catapulting women into poverty (Hutchens 1996: 4). While higher wages for women, safe and affordable child care, and universal health insurance constitute a progressive solution to the problems caused by the fragility of marriage and selfishness of dead-beat dads, right-wing women demand the return of a mythologized vision of patriarchal marriage, ignoring the reality of social change (see Coontz 2000).

Moreover, their policy solutions suggest they are more interested in reconsolidating patriarchy than in solving social problems. For example, while fathers should certainly take economic responsibility for their children, it is important to note that the fathers of poor children are often quite poor themselves and cannot adequately support a family. Consequently, insisting that only they, and not the government, have a responsibility to support their children will not actually ameliorate the problem of childhood poverty.

"THE TRUTH IS, DAD IS MORE IMPORTANT THAN MOM": THE "COMPASSIONATE" AUTHORITARIANISM OF JAMES DOBSON

James Dobson, founder and president of Focus on the Family, speaks to the anxieties of conservative Christians through his books and popular radio show, which reaches four million listeners a day. He propagates the idea that feminism hurts women while patriarchy helps them. For example, he argues that feminists have undermined the traditional family by refusing to accept natural gender differences, rejecting the rightful authority of the husband/father as the head of the household, attempting to change the sexual division of labor, and propagating the idea that a woman can fulfill the role traditionally played by a man. Consequently, men have lost interest in fulfilling their traditional family responsibilities, and boys have no one to teach them how to become responsible men. Detached from the civilizing influence of the traditional patriarchal family, males increasingly cause a wide array of social problems, and everybody suffers (Dobson 2000).

Dobson believes that a breakdown of traditional gender roles within the family fosters homosexuality in children. The prevention of homosexuality among boys requires the involvement of a properly masculine heterosexual father, especially during the early years. Dobson quotes the work of Joseph Nicolosi, a leading proponent of the Christian right's "ex-gay" movement (Hardisty 1999, 117), who asserts that "the father plays an essential role in a boy's normal development as a [heterosexual] man. The truth is, Dad is more important than Mom. Mothers make boys. Fathers make men" (cited in Dobson 2000, 120). To ensure heterosexuality, the father "needs to mirror and affirm his son's maleness. He can play rough-and-tumble games with his son, in ways that are decidedly different from the games he would play with a little girl. He can help his son learn to throw and catch a ball. . . . He can even take his son with him into the shower, where the boy cannot help but notice that Dad has a penis, just like his, only bigger" (Dobson 2000, 122).

Fathers are also important because they are traditionally viewed as disciplinarians, and Dobson favors an authoritarian approach to childrearing that includes corporal punishment—an approach widely accepted by conservative Christians (Greven 1992; Milburn and Conrad 1996) and explicitly supported by the CWA (Arlia 2004). In the discipline chapter in Bringing Up Boys, Dobson says, "Let's begin by examining the role of authority, which is pivotal to the proper training of boys and girls—but especially boys. . . . Boys need structure, they need supervision, and they need to be civilized" (Dobson 2000, 228, 230). He believes that contemporary parents are "confused" about how to discipline their children because they "have been misled by the liberal tenets of postmodern culture, especially when it concerns naughty or rebellious behavior" (Dobson 2000, 228–29). He cites a public-opinion poll that found that "people have become less traditional over time with a shift from emphasizing obedience and parent-centered families to valuing autonomy for children" (Dobson 2000, 229). Dobson believes there are times when a parent has to say, "Do this—because it is best and because I say so. Parents have been given the authority by God. . . . They should use it!" (Dobson 2000, 233).

In The New Dare to Discipline (1992), Dobson stresses that respect for authority must be instilled in young children to avert teenage rebellion and ensure respect for traditional religious values. This message is best communicated, he believes, by spanking children with a switch or a paddle any time they show defiance or willfully disobey their parents. As he puts it, "A controlling but patient hand will eventually succeed in settling the little anarchist, but probably not until he is between three and four" (Dobson 1992, 27). Dobson stresses that a spanking must be severe enough to make the child cry genuinely from pain rather than simply from anger or humiliation. While ostensibly condemning child abuse, Dobson praises the childrearing practices of his wife, who once "stung" their *fifteen-month-old* daughter's "little legs" with a "switch" for disobeying an "order" (Dobson 2000, 35–36). Hardly a lone voice, Dobson seems to be leading a movement to reauthorize the corporal punishment of children. To many people, this authoritarian approach seems like an easy solution to the complicated social problems affecting today's young people.[8]

Although many studies have documented the detrimental impact of corporal punishment on children (Greven 1992; Strauss and Donnelly 2000), people of goodwill differ on the question of spanking. Nevertheless, one has to wonder why Dobson makes corporal punishment a central plank in his political agenda.[9] What message does paddling teach children? A study by Michael Milburn and Sheree Conrad finds that subjection to frequent, harsh corporal punishment during childhood directly correlates with punitive and authoritarian political attitudes. People with such backgrounds are "more likely to identify themselves as politically conservative and to hold conservative attitudes toward abortion, the use of military force, and the death penalty" and to express "prejudice and intolerance toward particular minority groups," including gays and lesbians (Milburn and Conrad 1996, 223, 227). Philip Greven concurs that "authoritarianism has always been one of the most pervasive and enduring consequences of physical punishment" (Greven 1992, 198), and many Protestant fundamentalists strongly endorse the harsh physical punishment of children (Greven 1992; Milburn and Conrad 1996). Perhaps these findings help explain the motivation behind Dobson's ostensibly nonpolitical views on childrearing, as well as illustrate the authoritarian political vision inherent in the Christian right agenda.[10]

THE NEOCONSERVATIVE ARGUMENT

The idealized vision of patriarchy also plays a central role in another major ideological movement that supports the Bush administration: neoconservatism.[11] While often associated with the Bush administration's foreign policy, neoconservatism has long included the defense of the patriarchal family in its political agenda. In 1965, Senator Daniel Patrick Moynihan laid out the neocon position in his report on the African American family, in which he linked "the absence of a strong father figure in many black homes to a 'tangle of pathology,' beginning with high rates of juvenile delinquency, teen pregnancy, and 'illegitimate' births, and leading to persistent poverty and welfare dependency" (Diamond 1995: 186). Then in

1985, Irving Kristol, the neoconservative founding father, drew attention to the very social problems that many neocons focus on today: "crime, drug addiction, family disintegration, sexual promiscuity and illegitimacy among teen-agers, rampant homosexuality, and widespread pornography." He argued that "secular, 'progressive' liberalism — in its modern versions, anyway — exacerbates our social problems, while creating a spiritual and moral void in which they proliferate as so many cancers" (Diamond 1995, 280).

The neoconservative argument about the decline of fathers and families essentially parallels the argument of Dobson and others who blame feminism for perceived dysfunctions in society. Louise B. Silverstein and Carl F. Auerbach describe (and dismantle) the neoconservative view of the family as follows:

> The best way to ensure that men will consistently provide for and nurture young children is to provide a social structure in which men can be assured of paternity (i.e., the traditional nuclear family). Without the social institution of marriage, men are likely to impregnate as many women as possible, without behaving responsibly toward their offspring. If men can be induced to take care of young children, their unique, masculine contribution significantly improves developmental outcomes for children. This is especially true for boys who need a male role model to achieve a psychologically healthy masculine gender identity. (Silverstein and Auerbach 1999, 398)

While this position accords with the common-sense beliefs of many Americans, Silverstein and Auerbach demonstrate that the position is actually more ideological than empirical. Their data reveal that "a wide variety of family structures can support positive child outcomes," and "neither a mother nor a father" in particular is "essential" to the production of healthy children (Silverstein and Auerbach 1999, 397–98). Despite empirical evidence that contradicts their assertions, however, neoconservatives have used their social-science credentials to push their ideological agenda (Silverstein and Auerbach 1999; Stacey 1996), an agenda that dovetails with that of the Christian right.

David Blankenhorn, founder and president of the Institute for American Values, whose www.MarriageMovement.org website is referenced on the Bush administration's Department of Health and Human Services website—is a major leader in the movement to reconsolidate patriarchy. Fatherlessness, he tells us, is "the engine driving our most urgent social problems, from crime to adolescent pregnancy to child sexual abuse to domestic violence against women." He blames the "declining child well-being in our society" not on growing levels of poverty, deteriorating public services, lack of safe and affordable child care, the lower income of women, child abuse, racism, or misogyny but, rather, on fatherlessness (Blankenhorn 1995, 1). While some conservatives argue that "the best anti-poverty program for children is a stable, intact family," Blankenhorn believes that child well-being requires "a married father on the premises" (Blankenhorn 1995, 43). He opposes same-sex marriage, seeks to deny unmarried people access to sperm banks, and advocates making divorce more difficult to obtain.

Like Dobson and others, Blankenhorn insists that children need not just two involved parents but, more specifically, *a male father and a female mother enacting traditional gender roles*. He condemns attempts to equalize the roles of mothers and fathers in childrearing and derides what he calls the new "like-a-mother father" who changes diapers and does other tradition-ally female tasks (Blankenhorn 1995, 99). Blankenhorn claims that "the needs of the child compel mothers and fathers to specialize in their labor and to adopt gender-based parental roles." Consequently, men and women should stick with traditional roles, Blankenhorn insists, even if this con-flicts with their "narcissistic claims" to personal autonomy (Blankenhorn 1995, 101).

Blankenhorn and others claim to focus on the well-being of children when they make their arguments for restoring fathers to their rightful place at the head of the patriarchal family. As Jyl Josephson and Cynthia Burack (1998) have demonstrated, however, their repeated misreadings of empirical studies of child well-being and their lack of advocacy for poli-cies to help children beyond calling for the return of the traditional family render their motives suspect. At the same time, their emphasis on reestab-lishing traditional gender roles within families, despite "extensive feminist analysis and empirical evidence" documenting the ways in which "gender role differentiation in families is connected to stratification in economic, political and social life" in a way that harms women, leads Josephson and

Burack (1998, 224–25) to conclude that their real agenda is the reconsolidation of men's authority over women in both private and public.

Peter Berkowitz, a fellow at the Hoover Institution, accepts the neoconservative vision of the family and argues that it forms the necessary foundation for liberal democracy—the theoretically occluded private realm, in which children learn to become citizens capable of exercising freedom responsibly (Berkowitz 1999). Echoing the comments Irving Kristol made in 1985, Berkowitz argues that the extension of liberal principles—self-interest, antiauthoritarianism, and choice—has undermined the conditions necessary for the flourishing of liberal society (Berkowitz 1999, 174–75; 2005) in the realms of "education, work, romantic love, family, faith, science, and elsewhere" (Berkowitz 2003).

In *Virtue and the Making of Modern Liberalism* (1999), Berkowitz advances the neoconservative position that roots the alleged demise of American democracy in divorce, unwed motherhood, and fatherless families and cites the traditional family and organized religion as "seedbeds of virtue" necessary to the proper functioning of a free society. For Berkowitz, "intact, two-parent families" are a vitally important source of the moral virtue upon which liberal democracy depends (Berkowitz 1999, 26). But "with more than half of all new marriages expected to end in divorce," he argues, "with unwed mothers accounting for 30 percent of all births, and with single-parent families becoming increasingly common, the family . . . cannot readily serve . . . as a steady reservoir of the necessary virtues" (Berkowitz 1999, 173–74). In arguing that "the public good in a liberal state depends upon moral virtue," Berkowitz asserts that "the sources of moral virtue in such a state are intact, two-parent families, a vibrant civil society, and active citizen participation" (Berkowitz 1999, 26). He does not actually demonstrate, however, why "intact, two-parent families," as opposed to other types of functional families, are the necessary source of moral virtue. He simply asserts it. He does not specify what exactly constitutes the "necessary virtues," nor does he explain why children cannot acquire such virtues in families headed by single mothers or same-sex couples.

THE HETEROSEXUAL MARRIAGE MOVEMENT

The arguments of neoconservatives and the Christian right come together in the "marriage movement," which in general espouses the virtues of heterosexual marriage while working to prevent the legalization of same-sex marriage. For example, Maggie Gallagher, president of the Institute for Marriage and Public Policy, whose work has been praised and reprinted by the CWA, idealizes the institution of marriage, portraying it as a virtual panacea for a host of societal and human shortcomings (Waite and Gallagher 2000). She sees marriage as the (obvious) solution to the problem of unwed motherhood and advocates inserting a pro-marriage message into sex-education programs for teens (Gallagher 2004, 11, 13). She advocates government-funded marriage counseling for the poor that explicitly advocates against divorce. She believes that people who want to get divorced should be subjected to mandatory divorce-education programs before they are allowed to end their marriages (Gallagher 2004, 20–21).

Even though *single mothers* are most likely to be impoverished, Gallagher explicitly advocates government-funded economic assistance for *married fathers*. She recommends the following:

> *Target job training and earnings supplements for low-income married fathers.* There is considerable evidence that male wages and job stability play a significant role in the formation and maintenance of stable marriages. While economic factors alone cannot explain all or even most of the decline of marriage, men and women are more likely to get and stay married when men are able to get and keep jobs. Male unemployment, low earnings, and job instability are cross-culturally associated both with lower marriage rates and with marital disruption. (Gallagher 2004, 25)

While not every pro-marriage advocate opposes gay marriage, many actively and vehemently argue against allowing same-sex couples to marry. For example, working against equal marriage rights for lesbians and gay men is a major component of Gallagher's political work. While she views marriage as a cure-all for a vast array of social and personal problems, she wants to bar lesbians and gay men from reaping any of its rewards, whether material or psychological (Waite and Gallagher 2000). Since most of the rewards laid out in *The Case for Marriage* seem to come from a married couple's ability to establish trust, pool resources, support each other, and expect their relationship to last forever, it is unclear why same-sex couples would not benefit from the institution as well (Waite and Gallagher 2000,

23–25, 187, 201, 203). In fact, the book even admits as much: "The state of social-science research, as it now stands, sheds little light on the question: Would gay couples (and their children) reap the same benefits from legal marriage that men and women who marry do? As social scientists, the most we can conclude is, Maybe, maybe not" (Waite and Gallagher 2000, 200–201). Yet while social-science research fails to provide evidence for the superiority of heterosexual marriage, Gallagher (but not her co-author, Linda Waite) still publicly opposes and works politically against same-sex marriage (Gallagher 2005).[12]

The arguments advanced by the Christian right and neoconservatives about the virtues of the gendered, hetero-normative family provide the ideological underpinnings for the Bush administration's Healthy Marriage Initiative (HMI). This program, administered by the U.S. Department of Health and Human Services, uses government money to publicize the importance of marriage to a wide array of people, including not only the poor (via the Temporary Aid to Needy Families Program), but also high-school students and the general public. Bush says his initiative will "help couples develop the skills and knowledge to form and sustain *healthy marriages*" — a term that remains undefined. The Department of Health and Human Services also sponsors a Fatherhood Initiative because "the President is determined to make committed, responsible fatherhood a national priority" (U.S. Department of Health and Human Services 2001). The department's website quotes Bush as saying, "Research has shown that, on average, children raised in households headed by married parents fare better than children who grow up in other family structures," even though empirical evidence does not support a causal relationship between the two variables (Silverstein and Auerbach 1999; Stacey 1996).[13]

ADDRESSING THE CHALLENGE OF DOMINANCE AND SUBMISSION

It has long been commonly accepted that democracy requires, at the bare minimum, equality for all adults (Dahl 1998, 38, 85), yet traditional gender roles can erode gender equality in the larger society. As Susan Okin points out, when women have to take or expect to take primary responsibility for home and family, this affects their willingness and ability to pursue educational and career opportunities (Okin 1989, 142). The need to balance work and family contributes to women's educational and job "choices" and the wage differential between male and female workers. Married women often find that their lower earning power gives them less leverage in their marriages vis-à-vis their husbands; economic dependence renders them more vulnerable to physical and sexual abuse; and their lack of job skills makes them less able to support themselves in the case of divorce (Okin 1989, 152). "Thus, inequalities between the sexes in the workplace and at home reinforce and exacerbate each other" (Okin 1989, 146). As second-wave feminism would put it, "The personal is political."

Okin also takes seriously the claim advanced by neoconservatives that the family plays a key role in the socialization of children for democratic citizenship. She points out, however, that advocates of the patriarchal family have yet to explain how, "within a formative social environment that is *not* founded upon principles of justice, children can learn to develop that sense of justice they will require as citizens of a just society" (Okin 1989, 17)—a point also made by John Stuart Mill in the nineteenth century. For example, "Unless the first and most formative example of adult interaction usually experienced by children is one of justice and reciprocity, rather than one of domination and manipulation or of unequal altruism and one-sided self-sacrifice, and unless they themselves are treated with concern and respect, they are likely to be considerably hindered in becoming people guided by principles of justice" (Okin 1989, 17). Thus, patriarchal and authoritarian family practices undermine rather than undergird democracy.

Despite these important insights, however, the framework Okin uses to address the question of familial justice problematizes feminists' attempts to speak to women who choose marriages of dominance and submission, like Beverly LaHaye. Okin uses the framework of John Rawls to determine what a just family would look like and excludes from the get-go the possibility that some people are attracted to authoritarianism and might choose marriages based on dominance and submission. "We need not, therefore, consider approaches to marriage that view it as an inherently and desirably hierarchical structure of dominance and submission. . . . Marriages of dominance and submission are bad for children as well as for their mothers, and the socioeconomic outcome of divorce after such a marriage is very likely to damage their lives and seriously restrict their opportunities" (Okin 1989, 175).

Okin makes a good point, but she overlooks a couple of important factors. First, she does not distinguish between coercive and consensual forms of dominance and submission—between the woman who is tyrannized by her husband and the woman who finds fulfillment through submission. Second, Okin conceptualizes a just family as one that does not recognize distinctions based on gender, just as her ideal society has moved beyond gender. She calls for us "to work in the direction of ending gender itself," yet we live in a time of radical gender proliferation, and many people have a strong sense of gender identity that they would not wish to give up, even if they could.

This is the classic problem with the Rawlsian model, which asks individuals to abstract themselves from their substantive beliefs in making determinations about justice. By stripping away everything that constitutes a particular subject as the person she or he is, the model poses a counterfactual that is not very helpful in real-life situations. While a philosopher in the "original position" may not in fact agree to terms in which he could end up a Christian right wife, required to be in submission to her husband "24–7," that does little to address the real-life desires of an actual woman constituted by the Southern Baptist religion or desirous of submitting to a strong, powerful man for whatever reason.

Okin is correct in arguing that what happens in the family has ramifications for what happens in the larger society, but she does not leave open the possibility of reconciling consensual relations of dominance and submission (D/s) in marriage with a commitment to a political system based on equality.[14] While many Christian right women may not in fact support gender equality in the larger society, as shown by their vehement opposition to feminism, they are not the only ones engaged in D/s relationships.[15] Although the idea has been controversial in the feminist community, many women find it possible to support feminism and democracy in the political realm and to embrace practices of dominance and submission, or other forms of consensual BDSM, in their personal lives.[16] While their motivations may differ significantly from those of conservative Christians, the principle is the same. While a potential coalition exists between supporters of religious liberty and sexual freedom, however, the Christian right opposes the right of consenting adults to engage in BDSM practices (Concerned Women for America 2002).

Consequently, while Okin makes some valuable points, her solution to familial injustice would be rejected not only by religious conservatives, but also by the many people involved in consensual D/s as a way of life. While Okin may very well be right that a marriage characterized by dominance and submission has a negative impact on the democratic socialization of children, people who embrace a D/s lifestyle, either because of religious beliefs, personal inclinations, or erotic desire, are not going to renounce what they see as an essential part of who they are. Consequently, criticism and condemnation, however well argued or heartfelt, will not solve the central problem. At best, it will be ignored; at worst, it will breed anger and resentment. So what do we do? If Okin is right that "rather than being one among many co-equal institutions of a just society, a just family is its essential foundation," we are in serious trouble (Okin 1989, 17).

Another approach to the problem my title refers to as the allure of authoritarianism would be to expand on the liberal solution to the problem of church and state by differentiating between what is acceptable as a personal choice and what is legitimate public policy. Consenting adults certainly have the right to choose relationships of dominance and submission for whatever reason. They are not free, however, to impose that type of relationship on others through law and public policy. So while the LaHayes are free to practice dominance and submission in their own marriage, they are not free to use the U.S. government to impose their ideals on everybody else—or to say that their way of doing D/s is acceptable but someone else's is not.

But does this liberal response adequately address the challenge that dominance and submission and authoritarianism in the family pose to political systems based on equality? Or is there a possibility that personal and familial dynamics of this sort might leak out of the private realm and erode the democratic principle of gender equality? This is a central problem for feminism and one that is particularly difficult to deal with. The central feminist principle that "the personal is political" rightly maintains that what happens in the private sphere has direct relevance for what happens in the public sphere. Women's subordination at home plays into women's subordination in the larger society. Yet how do we eliminate women's subordination in the family when women actively desire such subordination? A non-totalitarian society does not allow the law or governmental authorities to enter into the private realm to change the behavior of consenting adults — or, at least, it shouldn't. This has been done in an effort to criminalize homosexuality, but the 2003 Supreme Court ruling *Lawrence v. Texas* that overturned anti-sodomy laws declares such efforts illegitimate.

In my view, the best way to deal with this dilemma is by considering "the personal is political" from a different angle. That is to say, the phrase also implies that the personal desires we have derive from or are shaped by the larger political realm (Benjamin 1988; MacKinnon 1989). Yet while sexual desire is socially constructed, it cannot be changed easily or at will (Butler 1993). Consequently, although it is probably not completely effective, particularly in the short term, the best strategy for addressing women's attraction to patriarchal authoritarianism is through changing the culture in which sexuality is constructed. For example, laws that protect gender and sexual minorities — including not only Lesbian, Gay, Bisexual, Transgender, Queer folks (including those into butch–femme) but also people into consensual BDSM — protect the viability of a variety of genders and sexualities beyond the traditional two. This provides the opportunity for women who desire submission to think outside the box of heterosexual male dominance.

In addition, democratic and feminist theorists need to support a wide array of policies designed to protect gender equality from practices that might erode it, from the continuing attraction of people to patriarchy and authoritarianism. To bolster the equal position of women in society and ensure the democratic socialization of children, two policies are crucial. First, we need to make sure that women are able to exit relationships of domination if they decide that the practice is not as desirable as the theory, or if the relationship evolves in ways that they do not consent to, or whatever their reasons. Women need protection from domestic violence and marital rape, and they need to maintain the right to divorce. They also need policies that help them balance work and family responsibilities and protect them from economic destitution upon divorce.

The Christian right, however, actively opposes such counterweights, which suggests that it does favor the reconsolidation of male dominance and female submission in the larger society, and that, by definition, is antidemocratic. While religiously controlled or unequal family law in other countries has been criticized by feminists, many believe this issue has been settled in the United States. But the Christian right and the Institute for Marriage and Public Policy are currently pursuing the creation of "covenant marriages" as a legal category across the country, which essentially resuscitates a form of marriage that existed before no-fault divorce. Covenant marriage currently exists in some states as an option. It is designed as a solution to the fact that half of all heterosexual marriages end in divorce. But it seems to me that many young people may be inclined to choose this form of marriage because of naivete or wishful thinking—especially in light of the pro-marriage propaganda campaign—and consequently end up trapped in unhealthy marriages. "To me, I thought, 'OK, if a man is willing to enter into a covenant marriage with me, then that really shows me that he wants it to be forever,'" as one young covenant newlywed put it. "I think that it would be a pretty big red flag if you asked your mate or your fiancé, 'Let's do a covenant marriage,' and they said they don't really want to do that." She calls standard marriage "marriage light" (Lewin 2005). But people do not get divorced because they did not mean "forever" when they said it on their wedding day. Making divorce more difficult will not improve things, especially not for women, who initiate most divorce proceedings.

Second, we also need to make sure that growing up in an authoritarian family does not undermine the democratic socialization of children. If democratic self-government actually requires citizens who possess certain civic virtues, as neoconservatives maintain, we should not, as a society, count on the family to inculcate those virtues in children. Relying on the family as the primary "seedbed of virtue" has two problems. First, many families are dysfunctional and consequently may be unreliable producers of democratic virtues. For example, families riddled with violence or substance abuse cannot be counted on to teach children democratic virtues in the midst of fear and instability. And even families without such glaring problems often have their own pathologies.

Second, parents take a variety of approaches to childrearing, from permissive to authoritarian. In general, parents want to make sure that their children learn the basic moral and religious values they endorse, which may or may not line up squarely with democratic principles. People differ in their views of childrearing, and conservative parents have the right to run strict, authoritarian households (as long as they do not cross the line into child abuse). Again, a non-totalitarian society probably does not want the government micro-managing childrearing practices.

There is no reason to think, however, that such households will instill in children the types of virtues required by a pluralistic democracy. Many conservative parents will more likely focus on instilling moral absolutism, obedience, and respect for authority in their children, than on teaching them tolerance, autonomy, and critical thinking. Moreover, the patriarchal family models male dominance and thus does not teach children of either sex gender equality, a fundamental principle of contemporary democracy. Consequently, if liberal democracy needs particular virtues, society would be better served by deliberately instilling those virtues in children via institutions like the public schools—which the Christian right tends to oppose—rather than hoping that families will produce the necessary virtues.

CONCLUSION

The argument that democracy requires gender equality and that male-dominated families undermine that principle by socializing children and habituating adults into inequality is obvious yet increasingly obscured by a deluge of conservative activists who have found common cause in reconsolidating patriarchy. Their agenda is actively supported by the Bush administration, but it needs to be vigorously opposed by democratic and feminist theorists. While a free society leaves people free to engage in relationships of inequality in their familial lives, we must recognize the threat those practices pose to the health of American democracy and take precautions both to protect individual freedom and preserve the principle of equality for all.

NOTES

This essay builds on the argument I make in *Gay Marriage and Democracy: Equality for All* (Snyder 2006). I thank Rowman and Littlefield for permission to use some passages from that work. I also thank Michaele Ferguson, Lori Marso, and the anonymous reviewers for their helpful comments.

  1. President Bush lays out the mission of his Healthy Marriage Initiative on the U.S. Department of Health and Human Services, Administration for Children and Families, website:

> To encourage marriage and promote the well-being of children, I have proposed a healthy marriage initiative to help couples develop the skills and knowledge to form and sustain healthy marriages. Research has shown that, on average, children raised in households headed by married parents fare better than children who grow up in other family structures. Through education and counseling programs, faith-based, community, and govern-

ment organizations promote healthy marriages and a better quality of life for children. By supporting responsible child-rearing and strong families, my Administration is seeking to ensure that every child can grow up in a safe and loving home. (http://www.acf.hhs.gov/healthymarriage/about/mission.html#ms)

See also the text of the federal marriage amendment, which states: "Marriage in the United States shall consist only of the union of a man and a woman. Neither this Constitution, nor the constitution of any State, shall be construed to require that marriage or the legal incidents thereof be conferred upon any union other than the union of a man and a woman."

2. Family Research Council, "Mission," available online at www.frc.org/get.cfm?c=ABOUT_FRC (accessed January 10, 2006).

3. See Concerned Women for America, "About CWA," available online at www.cwfa.org/about.asp (accessed August 10, 2005).

4. Focus on the Family, "Our Guiding Principles," available online at www.family.org/welcome/aboutfof/a0000078.cfm; see also idem, "Government and Public Policy," available online at www.family.org/welcome/aboutfof/a0007486.cfm#government (accessed April 21, 2006).

5. See Concerned Women for America, "About CWA."

6. The Christian right is not exclusively authoritarian. It has egalitarian and populist impulses, as well. For a discussion of how these oppositional impulses play out, see Apostolidis 2000.

7. The Left Behind series provides a fictionalized account of the tumultuous events preceding the Second Coming of Christ. For more information about the series, see the website at www.leftbehind.com.

8. According to a *Wall Street Journal* editorial, "Spanking is making a comeback. A growing number of parents—many of whom were never spanked themselves—are shunning the experts, defying disapproving friends and neighbors, and giving their kids a slap on the bottom, the hand or the leg. Websites popular with parents, such as iVillage.com and Oxygen.com, are filled with chat-room buzz from pro-spankers" (Costello 2000).

9. Although he does not publicly take a stand on parental spanking, President Bush does support protecting teachers who administer corporal punishment from lawsuits and included the "Teacher Protection Act" as part of his No Child Left Behind bill, signed into law in 2002 (Simpson 2003). According to the Center for Justice and Democracy, "There is a strong correlation between states that immunize teachers for corporal punishment and the number of children that are hit": Center for Justice and Democracy, "Federal Immunity for Corporal Punishment—Why It's a Bad Idea," n.d., available online at www.nospank.net/federal.htm (accessed January 12, 2006).

10. For an interesting and insightful discussion of the political work done by the ostensibly nonpolitical activities of Dobson, see Apostolidis 2000.

11. Although often "associated with a core group of standard bearers," neoconserva-

tism is best understood as "a commitment to a set of policy preferences" rather than as a list of particular people (Diamond 1995, 180–81).

12. In 2005, it was revealed that Gallagher's activism was secretly underwritten by Department of Health and Human Services and Department of Justice contracts. When her funding sources were exposed, Gallagher "apologized . . . for failing to reveal her contract to assist [Health and Human Services] while writing about the marriage initiative in articles and columns, one of which referred to Bush's 'genius.'" In her words, "It was a mistake on my part not to have disclosed any government contract. It will not happen again." This exposure of undisclosed funding to Gallagher and others prompted the president to denounce his administration's practice of secretly paying pundits to support his agenda (Kurtz 2005).

13. See the home page for the Healthy Marriage Initiative on the U.S. Department of Health and Human Services, Administration for Children and Families, website, at www.acf.hhs.gov/healthymarriage/about/mission.html (accessed August 10, 2005).

14. Elizabeth Wingrove (2000) suggests that democratic self-government necessarily requires dominance and submission, since citizens must both make law and be subjected to it.

15. For an interesting study of how conservative women actually negotiate between their religious and feminist values, see Manning 1999.

16. BDSM is an umbrella acronym that includes bondage and discipline (BD) and sadomasochism (SM) and that sometimes includes dominance and submission (D/s). Some practitioners of D/s put it in a separate category from BDSM because they view D/s as a way of life, not just as a sexual or somatic practice. My usage of the term "BDSM" includes D/s. For an introductory overview, see the entry for "BDSM" in Wikipedia, available online at http://en.wikipedia.org/wiki/BDWHO. For the debate over feminism and BDSM, see Linden et al. 1983; Samois 1981.

wwwwwww
Karen Zivi
wwwwwww

The Politics of Compassion in the Age of AIDS

In the past decade, the number of women infected with HIV has skyrocketed; women now account for more than 50 percent of the 40 million individuals living with the virus worldwide and almost 60 percent of the adults living with HIV/AIDS in sub-Saharan Africa (UNAIDS/World Health Organization 2005). This fact comes as little surprise to those AIDS activists and women's health advocates who have long argued that women represent one of the most vulnerable and fastest-growing groups of individuals to be infected with HIV. Indeed, concerns about the growing impact of HIV on women led the UN General Assembly (UNGA) to include specific language in its *Declaration of Commitment on HIV/AIDS* (2001), noting that women and girls were "disproportionately affected by HIV/AIDS" and calling on nations to adopt strategies that would "promote . . . women's full enjoyment of all human rights" by "empower[ing] women to have control over and decide freely and responsibly on matters related to their sexuality."[1] The United Nations is not alone in regarding the AIDS crisis among women as a significant health issue that is inextricably linked to rights. Indeed, many organizations concerned about AIDS and women's health, including the World Health Organization (WHO), have been treating the threat of HIV as a rights issue for some time now (e.g., World Health Organization 2000).

In the United States, however, responding to the AIDS epidemic in general, and the problem of women and AIDS specifically, has recently been identified as an issue of compassion. President Bush has described the AIDS epidemic as "a direct challenge to the compassion of the country" and has called on individuals, faith-based organizations, and the government to craft health policies that are motivated by and illustrative of our nation's care and concern for "the weak" (Bush 2004d). At the heart of the administration's vision of a compassionate response to HIV/AIDS is the President's Emergency Plan for AIDS Relief (PEPFAR), a package of policy initiatives designed to make $15 billion available to prevent and treat HIV/AIDS around the globe. PEPFAR, according to President Bush, will fund crucial research, prevention, treatment, and care nationally and internationally (Bush 2003b), enabling members of the "armies of compassion" (Bush 2005c) to do the "work of mercy" (Bush 2003a). This includes radically reducing the incidence of mother-to-child HIV transmission through the "Mother and Child HIV Prevention Initiative,"[2] an initiative that sets $500 million aside to fund programs that make AIDS drugs available to pregnant women and to support programs like "Mothers to Mothers-to-Be," which encourage pregnant women to be tested for HIV. According to the president, such efforts to reduce the spread of HIV from mother to child are quintessential examples of compassionate public policy, made possible by science, demanded by conscience (Bush 2002f), and evidence of the United States' commitment to advancing democracy by reaching out to friends in "desperate need" and serving as "a partner for a better life" (Bush 2006).

While the PEPFAR initiatives represent an important advance in the United States' efforts to fight AIDS globally, nearly tripling the amount of money spent to fight the disease and making the United States a central partner in the global response to HIV/AIDS, the Bush administration's response to the epidemic has not gone unchallenged.[3] Critics are quick to point out that the president has scaled back or delayed release of money pledged for the Global Fund to Fight AIDS, Tuberculosis, and Malaria (Lacey 2004). They raise concerns about the compatibility between President Bush's conservatism—with its emphasis on promoting specific moral values—and the goal of AIDS prevention. For example, critics argue that the president's major HIV prevention initiative, the promotion of the ABCs (Abstinence, Be Faithful, Use Condoms), emphasizes abstinence and "moral responsibility" over condom usage and thus does little to slow the rates of infection among married women whose husbands are already infected (e.g., Altman 2005). Moreover, critics call into question President Bush's commitment to helping women and children in light of calls to circumscribe women's reproductive rights or proposals to cut money for child care for mothers trying to leave welfare (Dionne 2003). By raising such concerns, critics do much to illuminate the gap between the rhetoric and the reality of the Bush administration's AIDS policy and to make visible the high costs paid by HIV-infected and at-risk individuals, particularly women. For many, these problems are rooted in the president's conservative political ideology, with its emphasis on fiscal responsibility and moral discipline (e.g., Smith 2004).

In this essay, I suggest that the problem with the administration's response to the global AIDS epidemic is problematic not simply because it is "conservative," but also, and perhaps more so, because it is "compassionate." Compassion, the emotional response to the suffering of others, I argue, may actually undermine efforts to advance women's equality and freedom in ways that compromise their health. As I suggest later, compassion, though often credited with promoting equality, actually has a stake in maintaining relations of inequality. It perpetuates inequality in part by basing a responsive action on an assessment of worth: if someone is not to blame for his or her suffering, then he or she is worthy of compassion. In the context of AIDS policymaking, the assessment of women's worthiness turns on evidence of a self-sacrificing maternalism, a requirement, I contend, that makes it difficult, if not impossible, to place certain concerns on the policy agenda. Thus, in elevating compassion to the foundation of health policy, and by placing it at the center of efforts to advance democracy, we may actually entrench a set of expectations that compromise women's health and status as citizens. And this can happen whether a politics of compassion is attached to a conservative or more progressive political agenda, whether it is advanced by conservative Republicans or liberal Democrats, and even if it is promoted by those struggling to advance women's equality. What is called for in this case is, then, a return to the language of rights, with its promise of an equality that is abstract, an equality that avoids assessments of worth and fault.

THE DEMOCRATIC PROMISE OF COMPASSION

That the Bush administration links the advancement of democratic equality to a politics of compassion is not without precedent. Throughout Western history, scholars and policymakers with varied and often conflicting political and philosophical commitments have turned to compassion in their efforts to understand and to reinvigorate democratic communities. The eighteenth-century political philosopher Jean-Jacques Rousseau, for example, posited compassion as foundational to social harmony and egalitarian citizenship. Rousseau, perhaps the best-known advocate of compassion, has been joined of late by contemporary scholars such as the political scientist Kristin Monroe (2004), who argues that compassion was crucial to a just response to the Holocaust; the sociologist Robert Wuthnow (1993), who suggests that compassion can mediate the fragmentation and individualism characteristic of modernity; and feminist theorists like Joan Tronto (1993), who contend that advancing women's equality requires more care and compassion in politics.[4] What attracts scholars of democracy to compassion is its supposed ability to draw individuals together in efforts to alleviate suffering, and thus its ability to create a sense of commonality among disparate and often unequal individuals. Compassion, according to this argument, is a multipurpose affect essential to democratic politics and citizenship, one that engenders an active and responsive citizenry, strengthens communal ties, addresses social problems, and rectifies relations of inequality.

In one of the most detailed philosophical defenses of compassion, Martha Nussbaum (1996) describes it as a "basic social emotion" essential to healthy democratic decision making. Compassion, she explains, can shape private action, public choice, and public policies in positive ways by providing a "good foundation for rational deliberation and appropriate action" (Nussbaum 2001, 299). The ability of compassion to advance democratic goals has a great deal to do with what Nussbaum calls the "structure" or the "cognitive requirements" of this emotion. Compassionate action begins with the onlooker assessing the degree of suffering to which another individual or group is subjected. Once the suffering is deemed "serious" rather than "trivial," the next step in the cognitive process of compassion is to assess culpability. Is the person who suffers to blame for that suffering? Is he or she at fault? If he or she is not to blame for the suffering, then the individual is a worthy object of compassion, someone who deserves *not* to suffer, someone on whose behalf it is necessary to act (Nussbaum 2001, 311–14).

Through the cognitive process of compassion, then, we become connected to other members of our community. Compassion, as the ancient Greeks suggested, serves as "our species' way of hooking the interests of others to our own personal goods" (Nussbaum 1996, 28). It connects us, in part, by enabling a moment of identification between the onlooker and the sufferer, a momentary recognition of commonality or of a shared "weakness and vulnerability" (Nussbaum 1996, 34). And it is this awareness of commonality that has such positive implications for democratic society. By connecting previously disparate individuals, compassion provides a necessary and powerful bulwark against self-centered individualism and political indifference (Nussbaum 1996, 57). If "followed through rigorously enough," Nussbaum argues, it promotes equality and justice by acknowledging "the value to each person of having a choice in his or her way of life" while also "concern[ing] itself at least with the provision to all of basic minimum welfare" (Nussbaum 1996, 36). Not surprisingly, then, compassion has been described as a "civilizing passion," an emotion without which "our social relations would be . . . bereft" (Piper 1991, 731), an emotion capable of and necessary to countering the "uncivilized passions" of selfishness, indifference, and greed (Alford 1993).

President Bush alludes to the civilizing potential of compassion when discussing AIDS policy. According to Bush, compassionate policies build social solidarity by engendering actions that bridge the distance between individuals locally and globally. Compassionate conservatism of the kind represented by PEPFAR reaches out across borders, oceans, and ethnic and racial differences through policies that express the kind of "love [for] our neighbors" that we would want for ourselves (Bush 2002e). Such promotion of global solidarity, with its corresponding rejection of a "sink-or-swim society" (Bush 2002e), is at the very heart of American democracy. Since the founding, the United States has been there "to feed the hungry, and rescue captives, and care for the sick" whether those in need, the weak, are found within our own borders or beyond (Bush 2005b). In addition, compassionate conservative policies promote the participatory citizenship so valued in American democracy. Such policies are designed, in other words, to enable active and effective citizenship. In supporting the efforts of faith-based organizations, for example, the Bush adminis-tration means to turn individuals from spectators or clients of the govern-ment into contributors to the health and vibrancy of their communities. Through their participation, such citizens respond to the needs of others, addressing social problems while touching hearts, even inspiring hope and behavioral change in those on the receiving end (e.g., Olasky 2000).

But does compassion really do this kind of work? Does it have such democratic promise? Answering these questions requires taking a more careful look at the relationship between the structure or cognitive require-ments of compassion and the practice of democracy. And for that I turn to the work of one of the most influential advocates of a democratic politics of compassion, Jean-Jacques Rousseau. Rousseau is often credited with in-augurating the modern-day politics of compassion and even deemed re-sponsible for putting "compassion . . . on the lips of every statesman" today (Bloom 1979, 18). And although Rousseau's eighteenth-century understanding of compassion may not coincide exactly with contemporary understandings, we can nonetheless expect similarities between the two, as his work clearly provides one of the many traditions of compassion on which we draw today.[5] We can learn a great deal about the benefits and limits of a politics of compassion by exploring his ideas.

ROUSSEAU AND THE POLITICS OF COMPASSION

Rousseau wrote during a time that philosophers were extolling the social benefits of the pursuit of a supposedly natural self-interest. If individuals were allowed to pursue their own interests in their own way, scholars like Adam Smith argued, a healthy, vibrant, and cohesive community, one of equality and justice, would result. Rousseau disagreed. Not only did he find the pursuit of self-interest to be corrosive to society, but he also believed that self-interest, of the kind advanced by Smith, was not natural. An in-stinct for pity or compassion, rather than egoistic self-interest, Rousseau argued, was natural to all human beings and served as the basis for the social virtues. Compassion, not self-interest, was the key component of democratic equality.[6]

Rousseau presents his insights about the nature and function of compassion in his "Discourse on the Origins of Inequality" (Rousseau 1987). There he suggests that if we want to understand and eradicate inequality, we must acknowledge and cultivate what is natural to human beings: compassion for others. Human beings, Rousseau argues, are not naturally self-interested in ways that put them into competition with others. While human beings admittedly have a love of self, an "ardor" for their own well-being, this self-love is not the same as the ruthless selfishness of an antagonistic egocentrism. Moreover, this instinctual, pre-rational love of self is accompanied by the moderating influence of pity or compassion. Pity, he explains, is that "innate repugnance" individuals have "to seeing [our] fellow men suffer" (Rousseau 1987, 53). It is evident in the "gut reactions" individuals have to "the sounds of complaints and cries, the sight of blood flowing . . . the convulsions of a dying animal" (Rousseau 1979, 222), as well as in the "tenderness" that mothers show for their children and "the perils they have to brave in order to protect them" (Rousseau 1987, 53–54). A natural instinct, compassion is also universal, common to us all: for "who does not pity the unhappy man whom he sees suffering? Who would not want to deliver him from his ills if it only cost a wish for that?" (Rousseau 1979, 221).

As Rousseau explains in Emile (1979), his treatise on civic education, the universality of compassion is rooted in the fact of our common humanity, our common vulnerability to suffering and death. "All men," he argues, "are born naked and poor; all are subject to the miseries of life, to sorrows, ills, needs, and pains of every kind. Finally, all are condemned to death" (Rousseau 1979, 222). When we acknowledge this fact, we acknowledge our commonality, for vulnerability is "what best characterizes humanity" (Rousseau 1979, 222). Thus, our compassion arises from the fact that we understand and imagine that the suffering of others could easily befall ourselves. Indeed, it is pain, not pleasure, and suffering, not self-interest, that bring us together: "We are attached to our fellows less by the sentiment of their pleasures than by the sentiment of their pains, for we see far better in the latter the identity of our natures with theirs and the guarantees of their attachment to us" (Rousseau 1979, 220).

Compassion's ability to generate connections between individuals is of great social and political value, according to Rousseau. Compassion gives rise to social ties; it connects us with others and connects us as equals, as capable of suffering the same fate. Compassion is, therefore, absolutely essential to the democracy. It is generative of sociality, moderating "in each individual the activity of the love of oneself" and "contribut[ing] to the mutual preservation of the entire species" (Rousseau 1987, 55). In fact, compassion gives rise to everything from "generosity, mercy, and humanity," to "benevolence and . . . friendship" (Rousseau 1987, 54–55). It is, as Judith Shklar explains, "the great equalizer. All men feel it and in much the same way. To illuminate it is to recognize the most common of human experiences and the most binding. That is why pity can hold us together" (Shklar 1985, 54).

Yet while Rousseau celebrates the democratic potential of compassion, he also gives us reason to question it. Keep in mind that Rousseau identifies compassion as a highly unstable emotion that requires relations of inequality for its generation. Pity is based, in other words, on a radical difference between the situation of the onlooker and the one who is the object of compassion; compassion is produced when the onlooker sees someone suffer in a way that he or she does not. But just the sight of suffering or inequality is not enough to generate a politically beneficial compassion. Compassion requires the faculty of imagination, that ability to put oneself in the position of another, to "transport him out of himself" to truly feel the suffering of others (Rousseau 1979, 223), and this imagination requires discipline and training. Compassion will only "bear sweet fruit if properly cultivated," if it develops under the appropriate conditions (Bloom 1979, 18). In fact, the cognitive processes of imagination and comparison required for the expression of pity can easily go astray if and when used prematurely or directed improperly. For compassion to generate social solidarity, careful cultivation is required. And, as I argue later, Rousseau illustrates that this careful cultivation may actually fail to solve the problem of inequality and antagonism, leading instead to its entrenchment.

It is in Emile that we come to see how and why the democratic potential of compassion is parasitic on an inequality that it never fully alleviates. Rousseau, through the characters of the tutor and Emile, suggests that compassion is generated not by showing individuals the joy of others, but by confronting them with the suffering of others. If a boy—in this case, Emile—is to grow into a man who feels compassion for others, a man capable of being a citizen, he must be raised with considerable attention to his surroundings and his experience. Emile must be "raised in a happy simplicity," unaware of and unexposed to the happiness of others that is manifest in everything from the "pomp of courts, the splendor of palaces, or the appeal of the theater," to the "circles of the great" and "brilliant assemblies" (Rousseau 1979, 221–22). If Emile were raised amid luxury, brilliance, and excess, he would learn to feel not pity but only the uncivilized passions of pride and vanity or jealousy and anger. The joy of others, Rousseau suggests, is deceptive, breeding and exacerbating envy: "The sight of a happy man, far from putting the envious man in his place, makes the envious man regret not being there" (Rousseau 1979, 221). Confronted with the happiness of others, Emile would feel cheated and desire what others had. He would be hostile rather than considerate toward others, and his actions would threaten rather than engender social solidarity and egalitarianism.

Rousseau's insight about what is necessary to cultivate proper compassion suggests that we feel compassion, generosity, and beneficence only toward those to whom we feel superior, to those who are not our equals. And though this recognition of inequality is supposed to give way to the recognition of a common vulnerability and thus equality, compassion clearly requires inequality: "It is not in the human heart to put ourselves in the place of people who are happier than we, but only in that of those who are more pitiable" (Rousseau 1979, 223). Moreover, we not only recognize, but revel in, our condition of relative prosperity: "Pity is sweet because, in putting ourselves in the place of the one who suffers, we nevertheless feel the pleasure of not suffering as he does" (Rousseau 1979, 221). We may recognize our common vulnerabilities, but we never completely let go of the important fact that we remain in a vastly superior situation.

It appears that compassion generates social solidarity, attaches us to others, not because we share common miseries, but precisely because we do not share suffering (Rousseau 1979, 220). We feel compassion only for those who are in positions worse than ours, and when we see suffering, the result is actually that we feel better about ourselves and our situation. Indeed, seeing joy and pleasure in others makes us feel envious rather than happy; we regret that we do not have what the other has. As one Rousseau scholar explains, what makes pity possible and "sweet is in good part because the delights of feeling that I don't suffer outweigh the discomforts of feeling that you do. . . . [I]t is pleasant simply to feel that we are free of the pain that afflicts others. . . . [And] we take pleasure in the victim's need of us" (Orwin 1997, 306). It is not, then, that we strive to help others, to respond to their suffering, because we wish to be of assistance and enable them to overcome the misery that is their lot. We do so, instead, because we strive "to be first: that is, to be better than others in whatever respect" (Orwin 1997, 304–305). Compassion, on this account, appears to be rooted far more in a kind of self-love than in any kind of benevolence. What is important is that I do not suffer rather than that I help you overcome your suffering, and to the extent that I do get pleasure from helping you, I have an interest, nonetheless, in remaining better off than you. Even Supreme Court Justice Antonin Scalia acknowledges that compassion is not always about alleviating another's suffering: "People sometimes identify with others' suffering . . . not because they particularly love the others or 'wish them well' . . . but because they shudder at the prospect of the same thing's happening to themselves. 'There, but for the grace of God, go I.' This is arguably not benevolence, but self-love" (quoted in Safire 2001).

It would seem, then, that social solidarity, and the social virtues attributed to compassion, could not flourish in a world of true equality because the experience of compassion requires the existence of inequality. Indeed, an extremely cynical reading would suggest that compassion requires a permanent victim, or, as Hannah Arendt puts it, a politics based on compassion "has a vested interest in the existence of the weak" (Arendt 1965, 89). In either case, it is clear that compassion is an emotional response that entails imputing a weakness to the other and maintaining relations of inequality. And if this is the case, one wonders what exactly a compassionate response is meant to do. To what extent is it meant to truly alleviate the suffering or disadvantage of another? If one feels only envy and regret at seeing someone living better than oneself, why would one ever seek to assist someone in transcending his or her unfortunate circumstances except, perhaps, to feel better about one's own lot in life? Self-esteem and solidarity, it would appear, require the continual reinforcement of inequality, even if some kinds of suffering are alleviated in the process.

Moreover, we must remember that theories of compassion teach us that not everyone who suffers is worthy of our emotional response. The cognitive processes of compassion, Nussbaum explains, entail assessments of fault, worth, and desert: "Insofar as we believe that a person came to grief through his or her own fault, we will blame and reproach, rather than pitying. Insofar as we do pity, it is either because we believe the person to be without blame for the loss or impediment, or because, though there is some fault, we believe that the suffering is out of proportion to the fault" (Nussbaum 1996, 33). Our compassion is, in other words, based not only on the onlooker's assessment of the severity of suffering (it must be "serious" rather than "trivial") but also on his or her assessment of the actions of the one who suffers. The one who suffers does not determine if and when action is to be taken; the onlooker does. And the onlooker's response is dependent on his or her own set of judgments about the role that the sufferer played in creating his or her own misery.

But who determines what counts as being worthy of compassion? While the onlooker is the one making the assessment, from where exactly do the standards of worth come? To return to Rousseau, it would be the job of someone like the tutor to cultivate compassion in particular directions, while in Nussbaum's argument, such education might be taken up by schools: public education ought to "cultivate the ability to imagine the experiences of others and to participate in their sufferings" (Nussbaum 1996, 50). In either case, the goal is to direct individuals, as one Rousseau scholar puts it, "to feel pity toward the right person to the right extent at the right time for the right reason in the right way," a goal that is often quite difficult to achieve (Alford 1993, 269). And even if it is achieved, it remains unclear what precisely a "right reason" for feeling pity would be and who would get to determine it.

THE COMPASSION OF AIDS POLICY

The project of educating people about "right" reasons, of cultivating compassion for worthy others, is a project from which the Bush administration has not shied away. As the president explained in his first inaugural speech, there are individuals who, like children in poverty, "are not at fault" for their dire circumstances and who deserve our compassion (G. Bush 2001a). Compassion is to be reserved for those who have met certain standards of desert, individuals like "single moms struggling to feed the kids and pay the rent. Immigrants starting a hard life in a new world. Children without fathers in neighborhoods where gangs seem like friendship, where drugs promise peace, and where sex, sadly, seems like the closest thing to belonging" (Bush 2000). Compassion is not meant for those who, as Representative Rick Santorum (2002) suggests, engage in or promote "illicit behavior" or "promiscuous sexual conduct."

In the context of women and AIDS policy, determinations of worth and fault are closely connected with a traditional maternal ideology that demands that women place the concerns of their children before their own. Infants at risk of or infected with HIV are the "innocent victims" of the epidemic and thus clearly deserving of compassion. Women, however, are a more difficult case. Those who do everything in their power to prevent mother-to-child HIV transmission are deemed worthy recipients of compassion, while those who do not are often the subjects of punitive policy proposals or of punitive policies themselves. For example, during the past two decades, the response to the problem of women and AIDS in the United States has focused largely on the issue of preventing mother-to-child HIV transmission through the implementation of mandatory HIV testing policies. The debate over implementation and proper response, moreover, centered on determinations of good and bad mothering. "Good" mothers, those who actively sought to prevent mother-to-child HIV transmission, would favor mandatory testing. Those who opposed mandatory testing were either "bad" mothers, incapable of properly caring for their children, or activists too lax in their expectations to be charged with drafting public-health policy. Efforts to mandate HIV testing were bolstered, in other words, by a public discourse that called into question the compassion and morality of HIV-positive women and rights activists. HIV-positive women who were caring and moral, policymakers suggested, would either avoid pregnancy altogether or certainly be willing to take an HIV test and use AIDS drugs if necessary to prevent mother-to-child HIV transmission. Those who failed to be tested or to take the necessary steps to avoid HIV transmission had to be "bad" mothers, uncaring and morally irresponsible women who were unnecessarily putting their infants in harm's way. Such depictions of women strengthened policymakers' conviction that mandatory testing of pregnant women and newborns was a proper response to the problem of HIV/AIDS. If women could not be trusted to engage in self-abnegating maternalism, the state had a duty to intervene. Though these efforts to regulate the reproductive lives of HIV-positive women through mandatory HIV testing were ultimately unsuccessful, they did much to shift attention away from concerns about women's own risk of infection and their specific prevention and treatment needs (Zivi 2005).[7]

Similar patterns are emerging in current global AIDS policy debates.[8] Non-punitive, compassionate state or social policies are considered appropriate responses only in very particular circumstances. Public-policy decisions, research agendas, funding allocations, and community practices are made in light of the presence or absence of evidence of women's self-sacrificing maternalism. Those women who put the needs of the children first are to be supported and praised; those who do not are either ignored or pressured to change. For example, PEPFAR, as I suggested earlier, provides support for programs designed to radically reduce the transmission of HIV from mother to child under the "Mother and Child HIV Prevention Initiative." This initiative makes antiretroviral drugs available to pregnant women and newborns and promotes voluntary testing and counseling of pregnant women. One of the administration's favorite examples of compassionate response to the AIDS epidemic is the "Mothers to Mothers-to-Be" program. This South African program "encourages mothers who are HIV-positive to counsel other mothers who are pregnant and to help them learn how to use the treatments that keep their children from having HIV when they're born," and it is being replicated in other African nations (Bush 2005c). The Ugandan ABC (Abstinence, Be Faithful, Use Condoms) approach to AIDS prevention is also touted as a successful compassionate response to the problem of HIV/AIDS and is being replicated in countries through the world.

While these programs and initiatives seem to be necessary and positive responses to the problem of mother-to-child HIV transmission specifically, and to that of women and AIDS more generally, their limitations become visible when one considers the requirements that attend a compassionate response. For example, the emphasis on preventing mother-to-child HIV transmission and protecting women from HIV by locating them in monogamous heterosexual relationships leaves women quite vulnerable. It suggests that the primary problems of women and AIDS have little to do with women's own health needs, particularly their need for female-controlled barrier methods, and far more to do with their roles as mothers and wives. The programs supported under the Mother to Child HIV Prevention Initiative in particular appear to be based on and to reinforce expectations of self-sacrificing maternalism, for only those who are "bad" mothers or those who are not bothered by women's negligence of their duty to their children could possibly oppose or question such efforts. Moreover, the emphasis on mother-to-child HIV transmission and a certain kind of sexual discipline—no sex before or outside of marriage—has the rhetorical force of directing attention away from women as individuals in ways that ultimately jeopardize their health.

Women's needs as separate individuals drop out of the equation almost completely. When claims to entitlements like health care and AIDS drugs for women are couched in the language of motherhood, their personhood becomes subordinate to that of the child.[9] And the focus on women as mothers obscures the complex web of social and political concerns in which pregnancy and AIDS infection is located in the first place. For example, to the extent that a woman receives health care and AIDS drugs, it is because of her role as the carrier of a child, a fact that often compromises a woman's own health care. Past research and current studies show that giving AIDS drugs to pregnant women to prevent mother-to-child HIV transmission is not necessarily good for women; they are likely to develop resistance to the AIDS drugs necessary to fight their own infection (Altman 2004). In addition, the preoccupation with mother-to-child HIV transmission often comes at the expense of attention to issues such as the provision of adequate pre- and post-test counseling, access to contraception, the development of female-controlled barrier methods, the importance of protecting women's confidentiality and preventing their abuse, and to any concerns about the woman's health and needs that may stand apart from her pregnancy or mothering.[10] And while women may not want to transmit HIV to their infants, they may have good reasons for engaging in behaviors that others would find objectionable—such as refusing to take AIDS drugs, failing to take an HIV test, or ignoring the possibility of transmission altogether. Unfortunately, compassion ties responsive action to determinations of worth and blame that place women in a vulnerable position. HIV-positive women who fail to take the necessary steps to prevent mother-to-child HIV transmission are easily dismissed as unworthy of compassion, their own health of little concern.[11]

The compassion motivating efforts to reduce transmission is not, then, a compassion for the full plight of HIV-infected women. Instead, the suffering worthy of compassion is the suffering that comes from having a child who might be infected with HIV. To reap the benefits of compassionate policies, women are expected to respond to their HIV status or pregnancy in very specific ways. Compassionate AIDS policies that focus on women as mothers and wives thereby perpetuate very specific understandings of good mothering behavior that compromises women's equality and health.

The link between compassion and maternal ideology is not surprising. Recall that for Rousseau, one of the clearest examples of natural compassion, the instinct of pity prior even to social cultivation, can be found in the response of mothers to their young. In the state of nature, mothers show a tenderness for their children and go to great lengths, braving considerable peril, to protect them (Rousseau 1987, 53–54). Rather than abandon their children, as other animals do, mothers will put their own lives at risk to protect their young (Rousseau 1987, 43). Indeed, it is not just mothers who have a natural compassion for their children; we all have a natural compassion for the plight of mothers, according to Rousseau. So obvious and natural is pity, Rousseau argues, that even Mandeville, a thinker famous for espousing a theory of individual self-interest, portrayed "man as a compassionate and sensitive being" to a certain extent. Mandeville recognized compassion in the mother–child relationship, and he believed that a prisoner watching a child being torn from a mother's breast would feel pity for both the child and the mother, pity being so powerful an instinct that even those with "the most depraved mores still have difficulty destroying" (Rousseau 1987, 54). And Rousseau is not alone is using an example of the mother–child relationship to illustrate the universal and instinctual qualities of compassion. Indeed, for a number of theorists, the most obvious example of a suffering that no individual could ever deserve is for a mother's child to be injured or killed in a way that was clearly not her fault (Nussbaum 1996, 37).[12] Compassion here is to be felt not simply for the child who may be hurt, but also for the mother who loses what is presumably her most precious concern. The repetition of such examples should make us pause to consider whether or not some kind of self-sacrificing maternalism is intrinsic to compassion itself. Such examples suggest that compassion is an emotion premised on and likely to perpetuate traditional notions of self-sacrificing motherhood that reduce women to the role of vessels of care rather than seeing them as distinct individuals.

CONCLUSION

In the context of the staggering implications of HIV infection in women around the globe, compassion might seem like an important and appropriate response. It would seem to be precisely what is needed to get the United States to recognize itself as part of a global community; to bridge the divides of race, poverty, and geography; and to become more active in AIDS-prevention efforts. Compassion, as President Bush and others suggest, promises to be a "civilizing passion" that directs our attention away from our own needs to the care and assistance of others. However, as I have suggested, placing compassion at the center of politics, particularly in the context of women and AIDS, has troubling consequences for women's health and status as citizens. With its reinforcement of inequality and its expectation of maternal sacrifice, compassion often obscures the social context of mothering and further compromises women's health.

The limits of a compassion justification can and should be rectified, I would argue, by a return to the language of rights. This, of course, is not a revolutionary insight. As I suggested at the outset, rights language has played an important role in debates about the proper responses to the global AIDS pandemic. That AIDS policy is a rights issue, in other words, is widely acknowledged. Major international organizations, including the United Nations and WHO, recognize it as such. In fact, several years ago, WHO recognized that the absence of attention to any one of the multitude of issues related to HIV and reproduction constituted a significant human-rights violation. Like many other women's health and rights advocates, WHO has raised concerns about the continual focus on women as vessels and vectors of contagion and care alone, and it sees even this as a human-rights violation (World Health Organization 2000). That is, WHO suggests that AIDS policy that fails to see women as distinct individuals, and that recognizes them only as a means to an end, threatens women's rights.[13]

Unfortunately, studies have shown that rights are often ignored at the policymaking level, and much scholarship certainly suggests that a politics centered on rights is neither helpful to women nor healthy for society. As a consequence, scholars and policymakers on the political right and the political left suggest that rights should be replaced—or, at least, complemented—by compassion and care. This move, however, obscures important advances in rights thinking and practice in the global arena. Indeed, in the international arena, women's coalitions often argue for better health policy by drawing on the language of rights rather than the language of compassion. In so doing, they adopt a revised understanding of rights, a conception of rights that acknowledges the intersubjectivity and complexity of individual lives. In other words, they adopt "a broad concept of reproductive and sexual health and rights that links sexual and reproductive freedom to women's human rights" in which "even the most intimate areas of family, procreative and sexual life are ones where women's human rights to self-determination and equality must prevail"(Bunch and Fried 1996, 1080).[14] The turn to rights language is not simply an embrace of traditionally liberal notions of atomistic and antagonistic rights-bearing citizens. Rights are an important and effective tool of political contestation, not only because they are universally recognized, but also because they allow women's groups to use a set of abstract and universal standards, rather than particular personal experiences, to articulate their political goals (Bunch and Fried 1996). Rights language is important, in other words, because it does not turn on assessments of desert, nor does it require that someone who suffers wait for another to act. Speaking in terms of rights, with their promise of abstract equality, is far more likely to make women present as individuals with needs and concerns of their own rather than just as mothers.

This does not mean, of course, that rights offer a solution to all the problems of AIDS or reproduction, or that a politics centered on rights will produce social solidarity, harmony, equality, and the end to suffering. Indeed, as Rosalind Petchesky (1997) reminds us, as important as human-rights language is in the context of reproductive freedom, women's sexual desire and bodily pleasure often falls off the agenda. However, it is quite clear that a politics of compassion runs into the same difficulty, and it is time to revisit and rethink the political potential of rights. It is the language of rights, albeit understood in terms other than those of traditional liberal individualism, to which we need to turn to protect women, children, and mothers in the age of AIDS.

1. The declaration also includes provisions stressing the importance of safe sex, the promotion of gender equality, and the protection and advancement of the sexual and reproductive health of women.

2. The goal of the initiative is to "treat one million women annually, and reduce mother-to-child transmission by 40 percent within five years or less in target countries" (Bush 2002f).

3. Organizations that have raised concerns about the Bush administration's AIDS policy include the Center for Health and Gender Equity, Human Rights Watch, the Sexuality Information and Education Council of the United States (SIECUS), and the Kaiser Foundation. They are joined by Stephen Lewis, U.N. Special Envoy for HIV/AIDS in Africa. See, for example, Altman 2005.

4. Joan Tronto (1993, 3, 161–62) argues that "the values of caring—attentiveness, responsibility, nurturance, compassion, meeting others' needs" are central to a good society and that the "practice of care describes the qualities necessary for democratic citizens to live together well in a pluralistic society." Care, she suggests, gets us beyond liberal individualism and acts as a complement to rights: "Care helps us rethink humans as interdependent beings. It can serve as a political concept to prescribe an ideal for more democratic, more pluralistic politics in the United States, in which power is more evenly distributed" (Tronto 1993, 21). If we want to make "citizens more thoughtful, more attentive to the needs of others, and therefore better democratic citizens," we should "include the value of caring in addition to other liberal values (such as a commitment to people's rights" (Tronto 1993, 169).

   See Balbus 2003 for a review of some of the recent feminist literature espousing different versions of the argument for care and compassion.

5. Compassion is clearly not a monolithic, ahistorical concept. Rather, it is one that evolves over time through engagement with various cultural traditions (Wuthnow 1993).

6. I follow Nussbaum here in her recognition that Rousseau's notion of pity is synonymous with compassion (Nussbaum 1996).

7. In "Contesting Motherhood in the Age of AIDS" (Zivi 2005), I explore these arguments in more detail and discuss the reasons that an HIV-positive woman might not want to be tested or use AIDS drugs. I also argue that such language not only reinforced the troubling norm of self-sacrificing maternalism, but it also effectively obscured the social and historical context that constrains the practice of mothering itself. Ultimately, women were erased from the discourse as individuals suffering from HIV infection. Their needs were subordinated to the interests of the children, and their bodies and freedom were constrained.

8. For compelling accounts of the role of maternal ideology in other policy debates,

see, e.g., Ashe 1993; Campbell 2000; Kline 1995; and Ladd-Taylor and Umansky 1998.

9. According to Rosalind Petchesky (1997), motherhood as an identity category plays an important role in the reproductive decision-making of women around the globe, and many use their status as mothers to make claims for their rights and freedom. Interviews with hundreds of women suggest that, "while most of them did place central value on marriage and motherhood and did see motherhood as a primary source of their identity, they were not willing to sacrifice their own decision-making autonomy or their own health and safety for the sake of traditional family and childbearing roles. In fact, many of the women we interviewed used their status as mothers to justify their autonomy over reproduction and sexual relations" (Petchesky 1997, 580). Petchesky identifies these different strategies of accommodation and resistance as "strategic accommodations" and "negotiated entitlements" (Petchesky 1997, 581–82).

10. For an excellent source on information on HIV/AIDS and women, see UNIFEM's Gender and HIV/AIDS web portal at www.genderandaids.org/modules.php?name=News&new_topic=23.

11. In addition, attention to women's sexuality is completely erased from the discussions of HIV infection in women. It is almost as if there is a willful forgetting of the activity required for women to become mothers, and certainly an avoidance of any discussion of sexual desire in women, particularly pregnant women. This can be understood partly in light of the politics of compassion—a politics that, according to Rousseau, takes great care to cordon off feelings of sexual desire and to keep them confined to a particular place and time.

12. A similar example of compassion can be found in Adam Smith's *The Theory of Moral Sentiments* (1984 [1759], 209–10): "Can there be a greater barbarity, for example, than to hurt an infant? Its helplessness, its innocence, its amiableness, call forth the compassion, even of an enemy, and not to spare that tender age is regarded as the most furious effort of an enraged and cruel conqueror."

13. This failure to treat women as ends, to recognize them as decision makers, is not confined to the realm of HIV/AIDS. It is a problem that confronts the larger arena of policy related to reproduction. As research by the International Reproductive Rights Research Action Group suggests, feminists often oppose population and family-planning policies because of "their failure to treat women's health and wellbeing as ends in themselves (rather than as means toward lowering or raising numbers) and their disregard for women as reproductive decision makers." Such failures, they argue, "constitute violations of women's human rights" (Petchesky 1998, 2).

14. Of course, "The concept of reproductive rights is by no means universally accepted among feminist groups around the globe. For some, it evokes a highly Westernized and narrow frame of reference that reduces reproduction at best to

fertility control and at worst to the single issue of abortion; or it evokes an even more devious scenario that masks racist and eugenic population control behind 'a feminist face.' For others, any rights discourse is suspect, if not objectionable, either on philosophical and political grounds . . . ; or on pragmatic grounds" (Bunch and Frost 2000, 6).

PART II

Bush's Masculinities

David S. Gutterman and Danielle Regan

Straight Eye for the Straight Guy

Nothing raises the specter and promise of normative masculinity quite like a war. The words "courage," "power," "honor," "duty," "strength," and "determination" reverberate throughout the land. Images of men in uniform resolutely looking off into the distance are commonplace. The manly status of these "warriors" is burnished by complementary images of wives, girlfriends, and children left safely at home. Today's soldiers bask in the reverential glow afforded to the "bands of brothers" who defended the interests of their nation in previous battles. Serving one's country in the military is often portrayed as the full measure of a man.[1] It is a standard that transcends the always present threat of death; indeed, it is the presence of this very fragility that lends this image of masculinity its nobility and its power.

George W. Bush has repeatedly declared himself a "war president." While Bush has long cultivated an image of rugged American masculinity, his desperate pursuit of this persona has been particularly focused since the events of September 11, 2001. In a nation feeling suddenly fearful and insecure, Bush quickly sought the familiar cultural ground of the cowboy in the white hat, calming people's fears and, with grim determination, swearing to get Osama bin Laden "dead

Figure 1. President George W. Bush at his ranch in Crawford, Texas, August 9, 2002.
(AP PHOTO/THE WHITE HOUSE, ERIC DRAPER)

or alive" (Bush 2001f; Figure 1). As the War on Terror has unfolded, Bush has claimed both power and refuge in the role of war president, the first man of America. Despite the broad cultural resonance of normative American masculinity, performing this role has proved to be difficult for the president. In the process, Bush has illuminated the growing challenges to the performance of normative masculinity and the political stakes of successfully navigating these choppy waters. In this essay, we first examine markers of normative masculinity in America and then discuss why appearing to embody this persona has been central to Bush's campaign strategy and his broader approach to presidential leadership. We conclude by arguing that the Bush administration's "straight eye for the straight guy" vision (including its version of the "Southern strategy") highlights the very fragility of masculinity in America it is designed to mask.

SIMULACRUM OF MASCULINITY

Masculinity is not something one is or possesses; it is always a process of becoming. It is a continuous struggle—never fully won. The standards of normative masculinity vary across time and place—and vary within time and place. Normative masculinity is an often contradictory amalgam of qualities, characteristics, and behaviors. Its elusiveness does not make it any less attractive or seductive; indeed, this elusiveness makes it that much more compelling. Becoming a "real man" means attaining almost a mythical status, yet one that is still somehow supposed to be "natural" to half of humanity. The paradox of masculinity thus poses a tantalizing cultural riddle, the purported resolution of which unites the extraordinary and the ordinary, the heroic and the mundane, the highest achievement and the most quotidian.

Masculinity, accordingly, is a ceaseless series of performances that are intended for public consumption as a vehicle for proving one's manhood. As participants and spectators we are trained and accustomed to settle for the appearance of masculinity—a simulacrum of the impossible ideal. Rather than a "depth" of masculinity, we have the accoutrements of masculinity—the uniform, the jaw, the gun, the ball, the truck. The exterior performance of masculinity stands in for the empty or absent interiority; what is left is a series of performative gestures toward an ephemeral "truth." Nevertheless, even while the phrase "act like a man" conveys the paradox that masculinity is a performance, there remains palpable in the culture the impossible longing to "be a man"—indeed, to be "The Man."

To be "The Man"—to have the recognizable authority, the confident demeanor, the air of accomplishment—is to enjoy a powerful but precarious place in American society. Attaining this status as "The Man," however, ultimately rests on the approval of an audience. Thus, an individual may claim, "I'm The Man," but this declaration becomes absurd or a statement of mere bravado unless someone else declares "You The Man." With his administration in precipitous decline, George W. Bush's attempts to gain this approval take on a tone of increasing desperation, even absurdity. For instance, in April 2006, Bush sought to defend Defense Secretary Donald Rumsfeld from critics by asserting, "I'm the decider, and I decide what is best. . . . And what's best is for Don Rumsfeld to remain as the secretary of defense."[2]

The performative quality of masculine authority evident here has significant cultural and political implications. Accordingly, this essay sits at a nexus of political and cultural analysis, and we move between analyzing cultural markers of masculinity and the politics of performing and appealing to masculine ideals. By exploring the performance of masculinity by President Bush—and the political implications of this performance—we illustrate the appeal and fragility of both normative masculinity and a presidency built on its impossible achievement.

PERFORMING MASCULINITY

The recognition that gender is a performance is, of course, nothing new. Long before Judith Butler invigorated academic analysis of gender, the performative quality of gender was amply illustrated in the realm of popular culture, often quite vividly, as in the example of the Village People. Conceived in the mid-1970s as a vehicle intended to reach gay audiences with a diverse image of the gay community, members of the Village People adopted the stage personas of iconic masculine identities: police officer, soldier, construction worker, cowboy, Indian chief, and biker. Of course, seeing the Village People sing "Macho Man" and "In the Navy" did not lead to the mass deconstruction of normative masculinity in America. If masculinity was a performance, then some men were determined to outperform other men and legitimate their status as "real men" for all to see. In a wonderfully Foucauldian sense, the discourse of gender performance produced both a deconstructive and a reconstructive impulse in American culture. The Village People helped generate KISS and Rambo, Queen and Schwarzenegger. What links these divergent impulses is the common acceptance of masculinity (and gender more generally) as a performance. Masculinity became more obviously a surface phenomenon, a sheen as deep as Gene Simmons's makeup, as "natural" as the steroid-induced bulk of a professional wrestler or a major-league baseball player. If the growing recognition of masculinity as a performance did not result in the broad dismissal of gender constraints, there has still been a loosening of norms of sex, gender, and sexuality. In turn, the (even tacit) recognition of the performative nature of masculinity gave rise to great performance anxiety.

The Bravo television program *Queer Eye for the Straight Guy*, which beginning in 2003 has been a surprising cultural phenomenon, demonstrates this point quite well. The show consists of gay men offering fashion, food and wine, interior design, grooming, and culture lessons to straight men in need of re-masculinization. These makeovers include new wardrobes, appliances, furniture, attitudes—in other words, "lifestyle choices." The test of the transformation is the success of a date at the end of each show—

and a final evaluation offered by the Fab Five. That is, while the straight guys acquire new ideas and accoutrements for their performances, they also acquire new audiences that must be pleased; not only do they need to perform well to please their female dates, they must also pass the critical eyes of the gay manhood coaches who view the proceedings via remote cameras. The performative quality of gender is thus the central premise of the hit TV show, and the experts in manhood training are the same gay males who would have been outcasts from the band of hetero-normative brothers in America. Of course, the straight guys are not even the stars of the show; that status belongs to the Fab Five. The straight guys are the clay, the vessel, molded, scripted, and directed by their gay gurus.

Amid the wonder of this "gay men as manhood guides" development, it is easy to lose sight of one fundamental aspect of the *Queer Eye for the Straight Guy* phenomenon: straight men are anxious and desperate enough about the inadequacy of their masculine performance that they are willing to turn to gay men for help. If we are to take *Queer Eye* as an important cultural marker for our times, we must appreciate the deep performance anxiety afflicting heterosexual men in America.

ANXIOUS DAYS

From the perspective of normative masculine expectations, there is good reason for this anxiety when we consider the perceived need to constantly perform masculinity—and the impossibility of ever completing this performance. Moreover, this anxiety is especially acute given social, political, and economic conditions in which traditional markers of normative male success are proving more difficult to meet. Stagnating wages, the loss of job security, the challenge of feminism and loss of clear gender roles, the emergence of queer critiques of norms of sexuality, the loss of prestige of the military (from the lingering effects of Vietnam to the current War on Terror), the diminution of traditional norms of married family life—all are prominent markers of the challenges to masculine norms. The point here is not whether these challenges represent normative benefits to American society as a whole—or even to the men in question—or whether or not men still hold disproportionate power in the United States. The point is that these challenges to normative masculinity are often portrayed and felt as threats. Consider four central markers of normative masculine performance in the United States: jobs/income, family, sexual virility, and military accomplishment.

Breadwinners

Over the past thirty years, the capacity of a man to serve as the "family breadwinner," the figure who works outside of the house and earns a salary sufficient to support a traditional household structure with the wife/mother raising the kids and keeping the home in order, has sharply declined. According to the Census Bureau, middle-class and working-class men's wages have stagnated: in the thirty-year period between 1973 and 2003, the median income (in 2003 adjusted dollars) for male, full-time, year-round workers has increased from $41,128 to $41,503, a change of $375, or less than 1 percent. By comparison, over this same thirty-year period, income (in 2003 adjusted dollars) for female, full-time, year-round workers has increased from $23,268 to $31,653, a change of $8,385, or 26.5 percent (U.S. Bureau of the Census 2003b). The comparative status of men and women in the workplace is also dramatically evident in changes in hourly wages over this thirty-year period. Since 1973, men's wages (again adjusted in 2003 dollars) have effectively stood still while women's wages have increased. In 1973, the median hourly pay was $14.60 per hour for all workers, but the average hourly pay for men was $17.71, whereas the average hourly wage for women was $11.18. By 2003, when the median hourly pay for all workers had risen to $16.48, men were making a median hourly income of $18.20 (a mere $.49 above the 1973 number) while women have been steadily increasing in wages to $14.73, a gain of $3.55 since 1973 (Economic Policy Institute 2005).[3] Indeed, Bureau of Labor Statistics data indicate that between 1970 and 2003, the contribution of wives' earnings to a married family income (median) has grown from 26.6 percent to 35.2 percent (Bureau of Labor Statistics, 2004a). Moreover, for "married-couple families in which both wife and husband had earnings from work" the percent of wives who earn more than their husbands has grown from 17.8 percent in 1987 to 25.2 percent in 2003 (Bureau of Labor Statistics 2004b). The economic stagnation of male earners and the corresponding economic reordering of the "American family" have resulted in the prototypical single male-earner family household becoming increasingly rare (U.S. Bureau of the Census 2003d).

Family Man

These economic trends are also reflected in the demographic changes in family and household structure that have developed in the United States. In 2004, less than 50 percent of total households in the United States contained married couples—down from 66 percent in 1975 and 75 percent in 1955 (U.S. Bureau of the Census 2003c). The average size of household has dropped from 3.33 in 1955 to 2.94 in 1975 to 2.58 in 2002 as both male and female "non-family" households have risen sharply.[4] In the short period between 1990 and 2001, the rate of marriage in the United States dropped from 9.8 per 1,000 to 8.4 per 1,000. The divorce rate has also dropped, as should be expected over time with a decrease in the marriage rate (U.S. Bureau of the Census 2003c). While nontraditional families and single-person households have become more common, there remains a longing for the "ideal" and an accompanying sense of dread (fed by the constant cries about the "crisis in the American family") about the state of families in America. Thirty-one percent of children in America do not live in households where two parents are present; of all children in America, 23 percent live with their single mothers, 5 percent with their single father, and 4 percent with a grandparent or other guardian.[5] Nontraditional families have thus become increasingly common in the United States, and while people tend to worry less about the threat of their nontraditional friends up the street, there is a more abstract fear about the "American family" that is all too commonly exploited. The cries of crisis convey a perpetual, low-level indication of the challenges to the traditional male performance of father while indicting feminists and other cultural forces for generating the fatherhood crisis in America and then dismissing its seriousness.[6]

Ready, Willing, and Able

The myths of the male breadwinner and head of the household are tightly entwined with notions of male strength and virility. Virility is measured in part by the capacity for an erection at any time, and losing this capacity is commonly understood as a diminution of one's masculinity. Erectile dysfunction is increasingly being treated in the United States with medication. Erectile dysfunction drugs offer the promise of restored potency to men, but the regimen is only a temporary solution rather than a cure for male impotence. The presence of deep-seated anxiety among men about virility is evident in the initial response to the introduction of the drug Viagra in 1998. "In its first three months $411 million of Viagra was sold and 160,000 physicians wrote prescriptions for the drug" (Herper 2004). Over 12 million men have tried Viagra ("Official partner of Major League Baseball"), and millions more have tried its competitors Levitra ("Proud sponsor of the NFL"), Cialis ("Official partner of PGA Tour"), and the increasingly prevalent generic erectile dysfunction drugs (Mostaghimi 2003).[7] Beyond the actual use of these drugs, there is the growing presence of erectile dysfunction as a cultural phenomenon. From Bob Dole ogling the adolescent Britney Spears in an infamous Pepsi advertisement to the inundation of television markets during the airing of sporting events, to the filling of e-mail in-boxes with spam (often seemingly in concert with invitations to porn sites and promises to add inches to one's penis), the discourse of erectile dysfunction and male inadequacy has saturated American culture.[8] All these medications and enticing promises have done is to further draw attention to the performative quality of masculinity—and likely raise the level of male anxiety. As Cialis's advertising asks—and threatens—men, the basic question is: "Will you be ready?"

Duty, Honor, Country

Being ready, like watchfulness, preparedness, and willfulness, is perceived as an attribute of being able to "act like a man"—especially in times of war. A lack of such preparedness has been widely recognized in the United States since the attacks of September 11, 2001. Not only, according to *The 9/11 Commission Report* (National Commission on Terrorist Attacks 2004), was the nation ill prepared to respond to the threat of terrorist attacks,[9] but the war on terrorism has been marked by a decided lack of readiness (to contain al-Qaeda; to pressure Saudi Arabia; to deal with nuclear threats in Pakistan, North Korea, and Iran; and, of course, to help develop a stable, democratic order in Iraq).[10]

The challenge to "be prepared" is particularly resonant in the War on Terror.[11] Not only is the nation facing military and political confrontations quite different than previous battles, but the soldiers deployed to meet these needs are also unconventional. Pentagon correspondent Pamela Hess (2004) has reported that "fully 43 percent of the roughly 110,000 soldiers who will be in Iraq through 2005 will be reservists." Soldiers are being asked to engage in situations of peacekeeping, reconstruction, and "nation-building" for which they have not received extensive training and are being required to stay longer than expected (Hess 2004). In addition, one of the underlying issues in the scandal regarding the abuse of prisoners and the use of torture by the United States is the lack of training given to soldiers responsible for handling prisoners in Iraq and Afghanistan (Human Rights Watch 2005). The perception of the American soldier has been further tarnished by the increased reliance on private military contractors hired to fulfill responsibilities (including the protection of L. Paul Bremer, former administrator of the Coalition Provisional Authority in Iraq), for which the U.S. military was apparently ill equipped. Congressman John Murtha, whose November 2005 call for the immediate withdrawal of U.S. troops from Iraq marked a dramatic shift in the public debate about the war, cited as one of his primary concerns the "demoralized" and "weakened" state of the American military. Murtha, a decorated Korean War and Vietnam War veteran who has been a "hawkish Democrat" intimately involved in military affairs during his tenure as a member of Congress, proclaimed:

> The future of our military is at risk. Our military and their families are stretched thin. Many say that the Army is broken. Some of our troops are on their third deployment. Recruitment is down, even as our military has lowered its standards. We must be prepared. The war in Iraq has caused huge shortfalls at our bases in the U.S. Much of our ground equipment is worn out and in need of either serious overhaul or replacement. George Washington said, "To be prepared for war is one of the most effective means of preserving peace." We must rebuild our Army. (Murtha 2005)

The idea of rebuilding the army as a foundation for peace and order is indicative of the broader problem we have been alluding to: the perceived need to "rebuild masculinity" to preserve the social order. In the face of stagnating wages, the loss of stable status in the familial order, the open questioning of male strength and virility, and a growing threat to the preparedness of the nation's military defense (beginning with the attacks of September 11, 2001), men in America face a serious challenge to their place in the social order.

Men have been de-centered, knocked off a privileged pedestal by social and cultural forces. This blow—which has left heterosexual men taking manhood lessons from queer men; which has undermined the notion of male breadwinner that had stood as a cultural ideal; which has led men to grasp for erectile dysfunction drugs and steroids in equal measure; which has left the military bereft, despite lower standards and a reliance on private military contractors—is hard to overstate. It is a shock to the social order akin to the shock to America's self-perception that occurred on September 11, 2001. It is a fundamental de-centering, a loss of stability, a loss of control. George W. Bush has sought to represent this beleaguered man as he has sought to represent the besieged nation. He has chosen a path that strives for the reassertion of power and prestige, the recapturing of a privileged status, by going on the attack from a position of the righteous victim against an enemy difficult to define or contain, but an enemy that in any case seeks to destroy "civilized" order.[12]

GEORGE W. BUSH: MAN AT WAR

George W. Bush staked much of his presidency on his capacity to confront these challenges. From his election in 2000 as a champion of moral virtue and traditional values to his adoption of the self-declared status of "war president," Bush explicitly adopted the traditional male role of providing order and security for the homeland. Yet, despite his desire to be a traditional war president and paragon of American manhood, George W. Bush has a problem. With his nicknaming informality; the stories of being a small businessman in hardscrabble Midland, Texas; his disdain of intellectuals; and the detailed reports of his athletic feats, George W. Bush has gone to great and sustained lengths to present himself as an all-around American guy. Nevertheless, Bush can only go so far to mask his uncommonness. As Kevin Phillips details, George W. Bush is a son of a president, grandson of a senator, and heir to old wealth and extraordinary connections. He broke rules, laws, and codes of conduct and led two companies into bankruptcy—yet always received not just another chance but a gilded helping hand. He is about as uncommon an American citizen as you could find (Phillips 2004).[13] Moreover, Bush has not always successfully navigated the challenging path of prototypical American masculinity—beginning with the ability of a son to "do better" than his father, for George W.

Figure 2. President Bush speaking about homeland security at Mount Rushmore National Memorial, August 15, 2002. (AP PHOTO/KEN LAMBERT)

Bush is not the athlete, the businessman, the student, the soldier, or the public servant George H. W. Bush was. To address these perceived weaknesses, George W. Bush has dedicated himself to an emotive performance of masculinity. He becomes the "Everyman," the God and country, mom-and-apple-pie exemplar of American manhood. As Paul Krugman has written:

> No administration in memory has made paeans to the president's character—his "honor and integrity"—so central to its political strategy. Nor has any previous administration been so determined to portray the president as a hero, going so far as to pose him in line with the heads on Mount Rushmore. (Krugman 2003; Figure 2)

The photograph at Mount Rushmore is one of many bold expressions of self-regard and assurance that Bush has conveyed during his time as president. For critics, it signifies astonishing arrogance (perhaps never more so than his famous unwillingness during the 2004 presidential debates to acknowledge any mistakes he made while in office), but for supporters of the president, such expressions are taken as illustrations of the clarity of his convictions. In either case, it is clear that Bush is trying very hard to demonstrate determination and certainty as a leader in difficult times. In this manner, Bush has sought to adopt the persona of the much cherished figure of Ronald Reagan, a figure who, as Lou Cannon explained, sought to

Figure 3. President Bush aboard the USS *Abraham Lincoln*, declaring the end of major combat in Iraq beneath "Mission Accomplished" banner, May 1, 2003. (AP PHOTO/J. SCOTT APPLEWHITE)

"restore national self-confidence by transferring his own self-confidence to his countrymen" (quoted in Jeffords 1994, 3).

And yet, unlike Reagan, Bush's efforts to convey self-confidence have all the markings of an actor trying too hard to compensate for frailties. It is hard to conceive of better testimony to the impossible performance of masculinity than the image of Bush speaking on the deck of an aircraft carrier under a banner proclaiming "Mission Accomplished" (Figure 3). The speech was delivered after U.S. troops "took control" of Baghdad from Baath Party leaders and was carefully orchestrated to present Bush in possession of his full powers as the "First Man of America"—a bold and successful military leader, a war president, surrounded by cheering uniformed soldiers on their way back home from the war. Instead, the Hollywood-directed photo-op was clearly premature and has, with the rising chaos and crisis in Iraq, become not, as intended, an emblematic image of leadership but, rather, a telling illustration of the shallowness of his leadership and the poor simulacrum of his masculinity. Not only has the mission in Iraq not been accomplished; the mission to perform hetero-normative masculinity also has not been accomplished—and the latter mission might be as intractable as the War on Terror.

BEING A MAN'S MAN AS POLITICAL STRATEGY

If masculinity is such a difficult and delicate performance, if it brings pronounced political risks, why would Bush go down this road? Answering this question requires more than the conclusion that Bush is trying to be the American Everyman; it also demands a more calibrated look at the American electorate. Bush does not want the approval of every American citizen or to win over every voter in America. Indeed, there are some votes that Bush does not want. He reaped the benefits of having particular portions of the electorate as opposition. For example, given the political dynamics in 2004, Bush (and John Kerry) gave up whole states and populations and concentrated their efforts not just on swing states, but on particular voters within those swing states. This election was won and lost on the degree to which each side animated its base and motivated the few swing voters left to go to the polls. Energizing these voters to go to the polls required a subtle political, moral, and psychological calculus.

Although national exit polls from 2000 are somewhat suspect (given their inaccurate use to incorrectly call the election), the numbers are stark enough to provide a general idea of the gender gap that provided a tactical framework for the 2004 election. Voter News Service reports from the 2000 election showed that Bush enjoyed an advantage among male voters of 10 percent, while Al Gore had an advantage of 11 percent among female voters. During the summer of 2004, this dynamic was showing signs of dramatically shifting.[14] In response to these threats, the Bush team reasserted its "straight eye for the straight guy" vision. Bush played the macho card as much to sustain the support of men as to attract women. And, indeed, this strategy worked: exit polls by Edison Media Research indicate that Bush increased his percentage of male voters from 53 percent in 2000 to 55 percent in 2004 and of female voters from 43 percent in 2000 to 48 percent in 2004 (Center for American Women and Politics 2004). As Paul Abramson, John Aldrich, and David Rohde (2005) report in their assessment of the 2004 election, Bush reversed the summer 2004 trend and preserved an 11 percent pro-Republican advantage among men. Even more starkly, Bush enjoyed a 25 percent support differential among white men.[15] This electoral endorsement from men—and especially white men—has proved to be a stable source of support during what has become a difficult second term for the president. Indeed, even as Bush's approval ratings have sunk to historic lows, he has maintained support among his core male supporters. For example, a March 22, 2006, Scripps Howard and Ohio University survey found that, while only "30 percent of women approve of President Bush's job performance . . . 44 percent of men approved of him." Moreover, the support among men "is much higher among more selected groups. Sixty percent of white men who describe themselves as spiritually 'born again' . . . say they approve of Bush's job performance. Among Midwestern evangelical white men, support rises still further, to 67 percent" (Hargrove 2006, 1).

This support is largely a response to the way that Bush has defended the continuing American military presence in Iraq by implying that critics of the war are not just cowardly, but are questioning the courage of the troops. Bush in turn asserts that his courage is akin to that of the soldiers. As he proclaimed in his November 30, 2005, speech at the U.S. Naval Academy in which he defended his administration's policies in Iraq:

> Setting an artificial deadline to withdraw would send a message across the world that America is a weak and an unreliable ally. Setting an artificial deadline to withdraw would send a signal to our enemies — that if they wait long enough, America will cut and run and abandon its friends. And setting an artificial deadline to withdraw would vindicate the terrorists' tactics of beheadings and suicide bombings and mass murder — and invite new attacks on America. To all who wear the uniform, I make you this pledge: America will not run in the face of car bombers and assassins so long as I am your Commander-in-Chief. (Bush 2005b)

In this remarkable speech, Bush, of course, once again invokes the specter of September 11. He also chooses to avoid mentioning not just the violence wrought by U.S. military forces, but also the reports of widespread torture and death squads among the Iraqi military and police forces (whose "courage" and determination Bush repeatedly hails as vital to the success of his military strategy). Indeed, this speech creates a tight figurative circle: supporting the troops equals supporting the president equals preserving our national self-image as innocent victim of violence equals celebrating the "masculine" virtue of "courage" as expressed by the pursuit of justice through acts of war and aggression (Figure 4).

There is fundamentally a great power, but also great danger, in this

Figure 4. President Bush speaking to Marines at Camp Pendleton, December 7, 2004. (AP PHOTO/DENIS POROY)

equation. If his plan in Iraq fails to bring freedom and democracy, if the military (as John Murtha suggested) or the American people or Bush's Republican base calls for the administration to withdraw troops in a way that can indeed be framed as "cutting and running and abandoning friends," then this failure to perform will not just diminish George W. Bush, but also the military, the nation, and peace and freedom around the world. As Bush said in conclusion to the U.S. Naval Academy:

> We will help the Iraqi people lay the foundations of a strong democracy that can govern itself, sustain itself, and defend itself. And by laying the foundations of freedom in Iraq, we will lay the foundation of peace for generations to come.
>
> You all are the ones who will help accomplish all this. Our freedom and our way of life are in your hands. (Bush 2005b)

The stakes for success are exceedingly high and generate, as should be expected, a pronounced level of anxiety.

The question that arises is what to do about this anxiety. Is Bush merely taking a page out of Machiavelli's playbook and creating a popular sense of fear that only he, as the "Prince," can resolve?[16] The answer to this question is not as unequivocal as one might think. Despite the rising and falling of color-coded security warnings and the manipulation of intelligence information to generate support for the war ("Facing clear evidence of peril, we cannot wait for the final proof—the smoking gun—that could come in the form of a mushroom cloud" [Bush 2002h]), Bush's attitude toward the anxiety is more subtle. As many have noted, Bush has stoked and utilized the fears of Americans to garner support, but he has also identified with these anxieties, not simply as one with the answer ("The Decider"), but also as one with a story of his own struggles.

MANHOOD AND THE SOUTHERN STRATEGY

Indeed, Bush, perhaps more than any other political figure, recognizes not just the great male performance anxiety in America, but also the political benefits that can result by identifying with this anxiety, by situating himself—despite his great uncommonness—as a regular guy, a "guy's guy," a soldier who can represent and appreciate straight guys' concerns, quite unlike liberal elites.[17] Indeed, the straight eye for the straight guy vision has incorporated a continuing Republican electoral approach—the "Southern strategy."

The Southern strategy has been widely noted as a cultural feature of the changing political landscape in the United States over the past forty years. For nearly one hundred years after Republican Abraham Lincoln led the Union forces in the Civil War, the Reconstruction-era response in the South was to support the Democratic Party. This era of the Dixiecrats began to fray in the 1960s when Democratic presidents John F. Kennedy and Lyndon Johnson began (haltingly to be sure) to support civil-rights legislation. Responding to the pull from Richard Nixon and Ronald Reagan to break from the Democratic Party in the name of "state's rights," Southern states have become increasingly Republican.[18] Southern Republicans have come to dominate the GOP majority in Congress—as shown by the leadership of Senator Bill Frist (Tenn.) and Congressman Tom DeLay (Tex.), and Senator

Trent Lott (Miss.) and Congressman Newt Gingrich (Ga.) before them — as well as the White House, where George W. Bush presents himself as a humble ranch owner tending to scrub brush in Texas.

The Southern strategy has also succeeded in more subtle and discursive ways in the United States. The Civil War is still commonly portrayed as a great "Lost Cause" — a legendary and noble effort to preserve a way of life against the inexorable meddling of foreign and elitist forces.[19] Losing a principled battle for the preservation of tradition has been romanticized as a model of glory and honor. This Southern strategy portrays losing a righteous struggle as a matter of principled — even religious — sacrifice. What matters is not losing a battle, but the way the event is remembered as a noble fight for a lost cause in the broader culture war. Such lost causes fuel commitment for tomorrow's battles.

The lost causes today's Republican Party champions share (at least) two features: (1) they represent a vision of traditional mores that are associated with conventional notions of gender; and (2) they are "impossible" to realize yet are dynamic enough to heighten often nostalgic longings that energize a vital political constituency. Witness, for example, the July 2004 debate in the Senate on the federal marriage amendment. As Thomas Frank argues, while this amendment was doomed to fail to gain enough votes to pass, it was successful in generating a "debate" about the loss of the "traditional American family" and the ensuing threats to American civilization.[20] The Republican intention was less the passage of the amendment than the "pseudo-populist" message about the crises in America in the ongoing culture war (T. Frank 2004). That Bush and some of his fellow Republicans nobly defended the honor of the American family against the meddling of liberal judges, cultural elites, and other proponents of the "homosexual agenda" was the point of the legislative charade.

The religiosity of the lost-cause rhetoric is, of course, no surprise. This positioning of normative masculinity as the subject of a holy war is a feature of a broader zeitgeist in the United States that the Bush administration utilizes and expands. Indeed, the current battle for the lost cause of normative masculinity is commonly portrayed in even more grandiose and righteous terms than the Civil War; today we can speak of "The Passion of the Lost Cause of American Masculinity," a vision perhaps best captured by Mel Gibson, who in films like the *Lethal Weapon* series, *The Patriot*, and

Braveheart has turned enduring persecution into macho martyrdom. In an interview with the *Los Angeles Times* on the eve of the release of his film *The Passion of the Christ*, Gibson asserted: "I'm subjected to religious persecution, persecution as an artist, persecution as an American, persecution as a man. . . . All I do is go and pray. For myself. For my family. For the whole world. That's what I do" (quoted in Abramowitz 2004). In Gibson's *The Passion*, Jesus is called to suffer a tortured, horrific death for righteousness. And yet, of course, despite losing the battle against the Jewish and Roman authorities of his day, Jesus wins the war for all time. The immediate loss reveals the evil and immorality of the enemies of God and is central to the holy and divine war for humanity. In his absolutist response to critics as "forces of Satan," Gibson depicts his own struggle to make and distribute the film as consistent with Jesus's own heroic martyrdom. Fighting the evil of challengers and skeptics may lead to his "persecution," but such a glorious battle presents the test of one's character as a man, a Christian, an artist, and an American.

Gibson is far from the first to claim the moral high ground that comes from the identity of "suffering innocent." Gibson's portrait of Jesus as a macho martyr is but a paragon of the broader cultural phenomenon in the United States.[21] Over the past thirty years, conservative religious forces in the United States have taken to portraying themselves as innocent victims of a culture of secular humanism.[22] And many Christian men have taken to portraying their fight as a lost cause—a likely doomed effort to re-create the mythical gendered social order in America. As the Christian right author Stu Weber nostalgically proclaims:

> If we're going to be healthy again, men are going to have to become healthy men again (and women healthy women). It's time for men to stand up, get a grip on biblical manhood, and quit apologizing for being men. What this culture desperately needs are men who are confident in their God-given masculinity and His intentions for it. . . . Remember when men were men? And women women and the differences were obvious? Remember when you didn't have to wonder? And you weren't criticized for being a man? (Weber 1995, 44)

During the Clinton years, these men thought they had lost the culture war.[23] With George W. Bush in the Oval Office, there has been a glimmer of hope that offers new dynamism to their lost cause. By identifying himself as a (once) beleaguered Christian man,[24] Bush, like Gibson, is seizing the opportunity to identify with men who believe that they have lost something that was rightly theirs: a particular understanding of America and their lives beneath the Stars and Stripes.

Bush is standing up for these beleaguered men. Even if he does not always successfully perform normative masculinity, his efforts still resonate because they show he recognizes the impossible plight of these men — and the coping devices they have often chosen to deal with the impact of the loss (from Bible study to Viagra). Ultimately, victory is demonstrated by the nobility and righteousness of one's mission, not by winning short-term temporal battles. This approach lends both a religiosity and a tragic sentiment to the struggle, an attitude that is amply evident in the struggle for the lost cause of American masculinity.

WHO'S THE MAN?

Bush's great and tragic determination to act like a man highlights both the resonance and the fragility of the normative performance of gender in America. The lost cause of "defending" a gender order is portrayed as a valiant fight, and when it fails, those who wish to see the myth will understand it as a grand battle for traditional values. Despite the reality that conventional markers of manhood are increasingly fleeting, crafting identification with the mythical man to excite potential male voters has been a vital tactic for the Bush administration. The great irony of Bush's efforts is that the electoral success of this "pro-family" conservative Christian man rests on his homosocial ability to endear himself to other straight men. If the Village People adopted personas to demonstrate the diversity of the gay community and appeal to gay men, George W. Bush has adopted similar personas to demonstrate a lack of diversity, a seeming consistency of hetero-normative notions of masculinity, to appeal to straight guys.

How then has the president chosen to reclaim the active and engaged support of straight male voters? By playing to, even heightening, their anxiety. Bush's policies and rhetoric are not intended to alleviate the causes of this anxiety. Rather, he acknowledges and identifies with this anxiety — but offers no substantive cures. It is a political strategy akin to erectile dysfunction drugs: exacerbate anxiety about the condition and offer palliatives. Indeed, the palliatives offered in each case require frequent repetition, so that the condition becomes a permanent part of the social landscape, and the patient/voter becomes dependent on the solace provided by the familiar recourse to a panacea. Viagra now offers a "frequent users" program: every time a user fills six eligible prescriptions, he gets the next one free. Bush, too, offers a frequent palliative plan for anxious voters: at moments of political weakness, he invokes the memory of September 11 and the specter of terrorism or makes public statements about the sacred status of heterosexual marriage as the foundation of American civilization. Raising anxiety by portraying men as subject to attack is intended to bring fearful men to a closer identification with the president and to become more dependent on the "restoration of manhood plan" offered by Bush. Although Bush sometimes appears ill equipped himself to successfully defend normative masculinity against these phantom attacks, this inadequacy actually helps with his short-term strategy. The inevitable defeat that is a product of defending the ephemeral qualities of manhood against reality is incorporated into a broader political strategy. The defeat, after all, is central to the noble myth of the "lost cause of American masculinity."

The War on Terror, as currently defined by the Bush administration, is shaping up as a profound illustration of such a lost cause. While to date Bush and Cheney have steadfastly resisted the temptation to portray the efforts in Iraq as a lost cause, preferring instead to insist that only "cynics" and "self-defeating pessimists" refuse to see the progress of freedom under way in Iraq, the groundwork for the depiction of the war in Iraq as a noble but tragic battle in an ongoing war has already been well established (Bush 2005a; Cheney 2005). As Bush declared in a speech on November 11, 2005:

> We don't know the course our own struggle will take, or the sacrifices that might lie ahead. We do know, however, that the defense of freedom is worth our sacrifice, we do know the love of freedom is the mightiest force of history, and we do know the cause of freedom will once again prevail. (Bush 2005a)

As he has done often, in this Veteran's Day speech Bush depicts the War on Terror as a noble cause and signals that he is willing to fight this heroic battle, despite the cowardly retreat of those unpatriotic individuals who lack faith in the mission. In many ways, the very framing of the mission as the "War on Terror" is a vivid illustration of both creating and using fear and anxiety. A "War on Terror" can only be imperfect and incomplete: no one can take all fears away or win a battle against a tactic rather than a nation or organization. It calls for courage but requires anxiety to be a permanent fixture in an unending war. But no matter: real men, real Americans, stand for freedom, and this honorable call will transcend whatever short-term failings Bush and other Republicans might encounter in coming years. And should the growing majority of American citizens joining the ranks of the "cynics" compel a retreat before the mission is accomplished, we should, in turn, expect the rhetoric of the lost cause to increase as a cover of a failed policy.

By arguing that the battle to defend normative American masculinity is a lost cause, we are introducing a note of optimism for those who would support the further deconstruction and de-centering of the hetero-normative imperative in the United States. This process is a long one, punctuated by amplified periods of instability and change. While the challenge to the firm grip of the masculine ideal comes in fits and starts, the trends are hard to ignore. In its claims to the status of the innocent victim fighting for a principled order, the right is both trying to capture a moral position and recognizing broad trends in America.

That said, a note of caution should also be sounded, because the de-centering of masculine ideals is not a simple, inevitable, linear process. The challenge to the normative gender order has excited the energy and focus of conservative cultural forces. If cultural trends regarding changes in conceptions of normative sex and gender are clear, so, too, is the powerful conservative cultural response on the Christian right (manifested, for example, in the rapid expansion of home schooling, the popularity of the Left Behind series, the expansion of abstinence-only sex education, and the nomination of John Roberts and Samuel Alito to the Supreme Court). Indeed, the Christian right has been so successful in acquiring political power and framing the terms of social debates that it is hard to take seriously the common claims of "victimhood" that serve to animate its moralizing politics.

As a president whose party has enjoyed control over Congress and the Supreme Court, George W. Bush has an even more difficult challenge maintaining the status of an "innocent victim." The attacks of September 11 have become less poignant a touchstone the more that Bush has sought refuge in the "ashes of American flags."[25] As the figure who promised to make the world safer and more secure, to fight the terrorists "over there" so we do not have to fight them "over here," Bush falls victim to his own rhetoric with each day that the war in Iraq drags on, with every prisoner-abuse scandal, with every dollar of profit enjoyed by Exxon–Mobil, with every General Motors plant closing, with every illustration that his performance of masculinity is palpably "artificial" rather than artificially "natural."

And yet, all is not lost for the Bush administration and its supporters. Bush's failings and the struggles of the War on Terror will only feed the broader narrative of the lost cause of American masculinity. The rhetorical beauty of the discourse of a lost cause is that no war is ever finished; every memory is contested, every cultural phenomenon is judged by the "principled standard" of a cherished—and often tragic—time. And in periods of instability, which challenges to normative standards always promise, a new champion will rise to represent a noble ideal for a beleaguered population. Such champions of nostalgia often lose their battles, but in the struggle they set the moral terms for future fights.

NOTES

For insightful recommendations, the authors thank Terrell Carver, Michaele Ferguson, Laura Fisher, Jill Locke, Lori Marso, and David Sumner.

1. The growing ranks of women in the U.S. military, and the shift in the nature of the battlefield in the War on Terror, have begun to change this dynamic. Nevertheless, consistent with the 1993 Department of Defense policy, women are still generally precluded from participating in direct combat. As a result, the Army and the Marines have more significant restrictions on the roles available to women than the Air Force and the Navy (see Segal and Segal 2004).

2. Quoted in New York Times, April 19, 2006. What makes the desperate bravado of the remark more poignant is the subtle mocking it received from the New York Times, which used the comment as its "Quotation of the Day" and the not-so-subtle mocking Bush received that night on The Daily Show with Jon Stewart, where the president was rendered as a caped superhero, "The Decider."

3. This table and other Economic Policy Institute data are based on the study The State of Working America, which is available online at: www.epinet.org/content.cfm/datazone_dznational.

4. A "non-family" household here means a household where neither children nor a married couple are present.

5. Thus, 69 percent of children in America still live in a two-parent household. However, 42 percent of children who live in two-parent households have both parents in the workforce. See U.S. Bureau of the Census, 2003a.

6. The literature on fatherhood is growing rapidly. For an introduction to this politically charged literature, see Daniels 2000.

7. While Viagra was the first erectile dysfunction drug on the market and enjoys the greatest name recognition, it has lost some of its market share in large part because it is outperformed by the other drugs, especially Cialis, whose effects start faster and last longer (thirty-six hours rather than Viagra's four-hour impact): see Mostaghimi 2003.

8. This relationship is seen most acutely in the figure of Rafael Palmeiro, the All-Star first baseman for the Texas Rangers and Baltimore Orioles, who was a prominent spokesperson for Viagra—and tested positive for steroid use.

9. See National Commission on Terrorist Attacks 2004, esp. chaps. 8–9.

10. One response to this state of unreadiness was the Department of Homeland Security's declaration that on September 9, 2004, the United States would officially begin "National Preparedness Month"—a phase that, conveniently, coincided with the conclusion of the Republican National Convention in New York and the start of Bush's and Cheney's barnstorming reelection tour of the nation.

11. It is worth noting that the Boy Scouts of America, for whom "Be Prepared" is the motto, emerged in the United States and Great Britain in the early twentieth century out of a concern for the "sissification" of boys and the dangerous threats to normative masculinity. On the early history of the Boy Scouts, see Putney 2001.

12. For a compelling discussion of responses to the attacks of September 11, 2001, that makes a similar argument to the one we make here, see Butler 2004.

13. As Frank Rich reported

> On the eve of his visit to London this week, [Bush] hit a characteristically phony note when he told an interviewer, "I never dreamt when I was living in Midland, Texas, that I would be staying in Buckingham Palace." Mr. Bush, who was born in New Haven, lived in Midland until only the age of 15 before moving on to such hick venues as Andover, Yale, and Harvard when not vacationing in family compounds in Kennebunkport, Me., or Jupiter Island, a tony neighbor of Palm Beach. (Rich 2003)

14. For example, polls conducted among registered voters by the *Washington Post* and ABC News between July 30 and August 3, 2004, indicated that Kerry and Edwards enjoyed a 17 percent advantage among female voters, while the advantage among male voters for Bush and Cheney had shrunk to 6 percent—a dangerous sign for Bush's reelection at that point. These numbers changed dramatically over the course of the summer as Kerry faced scathing challenges from the Swift Boat Veterans and the Republican Party focused on his "flip-flopping" on the War on

Terror—two sources of criticism designed to diminish Kerry's status as a traditionally masculine figure. See Morin and Balz 2004.

15. See esp. table 2. Their data are from a poll conducted by Edison Media Research and Mitofsky International and "completed by 13,110 voters as they left 250 polling places throughout the United States on Election Day and 500 telephone polls with early voters" (Abramson et al. 2005, 47). Abramson, Aldrich, and Rohde also report that Bush enjoyed a 15 percent advantage among married voters (who represent 63 percent of voters polled), and Kerry had a 12 percent advantage among unmarried voters.

16. Machiavelli 1992 (1515), esp. chap. 20.

17. On the efforts of Bush to portray himself as both a "regular guy" and a "tough guy" in the 2004 campaign, see, e.g., Axtmen 2004.

18. On the Southern strategy, see Black and Black 2002.

19. On the history and concept of the lost cause, see Reagan 1980.

20. For an example of this theme, see Santorum 2003.

21. On the evolution of the persona of Jesus in America, see Moore 2003; Prothero 2003.

22. Ever since Hal Lindsay, author of the influential 1971 best seller *The Late Great Planet Earth*, declared, "God didn't send me to clean the fishbowl; he sent me to fish," Christian conservatives have measured their success in terms of saving a worthy remnant of eager fish rather than arresting the declining morality of the nation as a whole. In other words, the mission of the messianic Christian is not to contribute to the betterment of the world, the fishbowl, but to save a few worthy fish stuck swimming in murky waters. On Lindsay, see Boyer 1992.

23. For example, the failure to remove Clinton from office led Paul Weyrich of the Free Congress Foundation to write an open letter to supporters calling for a retreat from a fundamentally corrupt nation:

I believe that we probably have lost the culture war. This is why, even when we win in politics, our victories fail to translate into the kind of policies we believe are important. Therefore, what seems to me a legitimate strategy for us to follow is to look at ways to separate ourselves from the institutions that have been captured by . . . other enemies of our traditional culture. (Weyrich 2006)

24. On Bush's rhetorical use of his conversion to Christianity, see Gutterman 2001.

25. The phrase is from the haunting song "Ashes of American Flags" (Wilco 2002).

wwwwwwwwww
Andrew Feffer
wwwwwwwwww

W's Masculine Pseudo-Democracy: Brothers-in-Arms, Suicide Bombers, and the Culture of Life

Ronald Reagan taught us that political power in contemporary America often involves the ability to encompass seemingly disparate figures in the national imaginary, bringing at once elitist and egalitarian characters—soldiers, genial grandfathers, lone gunmen, ordinary suburbanites, and Hollywood aristocrats—into a field of view that Americans routinely mistake for a democratic vista. The Republican Party has excelled in constructing such political landscapes, as we once again have learned in George W. Bush's regime, which through most of its existence has preserved much of the Reagan coalition by rhetorically and visually improvising on the archive of cultural images that his predecessor made familiar. Like the imaginary figures Reagan used so effectively, Bush's rhetorical commonplaces are substantially cinematic, inherited from the visual and narrative archive on which the rhetorical construction of American regimes has increasingly depended since World War Two.

One could see this method at work in W's notorious "Mission Accomplished" landing on the aircraft carrier U.S.S. *Abraham Lincoln*, the visual and rhetorical elements of which composed a picture of a presidency at once powerful and humble, descending from the remote reaches of the sky to the familiar adulation of a crowd of welcoming sailors and marines. Focusing on the comic hypocrisy of the banner stretched across the Lincoln's conning tower, many critics overlooked the actual achievement of the event, the ways in which Bush's image, action, and words enabled the kind of simultaneously authoritarian and pseudo-democratic masculinity that constitutes W as both commander-in-chief and one of the many ordinary soldiers protecting Americans from the deadly missionaries of Osama bin Laden.[1]

The speech on the Lincoln typified those given by presidents in times of war: Bush honored decent men and women for protecting the nation against indecent enemies. W, however, went further, drawing a stark contrast between the hetero-normative and the abnormal on the terrain of battle. The assembled sailors and marines did not just protect America against the interests of another nation; they defended it against the depredations of another culture, and they did so not only with force of arms, but with force of character as well. The attack of the "nineteen evil men" was met, Bush declared, by the "decency and idealism" of men and women who naturally reproduced the "daring of Normandy and the courage of Iwo Jima." Like the members of that "greatest generation," American soldiers in Iraq ennobled their sacrifices for the nation (and their acts of violence) with "strength, kindness and goodwill" (Bush 2003c). In other speeches, Bush made that contrast even more explicit, deriving the moral resources of American soldiers from the "culture of life" in which they were raised: the communities of love and faith, "courage and caring," the families of decent, hardworking people to which they belonged, shaped strong characters that prevailed regardless of one's circumstances, or one's actions. Such a culture of life was visually implicit in the assemblage before him on the Lincoln, in the membership of each individual soldier in a "band of brothers," a collection of "citizen soldiers" metonymically representing a diverse yet cooperative and democratic nation (Bush 2001h).

Bush juxtaposed this "culture of life" to a "culture of death," a refrain in Bush administration and journalistic rhetoric on a wide range of issues including the Middle East since before September 11, 2001. The suicide bombers against whom the soldiers on the Lincoln presumably defended Americans were raised in a culture that naturally produced "the shock troops of a hateful ideology" that forced young men "without conscience" into ignoble and bestial acts, killing "innocent civilians" and, as a clearer signifier of their evil, themselves. "Our enemies send other people's children on missions of suicide and murder. They embrace tyranny and death as a cause and a creed," Bush declared in his 2002 State of the Union address. Americans, in contrast, "stand for a different choice, made long ago, on the day of our founding. We affirm it again today. We choose freedom and the dignity of every life." Not only do we express that culture of life, but we improve on it: "In the sacrifice of soldiers, the fierce brotherhood of firefighters, and the bravery and generosity of ordinary citizens, we have glimpsed what a new culture of responsibility could look like" (Bush 2002a).

Bush's melodramatic distinction between life and death, good and evil, could appear in some iterations to endorse the advancement of women's rights: under the arc of the culture of life, "respect for our women" contrasts sharply with the discrimination and violence against women of the Taliban and the Iranian mullahs. The "freedom" presumably fostered by the culture of life includes the ostensibly full participation of women in civil society, in the economy, and in state institutions (even in the military). The GOP uses such comparisons to recruit women, employing campaign slogans like "W Stands for Women" and promoting key administration figures like Condoleezza Rice (Ferguson, in this volume). Yet even if Bush's opportunism rhetorically elevates the stature of women's rights and chivalrously protects their dignity at home and abroad, I would argue that the melodramatic frame promoting and defending "respect," "freedom," and participation for women undoes whatever gains, if any, might have been made for gender equality.

Exploiting melodrama as a cinematic and literary genre in which families, communities, and nations are defended against pathological outside threats, the rhetoric of the "culture of life" authorizes, at home and abroad, the sort of normative heterosexuality that ties the fate of women to patriarchal forms of political, cultural, and social power. The hetero-normative point of this rhetoric was made clear by Pope John Paul II, who introduced the phrase in August 1993. The Pope aligned the "culture of life" not just with the principle that "life is always a good" (i.e., that abortion and euthanasia are evil), but with the notion that the role of the conventional heterosexual family "in building a culture of life is decisive and irreplaceable."

The responsibility of the family, the Pontiff reminded his listeners, "flows from its very nature as a community of life and love, founded upon marriage." Only on the conjugal union and the parental bond, he insisted, can genuine social solidarity, equality, and, above all, democracy be grounded. The "culture of death," as the Pope understood it, promotes abortion, homosexuality, and the breakup of heterosexual families because it fosters "a notion of freedom which exalts the isolated individual in an absolute way, and gives no place to solidarity, to openness to others and service of them" (Pope John Paul II 1993).[2]

Applying the Pope's rhetorical contrast to justify sacrifices on the field of battle, Bush implicitly normalizes the families of the soldiers to whom he speaks (on the *Lincoln* and elsewhere), as well as those of the citizens who support them: wives wait for husbands, mothers sacrifice sons for war, their courage manifest at the dinner table, Sunday services, and the military rally. This is the common figure of an orderly society for the right wing with whom Bush cultivates a primary relationship. "So many of my generation, after a long journey, have come home to family and faith, and are determined to bring up responsible, moral children," he declared in his 2005 State of the Union. The sorts of heroic sacrifice with which Bush justifies his version of the national culture in turn remind us that the apparently democratic community Bush has in mind is a fundamentally masculine affair, one that requires the presence of women, yet excludes them from the central sacrificial act of belonging in which manhood is declared and true citizenship achieved.

Bush's rhetorical effect requires the maintenance of a clear boundary between the normal and the pathological that validates his masculine pseudo-democracy at home while vilifying its opposite abroad. His regime maintains that boundary using rhetorical resources found in two places, both of which I explore in this essay. The first is the field of "terrorism studies," regularly cited in the American press, that traces the pathological roots of suicide bombing to a culture of death located in the alien terrain of the Middle East. The second is the archive of cinematic commonplaces that shape the expectations of American audiences and their reception of melodramatic narratives that reaffirm the culture of life while marking and excluding its pathological exceptions. Over the past half-century, Hollywood cinema has forged among American audiences an identification with the forms of heroic self-sacrifice and masculine solidarity that the Bush regime successfully exploits. The narrative expectations of that cinematic audience will endure long after the Bush administration is history.

THE CULTURE OF DEATH

In its application to the War on Terror, the hetero-normativity of the culture of life becomes evident in its contrast to the culture of death, especially as the latter is manifest abroad. It is because "death" seems so prominent in the cultural geographies of America's enemies that Bush need not deal with inconvenient facts such as homosexuality in the ranks and can pay lip service to the growing number of women in uniform, both of which undermine the affirmative masculinity of the "band of brothers" and the image of tens of thousands of Mrs. Ryans waiting for the return of their heroic sons. He need only refer to the abnormality, the failed heterosexuality of suicide bombers whom he sends those sons against.

Here Bush is supported by much of the recent sociology and psychology of terrorism studies, which supply many of the commonplaces littering the landscape of the culture of death. As Jasbir K. Puar and Amit S. Rai point out, such studies serve a concerted effort to reinforce Bush's brand of "aggressive heterosexual patriotism" (Puar and Rai 2002, 117) by representing the terrorist as the sort of socially excluded "monster" that Michel Foucault (2003) considered a crucial element in the modern history of psychosexual normalization:

Indeed, an implicit but foundational supposition structures this entire discourse: the very notion of the normal psyche, which is in fact part of the West's own heterosexual family romance—a narrative space that relies on the normalized, even if perverse, domestic space of desire supposedly common in the West. Terrorism, in this discourse, is a symptom of the deviant psyche, the psyche gone awry, or the failed psyche; the terrorist enters this discourse as an absolute violation. (Puar and Rai 2002, 123–24)

Much in recent terrorism studies tends to support Puar's and Rai's conclusion. In the widely quoted work of the psychologist Jerrold Post, for instance, the suicide bomber does indeed offer an example of failed heterosexuality, emerging from the sexually confused social isolates produced by the breakdown of the normative heterosexual family—abandoned husbands, divorcees, unmanageable and delinquent children. The admitted limitations of his data did not stop Post from concluding that for a large group of terrorists (what he called the "anarchic-ideologue" type [Post 1984, 241]), loss or discrediting of a father or father figure in childhood or adolescence leads to marginalization and a narcissistic revolt against parental authority. Moreover, Post argued, "insufficient socialization in incomplete families" provokes a "strong need to affiliate with a group" (i.e., a terrorist cell) as a substitute family (Post 1984, 245).[3] The fact that Post attributed specific psychosexual pathologies to specific terrorist types did not prevent him from drawing conclusions about terrorists in general; nor did it stop others from generalizing his or similar psychodynamic models based on equally limited data, especially as the problem of the suicide bomber became more acute in the late 1980s.[4] Thus, one group of researchers in 2004 concluded that the suicide terrorist comes from a social order that is too restrictive and repressive—the suicide bomber is "overly integrated into his society and overly regulated." Those writers traced the psychopathology of the suicide bomber to perceived Middle Eastern social pathologies. Arabs, they argued, tend to have "borderline personality disorder," are dominated by shame, are habitually envious, have "defective bonding and dependency needs," are "prone to retaliate," and "use defense mechanisms that involve blaming others." They attributed these pervasive disorders to "Islamic child-rearing practices that frustrate the child's dependency needs and view personal desires as signs of weakness and failure." The absence of fathers in Arab communities and the oppression of mothers who retaliate against sons, they concluded, "facilitate the development of the authoritarian personality." And it is that authoritarian personality, especially in moments of social disintegration, that tends toward self-destructive acts of frustrated and narcissistic rage, such as suicide bombing (Lester et al. 2004, 285–87, 291–92).[5]

It is in this family culture, especially as it has been distorted and exaggerated by war and occupation, that the culture of death supposedly is formed. In her recent account of female suicide bombers in Palestine, the journalist Barbara Victor cites the Palestinian psychologist Shafiq Masalqa's discovery that this culture of death has "permeated" Palestinian society (Victor 2003, 8). In a 2001 study of three hundred Palestinian eleven year olds, Masalqa reportedly discerned an "atmosphere" on the West Bank that allows a "plan of suicide to flourish" and an inclination to martyrdom to prevail (Victor 2003, 27). Even opponents of the Israeli occupation attribute the political violence to social and cultural pathologies. One hears echoes of the Pope's homilies and Post's psychopathologies in the oft-quoted words of the Palestinian psychologist Eyad el Sarraj, whose face and voice should be familiar to viewers of CNN or listeners to National Public Radio. Israeli dominance has not only created despair, Sarraj contends, but has caused the "demolition of the father image in the eyes of the children," who then seek compensation in martyrdom (Butler 2002, 72–73; see also Moghadam 2003, 71; Oliver and Steinberg 2005, xxii, 122). Sarraj bitterly criticizes the Israeli occupation, which he argues places Palestinians in a no-win situation that leads to rage and aggression. But he also blames authoritarian Palestinian childrearing practices that presumably authorize violence, especially among boys. The combination of authoritarian patriarchy and Israeli humiliation thus creates the culture of death as a psychosexual nightmare of brewing social pathology: "the environment today is an environment that glorifies martyrdom, glorifies the martyr as a symbol of power, in comparison to the father image that has been demolished by humiliation and impotence and helplessness" (CNN 2004a).[6]

One need not excuse Palestinian patriarchy to question the notion that a *distinctively* Palestinian "culture of death" produces suicide bombers as pathological symptoms of Middle Eastern patriarchy (to a degree that distinguishes the culture of the West Bank from, say, that of West Texas or Flint, Michigan). It is on that ability to maintain a clear distinction between the violence of the suicide bomber and other forms of violence (such as an Israeli missile attack or American death sentences) that Bush hangs his rhetorical device, the "culture of death." The distinctiveness serves the rhetorical reduction of suicide bombers to "monsters" and at the same time allows the normalization of *similar behaviors* (i.e., similar expressions of violence and rage) in non-marginal or "democratic" spaces—for instance, in the American army of occupation in Iraq or on a high-school football team. It is precisely in that sort of absurd inconsistency, what Foucault (2003, 11–13) calls the "Ubu-esque," a form of the grotesque that combines science and nonsense, reasoned argument and preposterous displays like the landing on the *Lincoln*, that one finds the most effective discursive manifestations of power.

Yet such representations are also the point of greatest instability in

Bush's rhetorical strategy, for once the distinction is questioned (as hypocrisy, for instance) then the rhetoric becomes less persuasive. The field of terrorism studies is a good example. In addition to the normalization discerned by Puar and Rai, terrorism studies offers many critiques warning against indiscriminate psychopathological diagnoses, noting the lack of ethnographic evidence for the sorts of generalizations made by Post or Sarraj, and underscoring the limits of psychological autopsy as a basis for understanding motivation. Puar and Rai fail to mention that much of the field is committed to a rational choice or strategic model that exposes many of the hypocrisies and inconsistencies of Bush's distinction. The most recent, most comprehensive, and most convincing of these arguments is that of Robert Pape (2005), who maintains that suicide attacks are a rational strategy in an asymmetrical conflict that forces poor nations or sub-state groups to use what appear to be relatively drastic measures against an overwhelmingly superior force of arms. Following similar arguments by Martha Crenshaw and others, Pape draws on an enormous body of data to dispute poorly substantiated generalizations about the social psychology of suicide terrorism: if one widens the field of view to include all parts of the world, one sees that suicide bombers are neither sexual and social isolates nor "overly integrated" fanatics. Suicide bombers are not even overwhelmingly male (the Tamil Tigers, whose campaign of suicide bombings in the 1980s and 1990s make up the largest percentage of the total, prefer women for the task). They also tend to be older and middle class and work in well-coordinated teams, all characteristics that do not fit with the psychodynamic profile of the young, sexually and economically frustrated Islamic extremist (Pape 2005, 5, 17, 22, 171–172; see also Miskel 2004; Ruby 2002).

Thus, while terrorism studies as part of a regime of normalization contributes to the characterization of suicide bombers as monsters, the literature nonetheless offers a contradictory view that potentially undermines the constitution of the normal, especially of the hetero-normative. This body of literature poses a problem for Bush. In strategic terms, the suicide bomber of rational-choice studies looks (as Pape puts it) uncomfortably similar to "a politically conscious individual who might join a grassroots movement" (Pape 2005, 200) (e.g., a pro-life activist), an American soldier, or the leader of a powerful nation:

The heart of suicide terrorism's strategy is the same as the coercive logic used by states when they employ air power or economic sanctions to punish an adversary: to cause mounting civilian costs to overwhelm the target state's interest in the issue in dispute and so to cause it to concede the terrorists' political demands. (Pape 2005, 30)

Rather than conform the suicide bomber to a psychological and ethnographic profile, the approach of Pape and others brings him or her into an ethical and political discussion. As Mahmood Mamdani argues, suicide bombing is not, as Bush would have it, a *cultural* phenomenon. Rather, "terrorism is born of a *political* encounter" (Mamdani 2004, 62). Regardless of whether one condones suicide bombing, one begins to suspect that the bombers are acting as other people would under similar circumstances with similar resources. Though the preponderance of men among Palestinian and Iraqi suicide bombers reflects cultural and political differences, the motive for the act may have less to do with manhood than with the degeneration of political disagreement into armed struggle.[7]

CINEMATIC SNIPERS, RECKLESS PILOTS, AND SUICIDE BOMBERS

The success of Bush's rhetoric does not hinge merely on using the disputed claims of terrorism studies to demonize suicide bombers in presidential speeches. Long before the 2000 election, Bush's audience was already receptive to the notion that a heroic boundary exists between something like the "culture of life" and the "culture of death." The receptivity of Bush's audience to a large degree is a matter of recognizing generic character types whom they can counterpose to the failed heterosexuality of the suicide bomber: ordinary guys in civilian and military life whose sacrifices are noble, heroic, and, above all, masculine. The opposition of those two character types can be found in many cultural artifacts. However, since World War Two they are perhaps most familiar from their iconographic representations in Hollywood film.

Over the course of its history, Hollywood film has elaborated the contrast between something like the "culture of death" and the "culture of life" in political thrillers and war stories that explore the character of the suicidal political terrorist as melodramatic threat—that is, as an external menace to the stable order of the normative family. These cinematic characters resemble the suicide bomber of terrorism studies to a remarkable degree. They suffer from inadequate ego formation due to the breakdown of normative families (especially the absence or weakness of a father); they are either social isolates or overly integrated obsessive compulsives; and they suffer from one sort or another of male sexual crisis.[8] In the following readings of some representative films, I suggest that such cinematic spectacles align the political with the melodramatically hetero-normative in the sense shared by Bush, the Pope, and terrorism experts in their opposition of the cultures of death and life. I then provisionally explore that part of the film archive that we know Bush and his advisers consider a valuable source of rhetorical commonplaces.

The 1954 home-invasion sniper thriller *Suddenly* (directed by Lewis Allen) is a good example of Hollywood developing a melodramatic narrative tension around the problems of male identity formation in modern society and aligning them with political threat. *Suddenly* takes place in a small town in California on the day that the president is to arrive unannounced. The town is a perfect place to attempt an assassination, which is what John Baron (Frank Sinatra) and his assistants do, invading a home overlooking the train station where the president will disembark, holding its inhabitants hostage, and setting up a sniper's nest. The house, however, belongs to a retired Secret Service agent (Pop Benson, played by James Gleason), who lives with his widowed daughter-in-law, Ellen (Nancy Gates), and her son, Pidge (Kim Charney). The assassination plot is almost foiled when Pop's former subordinate in the Secret Service pays him a visit, accompanied by the local sheriff, Todd Shaw (Sterling Hayden), who we already have learned has been unsuccessfully courting Ellen, a bitter war widow who refuses to replace the husband "blown to bits on some godforsaken battlefield thousands of miles from where he was born." Baron and his colleagues kill the Secret Service agent but only wound Todd.

At this point, a melodramatic struggle ensues over the fate of Ellen's family, concerning issues that were raised in the opening scenes of the film. The main bone of contention is a gun, a toy desired by Pidge but denied him by his mother, who refuses to expose him to the violent masculine world that killed his father. Her rejection of male acculturation, which enrages Pidge and risks marginalizing him as a "sissy," is symptomatic of her more encompassing refusal to accept the reality that "there's cruelty and hatred and tyranny in the world." One cannot just end war by disavowing that truth, Todd (who bought the gun for Pidge anyway) paternalistically counsels her: guns are tools that in the hands of tyrants kill young husbands (or presidents) but in the hands of sheriffs protect the law and the community. An overly controlling mother, Ellen risks isolating Pidge and denying him his manhood, as the struggle over the gun symbolizes. "He's got to know that these things exist," Todd insists. "Then he can fight against them when it's his turn. You can't wrap the boy in cellophane." Pidge's problem is not just his mother's trauma but the fact that he has no adult "male role model" to balance her maternal protectiveness and sentimentality, the sort of absence that ten years later Daniel Patrick Moynihan would notoriously blame for inner-city riots. Will Todd (a man with a gun) fill that role, or will Ellen keep all guns out of her life?

Ellen's moment of truth comes from her exposure to Baron, whose pathological identity formation serves as an object lesson in what happens to boys raised without fathers. Baron is a Durkheimian and Freudian mishmash of anomic and narcissistic personality disorders. Like the suicide bombers of terror studies literature, he has no feelings. "They were taken out of me by experts," he tells Ellen. "Feeling's a trap. Show me a guy with feelings, and I'll show you a sucker. . . . If I had any feelings left in me at all it would be for *me*. Just me!" Baron is, as Bush might have declared, without conscience, because he is without human connection, without family, love, or faith. His mother "wasn't married"; his father "was a dipso." Abandoned and raised in an orphanage with other anonymous dead-end kids, he loves to kill as an expression of a narcissistic rage shaped by the suffocating anonymity of "the crowd."

> Baron: Before the war I drifted and drifted and ran, always lost in the great big crowd. I hated that crowd. I used to dream about the crowd once in a while. I used see all those faces scratching and shoving and biting. And then the mist would clear, and somehow all those faces would be me. All me and all nothin'.
> Todd: But the war changed everything, huh, Baron?
> Baron: I ain't no traitor, Sheriff. I won the Silver Star.
> Ellen: And learned how to kill.[9]

These exchanges confirm Ellen's worst fears. The gun, for which Baron has great affection, replaces Baron's absent father and mother, offering a distinctive identity as a war hero, a winner of the Silver Star, officially recognized as a "man" for killing other men in the same war that killed Ellen's husband. Yet Baron is also court-martialed for confusing killing with sexual desire. "I knew guys like you," Todd declares. "Killin' was sweet. Rather kill a man than love a girl."

That Baron's is a phony masculinity ("I'll bet you stole it," Pidge says of the medal, for which Baron hits him) is less important than Ellen's implicit (though absurd) realization that because of her smothering control and her liberal pacifist disconnection from reality, Pidge could end up like Baron, sexually confused and frustrated in a sniper's nest waiting for the president's train to arrive. Baron loses control of the situation, undone by the cooperative efforts of Todd, the family, and a young television repairman (there to fix their set) who dies for his part (yet another echo of Ellen's dead husband). His partners dead, Baron tries for one last shot, but the exposure of the plot cancels the train stop. As he laments his lost chance to "be somebody," Baron is shot—by Ellen, who finally learns that the gun is a useful tool.

The struggle that unfolds in the house is not only between Ellen and Todd over Pidge; nor is it just between Todd and Baron over the gun as primary signifier of masculinity. It is also over the meaning of self-sacrifice in war, the sociological obverse of the psychological matter of identity formation—that is, the giving up of self for the nation that gave one identity in the first place, the act performed in the back story by Ellen's husband and on screen by Judd, the young repairman. For the issue that prevents Ellen from allowing Pidge a "normal" masculinity is the question of whether her husband's death was useless sacrifice or a heroic fulfillment of his duty as a citizen and therefore as a man. The liberal pacifist notion that death in war is useless sacrifice is aligned melodramatically in the film with the sexually perverse pathology of the sniper or suicide bomber. With each, the culture of death threatens the stability of the normal family. Death in war as heroic self-sacrifice is aligned in the film with the sheriff's masculinity, heterosexual families, and boys whose normative masculinity is shaped by the presence of a real father figure. This truth Ellen recognizes, too. The film ends with her asking Todd along to church. The culture of life is back on track.

The guys like Baron who would rather "kill a man than love a girl" were the subject matter of many films after World War Two. Unlike Baron, who struggles to survive, many of these characters are also suicidal or, at least, so reckless that they are unable to sense the line between the heroic and the pathological. Steve McQueen, an actor who shaped the boundaries of masculine identity for W's generation, excelled in roles that skirted the boundary between heroic individualism and narcissistic personality disorder, often as insubordinate soldiers whose recklessness jeopardizes the mission.[10]

The pathological motivations of this character type are especially well explored in Buzz Rickson (McQueen), a daredevil B-17 bomber pilot flying missions over German-occupied Europe who is the central character of *The War Lover* (Phillip Leacock, dir., 1962).[11] It is quickly evident that, as with Baron, Rickson's real love is killing. "Lady," he declares proudly, "I belong to the most destructive group of men the world has ever known. That's my work." And he likes his work, in part because he is extremely talented at it. That it also gives him sexual pleasure is evident from his erotic response to the dropping of bombs in the first action scene. Rickson's eyes orgasmically widen as the blasts rock his low-flying plane. He then hands the controls over to his co-pilot, Boland (or "Bo" for short, played by Robert Wagner), and goes to sleep.

Buzz and Bo vie for the attention of Daphne Caldwell (Shirley Anne Field), an English woman who crosses their path one night at the officers' club. She falls in love with Bo but is still drawn toward Rickson, who reminds her of Rusty, the reckless paratrooper she loved and lost in the early years of the war. It is because of this earlier romance, however, that she knows Rickson's type, and even though she is cynically realistic about the prospects of an American airman like Boland marrying his English "war girl," she resists Rickson's blunt seductions when he tries to step in. She knows that women and planes are just the tools of Rickson's sexually perverse violence. As she explains to Bo, "It's almost as if [Buzz and Rusty] like fighting more than the things they're fighting for. . . . You don't like what you do, but you do it because you think something good will come of it." Bo objects, "I don't believe the things they tell us. All that propaganda and stuff." "I know you don't," Daphne replies. "But you are on the side of life."

Marty Lynch, Rickson's navigator, is his hetero-normative foil, representing life against Rickson's "culture of death." Like Daphne, Lynch, a father and a family man, sees through Rickson's pseudo-masculine daring and technical competence to the sociopath inside. If given a plane, Lynch tells Bo, Rickson would fight for anyone, the Americans or the Germans. Daphne thinks she understands this social pathology thoroughly. "I once knew a man like you," she says. "You take and give nothing back." Like Baron, Rickson finds justification in egoistic cynicism: "get wise, Daphne; the world belongs to the takers." Rickson easily crosses the line between reckless egoism and narcissistic rage, both murderous and suicidal. He "loves to drop bombs, smash cities, kill." He also loves to risk his life and the lives of others (one reason Lynch, who wants to return home, did not like him). After Rickson buzzes the base in the B-17, angry about having to drop propaganda leaflets instead of bombs, the commanding officer (CO) asks the medical officer for a psychological review.

> Doc: Rickson is a good example of the fine line that separates the hero from the psychopath.
> CO: Which side of the line do you put Rickson on?
> Doc: Time will tell. I suppose we're running a risk, but that's the nature of war.

War makers who need killers for pilots are willing to excuse Rickson for perpetuating the culture of death; the filmmakers are not. Like Daphne and Lynch, they are "on the side of life." They trace Rickson's suicidal violence and narcissistic rage to the same social pathologies as Baron's—a broken home and absent parents. "I could get knocked off over here," Rickson laments, and "nobody'd ever know about it." Boland asks, "When were you home last?" Rickson turns angry: "Home? You tell me where it is, Boland, I'll tell you how long ago it was." From the point of view of this film, Rickson's hypersexuality complements his suicidal rage; together they constitute a "failed heterosexuality," not because Rickson is unable to conquer women, but because he does so too easily and without forming the attachments necessary for a hetero-normative family of the sort Lynch has and Daphne wants.

Viewers, of course, wonder whether Bo is cut from some of the same cloth as Rickson. Will he marry Daphne? Will she help him embrace "life" and reject "death?" Rickson draws the line himself in the last scenes, as the plane returns smashed up from a terrifying mission. Dropping rapidly in altitude, Rickson is determined to fly the plane home anyway. As they approach Dover's white cliffs, Bo demands that they bail out. "Afraid to die Boland?" Rickson asks. "You're damn right I am," Bo replies, "but you're afraid to live." Letting Bo embrace the culture of life, Rickson orders him to call air-sea rescue and help the rest of the crew parachute to the channel below. He then pushes Bo out of the plane, returns to the cockpit, and tries to fly home. He crashes into the cliffs as Bo and the rest of the crew watch from the water below.

Unlike Baron, Rickson does not quite fit the model of the terrorist. But they share a cinematic psychopathology that Hollywood continued to explore through the 1960s and 1970s in such terrorist thrillers as *The Manchurian Candidate*, *Two Minute Warning*, *Rollercoaster*, and *Black Sunday*.[12] In the last of these examples, we get a study of a former soldier become suicide bomber at the point where the boundary between heroic self-sacrifice and suicidal psychopathology is crossed. As in other films of this sort, that boundary corresponds to the one drawn by Bush, Pope John Paul II, and others between the hetero-normative and the sexually perverse.

Resembling the post mortems of terrorist studies, *Black Sunday* (John Frankenheimer, dir., 1977) is composed of a series of profiles, each illustrating the etiology of terror in a culture of death. The film's central character, Michael Lander (Bruce Dern), is a psychopathic Vietnam veteran and former prisoner of war (POW) who conspires with Palestinian terrorists to float an enormous bomb on the bottom of the Goodyear blimp (of which he is the pilot) to the middle of the Super Bowl's fifty-yard line. The film largely blames the Vietnam War, his captors' brutality, and the political machinations and bureaucratic insensitivity of the U.S. Army and the Veterans' Administration for Michael's breakdown.[13] A hero (like Baron as winner of the Silver Star), Michael is fixated on that distinction at the expense of reestablishing a normal heterosexual life with his wife and children. Classically narcissistic, he blames everyone but himself for his problems: the Army for his court-martial, the American public for the consequent loss of his medals, his wife and the military counselor for the failure of his marriage.

Viewers can sympathize with Michael. But we begin to understand as well how far over the line between hero and psychopath Michael has strayed, and in which direction. Accusing the Navy of destroying his marriage, he tells a psychologist about how an officer "counseled" his wife:

And he told her that the life expectancy of a released POW is about one half the average. He also told her about the high rate of homosexuality and *impotence* among released POWs and *stressed* the impotence. . . . He was preparing her for what it was she was going to have to go through. *She* was going to have to go through?!

But that is "all water under the bridge now" he adds, flexing his arm in the universal sign of sexual potency, "because I don't have *that* problem anymore." When the psychologist remarks that "surely there were other factors involved," Michael retorts sullenly, "Yeah, she was getting a little dick on the side, if that's what you mean." Later we learn that Michael likely imagined this part of the story as a paranoid fantasy that haunted him in the Vietnamese prison; thus, it probably was his obsession with his lost masculinity that led to the divorce. As with the suicide bombers profiled by the terrorism experts, Michael's violence, then, is intimately entangled with his sense of failed manhood, his inability to hold his family together, and his perceived castration by women, paternal authority, and military power.

Though viewers join Michael in blaming Hanoi, the Navy, and the Veterans' Administration for his condition, this, of course, is where sympathy for him must end, because he is methodically preparing to murder eighty thousand football fans. And while we may share his contempt for the American public, which cares more about vicariously enjoying the violence of the gridiron than about taking responsibility for the destructiveness of the government's foreign policies, we draw the line at slaughtering American civilians. Here Frankenheimer plays effectively with the moral inconsistencies of American democracy and public opinion: the crowd's indifference to the slaughter of far more people in Vietnam is proportional to their fanatical attachment to their football stars. We know the horror of this culture of death from Michael's own cold-blooded interest in the killing itself, as he gleefully slaughters a watchman in a test of his device, a confabulation of plastic explosives and rifle darts that turn the man's body into Swiss cheese. His need for such effects is registered in his conception of his plan, an act of vengeance not only for the specific wrongs done him but also for his exclusion from the hetero-normative space of conventional American life:

> She took it away from me, every single one of them took it away from me. All those guys too, yeah, I see 'em every Sunday, I see 'em from up there (points to the sky), down in the mass, with their little up-

turned faces and their two little weenies and a Coke, watching the big game, cheering the big game, because they cheer all good things. They cheer the big game and they cheer court-martials, and they love the big event because it makes them feel big, and I was goin' to give it to 'em big. They'd a been talking about that goddamn game for the next five thousand years. And so would Margaret and so would the kids.

During most of the postwar period, it was hard for Americans to avoid these cinematic representations of problematic masculinity, suicidal reck- lessness, and terrorist psychopathology. Such character studies explored the boundaries between normative masculinity and something resem- bling the suicide bomber, whether it was the full-blown terrorist or just the anomic and self-destructive GI. These films conveyed to the viewers the importance of embracing "life" for the sake of personal happiness, but more important, for the nation's political health and well-being. While nations need to sacrifice citizens in war, they also need citizens to be will- ing to sacrifice themselves for the right reasons, as that sacrifice serves not only the strategic military effort, but also (as Ellen's case makes clear) the psychological formation of other citizens, their ability to recognize the boundary between the normal and the exceptional in daily life.

BANDS OF BROTHERS

While it was difficult for American moviegoers to avoid the various antici- patory shadows of the suicide bomber, it was equally hard to miss their counterparts, not just in the films where the Barons, Ricksons, and Landers appeared, but in those that independently celebrated heroic self-sacrifice in war and elsewhere as the measure of male citizenship. The images and the narratives of such films help political leaders like Bush turn a landscape of death (occupied Iraq, for instance) into the outer reaches of the "culture of life," where acceptable forms of male violence are distinguished from suicidal, fanatical, or evil ones. To illustrate the service of cinematic image to that rhetorical strategy, I will now discuss three recent films that that are favorites of the Bush regime.

Bush himself has expressed a personal preference for one of those films, Steven Spielberg's *Saving Private Ryan*, a movie about the horrors of war that nonetheless turns a suicide mission for the sake of military public relations into an honorable act of self-sacrifice (Associated Press 2005). Many Americans might have been satisfied with Spielberg's cinematically clichéd justification for the demise of so many men to save just one other: if the platoon, according to this way of thinking, as an ethnically diverse version of Shakespeare's "band of brothers," metonymically stands for the nation, then sacrifices for the sake of one's "comrades," regardless of the strategic goal, are justified in the name of egalitarian democracy.[14] The historian Stephen Ambrose (1997) makes just this case for the "citizen soldiers" who opened the Western Front in June 1944, thereby turning the cinematic cliché into a historical one (and then recycling it back to the screen as an adviser to Spielberg). Unlike the ideologically driven Nazis, American GIs, disillusioned by the betrayals of the previous world war, did not fight for "country and flag," Ambrose argues. Instead, they "fought because they had to. What held them together was . . . unit cohesion" (Ambrose 1997, 472). Ambrose traces an entire era of political accomplishments to GI solidarity (while absurdly excluding women and non-veterans from the building of postwar America). After learning in the war "to work together," this greatest generation "licked polio" and "developed the modern corporation." They "did more to help spread democracy around the world than any other generation in history" by recognizing that "the way to prevent war was to deter through military strength" (Ambrose 1997, 472–73).[15]

If Ambrose mines cinematic cliché to promote Cold War belligerence, he and Spielberg also tap into the equally jaded sentiments of the post-Vietnam generation, for whom protecting "the guy right next to you" became justification enough for conscripts and National Guardsmen to keep fighting in Vietnam or the Persian Gulf. One of Bush's rhetorical triumphs has been to convince the public to trust his radically self-serving foreign policy because he is just one of those guys, despite his actual origins as a scion of one of the wealthiest and most powerful dynasties of the twentieth century. Thus, the landing on the *Lincoln* signified a reassuring membership in and affirmation of the "band of brothers" before whom Bush's plane set down. In that performance, Bush represented himself in the absurd and contradictory position of simultaneously being a "brother" (who might save or be saved) and a sovereign commander-in-chief (who sends the other brothers to their deaths from the safety of the White House).

Bush's advisers and pundits had been preparing for the *Lincoln* event since the 1990s, when they began likening the president to Shakespeare's Henry V, who justified a "war of choice" against the French in 1415 as the honorable and divinely sanctioned struggle of ordinary Englishmen (the original "band of brothers") against an effete French aristocracy. They saw in Henry and W "dissolute" youths who became "war leader[s] of the first rank" in the face of national crisis. This analogy also served neocons eager to promote W as a man of the people, who use it (as one Shakespeare scholar said of Henry) to "blend vertical authority with horizontal camaraderie in a way that evokes the best of both worlds, or at least effaces the worst of each" (Newstrom 2003).[16] That horizontal connection of king and commoner is one main thrust of the king's St. Crispin's Day speech before the Battle of Agincourt, in which he invokes not merely God but also the democratic spirit as the sanction for battlefield sacrifice: "And Crispin Crispian shall ne'er go by,/ From this day to the ending of the world,/ But we in it shall be remembered—/ We few, we happy few, we band of brothers;/ For he to-day that sheds his blood with me/ Shall be my brother, be he ne'er so vile,/ This day shall gentle his condition" (Shakespeare 1914/2000 IV.iii.58–64).

Shakespeare suggests in other dialogues that this brotherhood of the battlefield offers only a false equality, instrumental to Henry's need to have his conscripts enter a hopeless battle on his behalf. It is Henry's pseudo-democratic message, however, that comes out especially clearly in Kenneth Branagh's sanitized film production of the play, reportedly a favorite in the Bush household in the early 1990s. As Robert Lane (1994) explains, the movie cuts out critically ambivalent elements that Shakespeare used to show Henry's hypocrisies and character flaws (not to mention the brutalities of war and aristocratic rule). Instead, Branagh (playing Henry) delivers the Crispin's Day speech with all the earnest boyishness of a young GI gaining a battlefield commission in Normandy. The atrocities and moral complexities of the historical Henry V's reign, some of which Shakespeare alludes to in the play, disappear from the screen. Not only does Branagh's version promote wars of choice; it changes the band-of-brothers motif from a rhetorical manipulation to a statement of principle rationalizing the letting of one's blood. In Shakespeare's version, one might conclude that there was little to distinguish Henry's apparently doomed commoners from fanatical suicide bombers—they were, after all, about to die for "God and country" in an unjust war (and it was largely luck that allowed them to defeat the French). In Branagh's version, they become ordinary heroes by virtue of their membership in the inaugural band of brothers, the archetype of a pseudo-democratic militarism that eventually would expand the British empire.

King Hal's speech is echoed in the half-time pep talk of Coach Gary Gaines at the climax of another of W's favorite films, Friday Night Lights, a translation of the band-of-brothers saga to the gridiron that shows how well Americans have incorporated these ideas of ennobling self-sacrifice into what they call "the American way of life." It also shows how dangerously W incorporates male violence into what he considers democracy's equivalent—the culture of life. This film dramatizes a single football season at Permian High School in Odessa, Texas, where W spent part of his early childhood.[17] Though based on Buzz Bissinger's (2000) superb journalistic study of educational failure, social violence, and discrimination in West Texas's troubled oil economy during the 1980s, the film sanitizes the original story, instead glorifying football's brutality as a confirmation of adolescent masculinity. With a gesture toward equality similar to King Hal's, Friday Night Lights elides enormous racial and economic gaps that actually existed among the players (as well as between the relatively powerless teenagers and the dictatorial and retributive coaching staff). Like Henry, Gaines (played contrary to fact with gentle but paternal simplicity by Billy Bob Thornton) invokes the sacrificial brotherhood of the gridiron, even though it is one that he, as coach, cannot share physically.

One of the characteristics of the Permian team is the relatively small stature and light weight of its members. What they lack in size, however, they make up for in effort and team spirit, winning by virtue of hard work and their shared willingness to sacrifice parts of their bodies at the scrimmage line.[18] The teenage boys, lacking the "opportunities" already exploited by their fathers' generation and turning instead to football as a way out of Odessa, willingly shed blood and ruin their bodies for the sake of the coach, the game, and the town, which sees in the efforts of its heroic youth evidence of its own dying virtue. Their sacrifices, then, emerge from a shared "feeling" and as public evidence of whether one's heart is in the task of, as the townspeople repeatedly put it, "getting the job done."

Gaines's version of masculine pseudo-democracy, a fatherly sermon on the meaning of achievement, elides the brutality of this relationship and masks his own authority over the players by invoking and (he hopes) evoking this heroic solidarity of mutual effort:

> To me, being perfect is . . . about you and your relationship to yourselves and your family and your friends. Being perfect is about being able to look your friends in the eye and being able to know that you didn't let them down, because you told them the truth. And that truth is that you did everything that you could. There wasn't one more thing that you could have done. Can you live in that moment, as best you can, with clear eyes and love in your heart? With joy in your heart? If you can do that, gentlemen, then you're perfect. I want you to take a moment, and I want you to look each other in the eyes. I want you to put each other in your hearts forever, because forever is about to happen here in just a few minutes. (Transcribed from the film.)

Unlike King Henry, Gaines cannot participate by spilling his own "blood." Instead, he must sustain the brotherhood of the team (and the team's service to the town) on the basis of "heart," something he (and the community) can share. "And I want you to put that into your hearts," he says. "Boys, my heart's full. My heart's full." If this looks like evangelical hard core, it is—different from the nineteenth-century enthusiasms of the Burnt-Over District only in volume and the gender of its core enthusiasts. More important is the manner in which this film replicates on the psychological and seemingly secular level the emotional form of an evangelical politics, one in which the collective feelings of a community are the content of the presumptive democracy.

This muscular and hetero-normative evangelicalism, however, is largely and paradoxically homosocial in its ritual affirmation, and that still needs explaining. In Shakespeare's play, the purpose of Henry's speech is to elicit sacrifices for the king from his assembled troop of commoners by establishing a bond of pseudo-democratic solidarity not unlike the one Bush proposes in the culture of life. It effects one kind of democratic substitution for *pro patria mori*, what I have been calling "masculine pseudo-democracy," the act of self-sacrificial solidarity among apparent equals (on the battlefield or the gridiron) that defines masculinity. In general, such sacrifices constitute nation-states as bodies politic and nations as territorially defined groups of people or cultures. The relationship is also reversed: the act of individual sacrifice on the battlefield for the nation constitutes individual identity, or, as Arjun Appadurai puts it, localizes a nation's subjects.[19] By shedding one's blood, one shares "brotherhood" with the king, enjoying a piece of his sovereign authority. The violence of battle then becomes a constituent of male identity and the price of membership in the democratic community (if it indeed exists), possibly even something we would call "citizenship." Others cannot enjoy that membership to its fullest extent: "And gentlemen in England now-a-bed/ Shall think themselves accurs'd they were not here,/ And hold their manhoods cheap whiles any speaks/ That fought with us upon Saint Crispin's day" (Shakespeare 1914/2000, IV.iii.65–68).

Such pseudo-democratic expressions of masculine collective violence exclude the feminine as an object of contempt even as they sentimentalize battlefield sacrifices through expressions of emotional attachment to one's brothers. Only a male character like Gaines, who plays surrogate father to at least one of the teammates, could ask the team to put one another in their hearts. In doing so, he turns individual sacrifice into a collective effort that affirms the identity of player, team, and community simultaneously. But to do so, all other suggestions of femininity must be banished or stigmatized, as is the case with any evidence of physical weakness or lack of effort (usually associated with female body parts or homosexuality). Alternatively, such sentiments must be compensated for with violence. One could argue, as Lane does, that Shakespeare likewise shows that dynamic in the deaths of York and Sussex, whose affections seem (in the play, though not in the movie) more than just brotherly (one kisses the other as they die). The tears their death raises in Henry are immediately followed by his order to kill the French prisoners. Thus, as Lane suggests, "The sentiment spawned by the intense male comradeship in war harbors within it a savagery, that the potential for tears is just as apt to produce blood" (Lane 2004, 44).

Yet at the same time, sacrifices are ennobled by the presence of women on the actual and metaphoric sidelines: as suffering mothers, loyal wives, admiring daughters, and other members of the community of life. This is the other side of the hetero-normative but one that is no more included in the brotherhood than "gentlemen in England now abed." Women's "primary civic task" is to produce and raise the men that will be sacrificed on the fields of battle (Elshtain 1991, 547). They are banished yet reimported to justify the bonds among men. Spielberg reminds us that for the modern era, at least, neither honor on the field of battle nor even simple brotherhood is enough. He measures the worth of Private Ryan (and thus the sacrifices of those who saved him) amid the headstones of the American cemetery in Normandy, in the loving gazes and earnest assurances of Ryan's wife and children, who tell him fifty years later that he has indeed "earned" his salvation. Whatever his accomplishments as a member of the greatest generation, we know at least that Ryan did what George W. Bush might call the "hard work" of leading a normal heterosexual life.[20]

CONCLUSION

If such stories ("passed down from fathers to sons") are accepted as the constitutive narratives of national identity (as Shakespeare intended *Henry V* and as Ambrose and Spielberg intend the story of the Normandy invasion), then democracy becomes a fundamentally masculine affair, regardless of the claims about the participation of women, their "dignity," or their prominent inclusion in powerful offices of state. The fact that women now occasionally die on the field of battle does not change the gendered distribution of heroic virtues in such melodramatic narratives. At the core of that melodrama are assumptions about the proper location and distribution of masculinity and its relationship to external threats like the demonized and failed heterosexuality of the suicide bomber. This politics endangers gender equality in the obvious manner of tying women's power to their status in traditionally patriarchal institutions and their adherence to hetero-normative family values. An even more sinister danger lies, however, in the violent forms of ritual self-sacrifice that demand the witness of women while simultaneously excluding them from the central act of pseudo-democratic solidarity. In such melodrama, women shift readily from being treated as protected objects of reverence to becoming threatening targets of violence.

Moreover, while we can take some comfort in the recent waning of W's popularity, we would be foolish to assume that with his demise will come an end to the popular tastes and expectations on which he built that support in the first place. We can expect others (including liberals and women) to tap into the same visual and narrative tradition that Bush exploits and refines, one that replaces politics with melodrama and reduces democracy to the collective spilling of blood. W paints a political landscape considerably darker and more threatening than the happy vistas of his Republican predecessors. Yet like them, he uses cinematic commonplaces to draw together the contradictory elements of a deeply problematic and deceptive presidency that exceeds constitutional authority while appealing to the most degraded aspects of the democratic tradition. In large part, that deception involves misrepresenting his own intentions, simultaneously exalting his sovereign stature while humbling himself as just one of the guys. In the culture talk that marks his presidency, however, W also reflects the intentions of a restive and self-deceptive public already receptive to melodramatic excess, a durable part of American political culture manifest most graphically and sustained most effectively in the visual and narrative rhetoric of Hollywood film. The persistence and pervasiveness of that rhetoric tells us that the excesses of W's masculine pseudo-democracy will last well past Bush's presidency.

NOTES

1. A video and photos of the event can be viewed at the U.S. Department of Defense's website at www.defenselink.mil/news/May2003/n05012003_200305018.html (accessed November 1, 2006). While there were women among the sailors stationed on the Lincoln, the vast majority of sailors and marines greeting Bush were men. Most of the publicity shots featured him in crowds of brothers-in-arms.

2. The Pope's most extensive discussion of the sacred forms of caring, dependence, and solidarity necessary for the "culture of life" can be found in his encyclical *Evangelium Vitae* (Pope John Paul II 1995).

3. His inferences are based on limited and dated biographical information about German terrorists (in the 1970s), about whom Post thought it noteworthy that a third had conflicts with their parents. On Post, see also Brannan et al. 2001, 6.

4. For a summary of those arguments, see Hudson 1999.

5. The habitual conflation of Arabs and Muslims is made by the authors cited.

6. Sarraj has no readily available body of writing in English. To save space, I am neglecting reports about Hizbollah and Hamas recruitment through promises of virgins in heaven and sexual fulfillment. On that subject, see Kelley 2001; Moghadam 2003, 71–73. Such a line of argument quickly reaches the ridiculous. One

psychiatrist, commenting on both the phenomenon and the literature about the phenomenon, goes so far as to characterize suicide bombing as a "massive explosive orgasmic catharsis" providing a "sexual outlet" for Palestinian youth made unmarriageable (and therefore sexually frustrated) by chronic unemployment (Gordon 2002, 288).

7. The anthropologist Emiko Ohnuki-Tierney's study of the Japanese *tokkotai* pilots (often cited as one of the modern precedents for contemporary suicide bombing) offers a model for combining cultural and sociological data with a political and gender analysis (Ohnuki-Tierney 2002).

8. The psychology of this cinematic terrorist (and his war-movie equivalents) was informed by the same foundational social psychology as terrorism studies a generation later, a popular amalgam of Freud, Emile Durkheim, and the crowd psychology of Robert Park's Chicago School of Sociology. On film melodrama, see Gledhill 1992; Landy 1991, 15–16; Schatz 1991.

9. On the role of the crowd in melodrama, see Gledhill 1992, 154. Following Andreas Huyssens (1986), Gledhill argues that the crowd, regularly figured as female, serves as the perfect villain in those family melodramas that concern male identity.

10. Films in which McQueen played such characters include *Never So Few*, *Hell Is for Heroes*, *The Great Escape*, and *Bullitt*.

11. Though born in England, where *The War Lover* was produced, Leacock by 1962 was a veteran of Hollywood screen and TV. The script was by the blacklisted screenwriter Howard Koch, most famous for scripting *Casablanca*, who moved to England to continue in the industry.

12. One can add to this list modified family melodramas from the 1950s like *Rebel without a Cause* (a juvenile-delinquent film) and *The Desperate Hours* (a home-invasion thriller).

13. In this respect, the movie was quite unlike the novel, which traces narcissistic rage and an obsessive compulsive disorder to his mother.

14. On the evolution of this metonym see Elshtain (1991, 551). See also Schatz (1998). The list of similar films is vast, including *The Longest Day*, *A Guy Named Joe*, *The Sands of Iwo Jima*, *A Walk in the Sun*, *Bataan*, and *Guadalcanal Diary*.

15. On Ambrose's role in the film's production (he is not officially credited), see Bremner 1998.

16. The neoconservative Kenneth Adelman (infamous for predicting that the Iraq invasion would be a "cakewalk") incorporated *Henry V* into leadership seminars at Aspen in the summer of 2003 and into his "Movers and Shakespeares" executive-training institute. The Shakespeare scholar Scott Newstrom reminds us that conservatives routinely get the play wrong, bringing back onto the stage bowmen whom Shakespeare for his own reasons had removed from the history as a lesson to listeners about the virtues of initiative and technological innovation. See also

Owens 2004; Thompson 2004. Arianna Huffington made the neocons regret their analogy the following year in a blistering reversal of their interpretation, reminding readers that in the end, like Henry, "George II has lost the war, emboldened our enemies and made America bleed" (Huffington 2004).

17. George Bush Sr. worked one year in Odessa in the late 1940s before moving on to a job one town over in Midland. On *Friday Night Lights* as a Bush favorite, see Associated Press 2005.

18. In real life, the team was indeed small, but also mainly white. The size comparison worked to the disadvantage of Permian on the gridiron but to the public disfavor of the black football players with whom Permian competed. In a conventionally racist manner, Odessa's white middle class believed that black players' talents were unearned consequences of genetics, while they were otherwise lazy and selfish (Bissinger 2000, 87, 92).

19. On the distinction between the nation-state and the nation as a geographical, demographic entity, see Appadurai 1996. I am eliding the distinction between citizen and subject because that is one of the consequences of the "culture talk" that Bush employs.

20. This is the message of Spielberg's most recent contribution to the screen, *War of the Worlds*, in which the dissolute life of an ordinary American Joe (Tom Cruise) is redeemed by his willingness to sacrifice himself for his children, not as a fruitless gesture for the sake of honor, but as an act that brings together at that moment yet another band of Americans in their struggle against an alien occupation army (the people with whom Cruise shares the aliens' version of a slaughtering pen).

PART III

Gendered War Logics at Home and Abroad

wwwwwwwwwwwww
Iris Marion Young
wwwwwwwwwwwww

The Logic of Masculinist Protection:
Reflections on the Current Security State

My most important job as your President is to defend the homeland; is to protect American people from further attacks.
—GEORGE W. BUSH (2002D)

Every man I meet wants to protect me. I can't figure out what from.
—MAE WEST PLAYING "FLOWER BELLE LEE" IN THE FILM *MY LITTLE
CHICKADEE* (1940) DIRECTED BY EDWARD F. CLINE, SCREENPLAY BY
MAE WEST AND W. C. FIELDS

The American and European women's movement of the
late 1970s and early 1980s contained a large segment
that organized around issues of weapons, war, and peace.
Creative civil-disobedience actions wove webs of yarn at en-
trances to the Pentagon and set up colorful camps on cruise-
missile sites in England's Greenham Common. Writings of
the women's peace movement tried to make theoretical connections between male domination and militarism, between
masculine gender and the propensity to settle conflicts with
violence, and these echoed some of the voices of the women's
peace movement earlier in the twentieth century. By the early
1990s, the humor and heroism of the women's peace actions
had been all but forgotten.

Organized violence, led both by states and by non-state actors, has certainly not abated in the meantime and has taken new and frightening forms (Kaldor 1999). Thus, there are urgent reasons to reopen the question of whether looking at war and security issues through a gendered lens can teach lessons that might advance the projects of peace and democracy. In this article, I analyze some of the security events and legal changes in the United States since fall 2001 by means of an account of a logic of masculinist protection.

Much writing about gender and war aims to explain bellicosity or its absence by considering attributes of men and women (Goldstein 2001). Theories adopting this approach attempt to argue that behavioral propensities of men link them to violence and those of women make them more peaceful and that these differences help account for the structure of states and international relations. Such attempts to connect violence structures with attributes or behavioral propensities that men or women supposedly share, however, rely on unsupportable generalizations about men and women and often leap too quickly from an account of the traits of people to institutional structures and collective action. Here I take a different approach. I take gender as an element not of explanation but, rather, of interpretation, a tool of what might be called ideology critique (cf. Cohn 1993). Viewing issues of war and security through a gender lens, I suggest, means seeing how a certain logic of gendered meanings and images helps organize the way people interpret events and circumstances, along with the positions and possibilities for action within them, and sometimes provides some rationale for action.

I argue that an exposition of the gendered logic of the masculine role of protector in relation to women and children illuminates the meaning and effective appeal of a security state that wages war abroad and expects obedience and loyalty at home. In this patriarchal logic, the role of the masculine protector puts those protected, paradigmatically women and children, in a subordinate position of dependence and obedience. To the extent that citizens of a democratic state allow their leaders to adopt a stance of protectors toward them, these citizens come to occupy a subordinate status like that of women in the patriarchal household. We are to accept a more authoritarian and paternalistic state power, which gets its support partly from the unity a threat produces and our gratitude for protection. At the same time that it legitimates authoritarian power over citizens internally, the logic of masculinist protection justifies aggressive war outside. I interpret Thomas Hobbes as a theorist of authoritarian government grounded in fear of threat and the apparent desire for protection such fear generates.

Although some feminist theorists of peace and security have noticed the appeal to protection as justification for war making (Stiehm 1982; Tickner 1992, 2001), they have not elaborated the gendered logic of protection to the extent that I try to do here. These accounts concentrate on international relations, moreover, and do less to carry the analysis to an understanding of the relation of states to citizens internally. My interest in this essay is in this dual face of security forms: those that wage war outside a country and conduct surveillance and detention inside. I notice that democratic values of due process, separation of powers, free assembly, and holding powerful actors accountable come into danger when leaders mobilize fear and present themselves as protectors.

Since the attacks of September 11, 2001, I argue, the relation of the leaders of the United States to its citizens is well illuminated by interpreting it under the logic of masculinist protection. The Bush administration has mobilized the language of fear and threat to gain support for constricting liberty and dissent inside the United States and waging war outside. This stronger U.S. security state offers a bargain to its citizens: obey our commands and support our security actions, and we will ensure your protection. This protection bargain between the state and its citizens is not unique to the United States in this period but, rather, often legitimates authoritarian government. I argue that the bargain is dangerous in this case, as in most others. The essay concludes with a gendered analysis of the war against Afghanistan of fall 2001. While the Bush administration initially justified the war as a defensive action necessary to protect Americans, its rhetoric quickly supplemented this legitimation with an appeal to the liberation of Afghan women. I suggest that some of the groundwork for this appeal may have been laid by feminist campaigns concerning the Taliban, which the Bush administration chose at that moment to exploit. I argue that the apparent success of this appeal in justifying the war to many Americans should trouble feminists and should prompt us to examine whether American or Western feminists sometimes adopt the stance of protector in relation to some women of the world whom we construct as more dependent or subordinate.

MASCULINISM AS PROTECTION

Several theorists of gender argue that masculinity and femininity should not be conceptualized with a single logic. Rather, ideas and values of masculinity and femininity, and their relation to one another, take several different and sometimes overlapping forms (Brod and Kaufman 1994; Hooper 2001). In this spirit, I propose to single out a particular logic of masculinism that I believe has not received very much attention in recent feminist theory: that associated with the position of male head of household as a protector of the family and, by extension, with masculine leaders and risk takers as protectors of a population. Over twenty years ago, Judith Stiehm (1982) called attention to the relevance of a logic of masculinist protection to the analysis of war and security issues, and I will draw on some of her ideas. Her analysis more presupposes than it defines the meaning of a masculine role as protector, so this is where I will begin.

The logic of masculinist protection contrasts with a model of masculinity assumed by much feminist theory: of masculinity as self-consciously dominative. In the male-domination model, masculine men wish to master women sexually for the sake of their own gratification and to have the pleasures of domination. They bond with other men in comradely male settings that give them specific benefits from which they exclude women, and they harass women to enforce this exclusion and maintain their superiority (MacKinnon 1987; May 1998, chaps. 4–6).

This image of the selfish, aggressive, dominative man who desires sexual capture of women corresponds to much about male-dominated institutions and the behavior of many men within them. For my purposes in this essay, however, it is important to recall another, apparently more benign image of masculinity, one more associated with ideas of chivalry. In this latter image, real men neither are selfish nor do they seek to enslave or overpower others for the sake of enhancing themselves. Instead, the gallantly masculine man is loving and self-sacrificing, especially in relation to women. He faces the world's difficulties and dangers to shield women from harm and allow them to pursue elevating and decorative arts. The role of this courageous, responsible, and virtuous man is that of a protector.

The "good" man is one who keeps vigilant watch over the safety of his family and readily risks himself in the face of threats from the outside to protect the subordinate members of his household. The logic of masculinist protection, then, includes the image of the selfish aggressor who wishes to invade the lord's property and sexually conquer his women. These are the bad men. Good men can only appear in their goodness if we assume that lurking outside the warm familial walls are aggressors who wish to attack them. The dominative masculinity in this way constitutes protective masculinity as its other. The world out there is heartless and uncivilized, and the movements and motives of the men in it are unpredictable and difficult to discern. The protector must therefore take all precautions against these threats, remain watchful and suspicious, and be ready to fight and sacrifice for the sake of his loved ones (Elshtain 1987, 1991). Masculine protection is needed to make a home a haven.

Central to the logic of masculinist protection is the subordinate relation of those in the protected position. In return for male protection, the woman concedes critical distance from decision-making autonomy. When the household lives under a threat, there cannot be divided wills and arguments about who will do what or what is the best course of action. The head of the household should decide what measures are necessary for the security of the people and property, and he gives the orders that they must follow if they and their relations are to remain safe. As Stiehm puts it, "The protector cannot achieve status simply through his accomplishment, then. Because he has dependents he is as socially connected as one who is dependent. He is expected to provide for others. Often a protector tries to get help from and also control the lives of those he protects—in order to 'better protect' them" (Stiehm 1982, 372).

Feminine subordination, in this logic, does not constitute submission to a violent and overbearing bully. The feminine woman, rather, in this construction, adores her protector and happily defers to his judgment in return for the promise of security that he offers. She looks up to him with gratitude for his manliness and admiration for his willingness to face the dangers of the world for her sake. That he finds her worthy of such risks gives substance to her self. It is only fitting that she should minister to his needs and obey his dictates.

Hobbes is the great theorist of political power founded on a need and desire for protection. He depicts a state of nature in which people live in small families where all believe some of the others envy them and desire to enlarge themselves by stealing from or conquering them. As a consequence, everyone in this state of nature must live in a state of fear and insecurity, even when not immediately under attack. Households must live with the knowledge that outsiders might wish to attack them, especially if they appear weak and vulnerable, so each must construct defensive fortresses and be on watch. It is only sensible, moreover, to conduct preemptive strikes against those who might wish to attack and to try to weaken them. But each knows that the others are likely to make defensive raids, which only adds to fear and insecurity. In Hobbes's state of nature, some people may be motivated by simple greed and desire for conquest and domination. In this state of nature, everyone has reason to feel insecure, however, not because all have these dominative motives, but because he or she is uncertain about who does and each person understands his or her own vulnerability.

In her contemporary classic *The Sexual Contract*, Carole Pateman interprets Hobbes along the lines of contemporary feminist accounts of men as selfish aggressors and sexual predators. In the state of nature, roving men take advantage of women encumbered by children and force them to submit to sexual domination. Sometimes they keep the women around as sexual servants; thus arises marriage. These strong and aggressive men force other men to labor for them at the point of a sword. In Pateman's account, this is how the patriarchal household forms: through overpowering force (Pateman 1988, chap. 3).

One can just as well read Hobbes's ideas through the lens of the apparently more benign masculinity of protection. Here we can imagine that men and women get together out of attraction and feel love for the children they beget. In this construction, families have their origin in a desire for companionship and caring. In the state of nature, however, each unit has reason to fear the strangers who might rob or kill its members; each then finds it prudent at times to engage in preemptive strikes and to adopt a threatening stance toward the outsiders. In this alternative account, then, patriarchal right emerges from male specialization in security. The patriarch's will rules because the patriarch faces the dangers outside and needs to organize defenses. Female subordination, in this account, derives from this position of being protected. As I will discuss in the next section, however, Hobbes does not think that it is a good idea to leave this armed power in the hands of individual male heads of household. Instead, the sovereign takes over this function.

Both Pateman's story of male domination and the one I have reconstructed depict patriarchal gender relations as upholding unequal power. It is important to attend to the difference, however, because in one relation the hierarchical power is obvious and in the other it is more masked by virtue and love. Michel Foucault (1988, 1994) argues that power conceived and enacted as repressive power, the desire and ability of an agent to force the other to obey his commands, has receded in importance in modern institutions. Other forms of power that enlist the desire of those over whom it is exercised better describe many power relations both historically and today. One such form of power Foucault calls pastoral power. This is the kind of power that the priest exercises over his parish and that, by extension, many experts in the care of individuals exercise over those cared for. This power often appears gentle and benevolent both to its wielders and to those under its sway, but it is no less powerful for that reason. Masculinist protection is more like pastoral power than dominative power that exploits those it rules for its own aggrandizement.

THE STATE AS PROTECTOR AND SUBORDINATE CITIZENSHIP

The gendered logic of masculinist protection has some relevance to individual family life even in modern urban America. Every time a father warns his daughter of the dangerous men he fears will exploit her and forbids her from "running around" the city, he inhabits the role of the male protector. Nevertheless, in everyday family life and other sites of interaction between men and women, the legitimation of female inequality and subordination by appeal to a need for protection has dwindled. My purpose in articulating a logic of masculinist protection is not to argue that it describes private life today but, rather, to argue that we learn something about public life—specifically, about the relation of a state to its citizens—when state officials successfully mobilize fear. States often justify their expectations of obedience and loyalty, as well as their establishment of surveillance, police, intimidation, detention, and the repression of criticism and dissent, by appeal to their role as protectors of citizens. I find in Hobbes a clever account of authoritarian rule grounded in the assumption of threat and fear as basic to the human condition, and thus a need for protection as the highest good.

Hobbes tells a story about why individuals and families find it necessary to constitute a sovereign, a single power to rule them all. In response to the constant fear under which they live, families may join confederations or protection associations. Such protection associations, however, no matter how large and powerful, do not reduce the reasons for fear and insecurity. As long as the possibility exists that others will form larger and stronger protective associations, the nasty state of war persists. As long as there is potential for competition among units, and those units hold the means to try to force their desires on one another, they must live in fear. Without submission to a common power to which they yield their separate forces, moreover, members of a protective association are liable to turn on one another during times when they need to rely on one another for protection from others (Hobbes 1994 [1668], chap. 17, 3, 4; cf. Nozick 1974, chap. 2). So Hobbes argues that only a Leviathan can assure safety and quell the fear and uncertainty that generate a spiral of danger. All the petty protectors in the state of nature give up their powers of aggression and defense, which they turn over to the sovereign. They make a covenant with one another to live in peace and constitute civil society under the common rule of an absolute authority who makes, interprets, and enforces the laws of the commonwealth for the sake of peace and security of subjects.

Readers of Hobbes sometimes find in the image of Leviathan a mean and selfish tyrant who sucks up the wealth and loyalty of subjects for his own aggrandizement. Democratic values and freedoms would be much easier to assert and preserve in modern politics if the face of authoritarianism were so ugly and easy to recognize. Like the benevolent patriarch, however, Leviathan often wears another aspect: that of the selfless and wise protector whose actions aim to foster and maintain security. What I call a security state is one whose rulers subordinate citizens to ad hoc surveillance, search, or detention and repress criticism of such arbitrary power, justifying such measures as within the prerogative of those authorities whose primary duty is to maintain security and protect the people.

The security state has an external and an internal aspect. It constitutes itself in relation to an enemy outside, an unpredictable aggressor against which the state needs vigilant defense. It organizes political and economic capacities around the accumulation of weapons and the mobilization of a military to respond to this outside threat. The state's identity is militaristic, and it engages in military action, but with the point of view of the defender rather than the aggressor. Even when the security regime makes a first strike, it justifies its move as necessary to preempt the threatening aggressor outside. Security states do not justify their wars by appealing to sentiments of greed or desire for conquest; they appeal to their role as protectors.

Internally, the security state must root out the enemy within. There is always the danger that among us are agents who have an interest in disturbing our peace, violating our persons and property, and allowing outsiders to invade our communities and institutions. To protect the state and its citizens, officials must therefore keep a careful watch on the people within its borders and observe and search them to make sure they do not intend evil actions and do not have the means to perform them. The security state overhears conversations to try to discover conspiracies of disaster and disruption, and it prevents people from forming crowds or walking the streets after dark. In a security state there cannot be separation of power or critical accountability of official action to a public. Nor can a security state allow expression of dissent.

Once again, Hobbes explains why not. It is necessary that the sovereign be one. The commonwealth can secure peace only if it unites the plurality of its members into one will. Even if the sovereign consists of an assembly of officials and not only one ruler, it must be united in will and purpose. It is the mutual covenant that each man makes to all the others to give over his right to govern his own affairs to the sovereign, on condition that all others do the same, that gives the sovereign both its power and unit of will (Hobbes 1994 [1668], chap. 17, 13). Sovereign authority, then, must be absolute, and it cannot be divided. The sovereign decides what is necessary to protect the commonwealth and its members. The sovereign decides what actions or opinions constitute a danger to peace and properly suppresses them. "The condition of man in this life shall never be without inconveniences; but there happeneth in no commonwealth any greater inconvenience, but what proceeds from the subject's disobedience and breach of these covenants from which the commonwealth hath its being, and whosoever, thinking sovereign power too great, will seek to make it less, must subject himself to the power that can limit it, that is to say, to a greater" (Hobbes 1994 [1668], chap. 20, 135).

Through the logic of protection the state demotes members of a democracy to dependents. State officials adopt the stance of masculine protector, telling us to entrust our lives to them, not to question their decisions about what will keep us safe. Their protector position puts the citizens and residents who depend on state officials' strength and vigilance in the position of women and children under the charge of the male protector (cf. Berlant 1997). Most regimes that suspend certain rights and legal procedures declare a state of emergency. They claim that special measures of unity and obedience are required to ensure protection from unusual danger. Because they take the risks and organize the agency of the state, it is their prerogative to determine the objectives of protective action and their means. In a security state there is no room for separate and shared powers or for questioning and criticizing the protector's decisions and orders. Good citizenship in a security regime consists of cooperative obedience for the sake of the safety of all.

The authoritarian security paradigm, I have argued, takes a form analogous to that of the masculine protector toward his wife and the other members of his patriarchal household. In this structure, I have suggested, masculine superiority flows not from acts of repressive domination but from the willingness to risk and sacrifice for the sake of the others (Elshtain 1987, 1991). For her part, the subordinate female in this structure neither resents nor resists the man's dominance. Rather, she admires it and is grateful for its promise of protection.

Patriotism has an analogous emotive function in the constitution of the security state. Under threat from outside, all of us, authorities and citizens, imagine ourselves a single body enclosed on and loving itself. We affirm our oneness with our fellow citizens and together affirm our single will behind the will of the leaders who have vowed to protect us. It is not merely that dissent is dangerous; worse yet, it is ungrateful. Subordinate citizenship does not merely acquiesce to limitations on freedom in exchange for a promise of security; the consent is active, as solidarity with the others uniting behind and in grateful love of country.

THE UNITED STATES AS A SECURITY STATE

A security state is what every state would have to be if Hobbes were right that human relations are always on the verge of disorder and violence, if only an authoritarian government that brooks no division of power or dissent can keep the peace, and if maintaining peace and security is unambiguously the highest value. Democratic theory and practice, however, question each of these Hobbesian assumptions. Democrats agree that a major purpose of government is to keep peace and promote public safety, but we deny that unquestioning obedience to a unified sovereign is the only means to achieve this, and we question whether values of freedom and autonomy must be traded against the value of security. In a non-ideal world of would-be aggressors and states that have imperfect procedural justice, transparency, accountability, and lax rights enforcement, every state exhibits features of a security state to some extent. It seems to me, however, that, since September 11, the United States has slipped too far down the authoritarian continuum. The logic of masculinist protection, I suggest, provides a framework for understanding how government leaders who expand arbitrary power and restrict democratic freedom believe that they are doing the right thing and why citizens accept their actions. It also helps explain this state's righteous rationale for aggressive war.

A marauding gang of outsiders attacked buildings in New York and Washington with living bombs, killing thousands in barely an instant and terrifying large numbers of people in the country. Our government responded with a security alert, at home and abroad. Many were frightened, and the heads of state stepped up to offer us protection. Less than a week after the attacks, the Bush administration announced the creation of an Office of Homeland Security to centralize its protection efforts. "Our nation has been put on notice: We are not immune from attack. We will take defensive measures against terrorism to protect Americans" (quoted in Roth 2001).

The events of September 11 are certainly a turning point for U.S. politics, for the relation of the government to its citizens and to the rest of the world. Americans learned that "oceans no longer matter when it comes to making us safe" (Bush 2002c), that we are just as vulnerable as people elsewhere who have long lived with the awareness that some people have the motive and means to kill and wound randomly. More than a year later, it appeared that little had changed, either in the fear that some Americans said they have of another attack or in the material ability of law enforcement to predict or prevent one (Firestone 2002). Much has changed in the letter and application of the law in the United States, however, and in the environment of democracy. The Bush administration has repeatedly appealed to the primacy of its role as protector of innocent citizens and liberator of women and children to justify consolidating and centralizing executive power at home and dominative war abroad.

It is arguable that, before September 11, airports and other public places in the United States were too lax in their security screening protocol. I welcome more thorough security procedures; this essay is not an argument against public officials' taking measures to try to keep people safe. The key questions are: how much power should officials have, how much freedom should citizens have, how fair are the procedures, how well do they follow due process, and how easily can citizens review official policies and actions to hold them accountable? With respect to these questions, there have been very large and damaging changes in the United States since fall 2001, although a direction toward some of them had been enacted by legislation and judicial action in the years before.

The U.S. security state has expanded the prerogative of the executive and eroded the power of the legislative and judicial branches to review executive decisions or to be independent sources of decision making. In the week after the September 11 attacks, for example, Congress passed a resolution effectively waiving its constitutionally mandated power to deliberate and decide on whether the state shall go to war. Months later, again with virtually no debate, Congress approved the largest increase in the military budget in twenty years. Since the war on terrorism has no declared ending, the executive may have been granted permanent legal discretion to do what it wants with U.S. military personnel and equipment at current taxpayer expense of over $400 billion per year.

Drafted quickly and passed with almost no debate, the USA PATRIOT Act (which stands for "Uniting and Strengthening America by Providing Appropriate Tools Required to Intercept and Obstruct Terrorism Act of 2001"), signed on October 26, 2001, severely reduces the power of courts to review and limit executive actions to keep organizations under surveillance, limit their activities, and search and seize or detain individuals. Under its provisions, individuals and organizations have had their records investigated, their assets seized, and their activities and correspondence monitored. Citizens' access to government files and records, which took so much struggle to achieve in the 1970s, has been severely reduced, with no fanfare and thus no protest (Rosen 2002).[1] Thousands of people have been detained, interrogated, or jailed at the discretion of law-enforcement or immigration officials, and hundreds remain in jails without being charged with any crime. Few have been allowed access to lawyers. Many foreign residents have been deported or threatened with deportation, sometimes without time to arrange their lives. Laws with similar purposes have been passed in other supposedly liberal democratic states, such as the United Kingdom and Australia.

The U.S. executive branch has taken other steps to enlarge and centralize its power and to put itself above the law. In November 2002, Congress approved the creation of the Department of Homeland Security, which merges twenty-two existing federal agencies. The Bush administration has flouted principles of a rule of law at the international level by holding captured citizens of many countries prisoner and declaring its prerogative to bring any or all of them before secret tribunals.

These and other legal and policy changes have far-reaching implications. The most ordinary and fundamental expectations of due process are undermined when search and surveillance do not require court approval, when people can be jailed without charge, and when there is no regularity or predictability to the process that a person in custody will undergo. The basic American principle of the separation of power has been suspended, with no reversal in sight. Legislatures and judiciaries at federal and more local levels have been stripped of some formal powers and (especially in the years immediately following September 11) declined to use much of what they had left to question, criticize, or block executive action. Most citizens apparently registered approval for the increased policing and warmaking powers, and the ability of those who did not to organize, criticize publicly, and protest in public streets and squares was seriously curtailed, not only by fear of peer and employer disapproval but also directly by official repression and intimidation.

How can citizens and their representatives in a democracy allow such rapid challenge to their political principles and institutions with so little discussion and protest? The process of limiting civil liberties, due process, and deliberation about war has itself been deeply undemocratic, a bold assertion of dictatorial power. One part of the answer lies in a conviction that most people hold that their own rights and freedoms will not be threatened. Aliens will be subjected to surveillance and deportation, and these enemies who have infiltrated deserve to be routed out by any means, and we can leave it to the discretion of police officers, immigration officials, and military personnel to determine who they are. Many of those whose records have been seized or who have been detained without charge are U.S. citizens, however, and the new legislation and guidelines do not make any citizen immune. Well, then, many of us tell ourselves, the ones whose privacy is invaded or freedoms limited by government action must be doing something wrong and deserve what they get. Since I am not doing anything wrong, I am protected. The move from a relatively free society to one over which the state exercises authoritarian domination often occurs by means of just this logic: citizens do not realize how easily they may find themselves under suspicion by authorities over whose decisions there is no public scrutiny. The principle of trial by a jury of peers in which the accused is presumed innocent is an important protection any person has from false charge and arbitrary power. The slippery slope from the fearsome outsiders, to the aliens within, to the bad fellow citizens is likely to end at my brother's front door.

The deeper explanation for why people who live in what promotes itself as one of the most enlightened democracies in history so easily allow, and even support, the erosion of basic rights lies in the mobilization of fear. John Keane (2002) challenges the opinion that democracies privatize fear. On the contrary, he claims, contemporary commercial communications media in democratic societies often exploit and incite fear. Although freedom of speech and press make possible such public accumulation of fear, the process threatens to shut down civic freedom. "Fear is indeed a thief. It robs subjects of their capacity to act with or against others. It leaves them shaken, sometimes permanently traumatized. And when large numbers fall under the dark clouds of fear, no sun shines on civil society. Fear saps its energies and tears and twists at the institutions of political representation. Fear eats the soul of democracy" (Keane 2002, 235).

Public leaders invoke fear, then they promise to keep those living under them safe. Because we are afraid, and our fears are stirred by what we see on television or read in the newspaper, we are grateful to the leaders and officers who say that they will shoulder the risk to protect us. The logic of masculinist protection works to elevate the protector to a position of superior authority and to demote the rest of us to a position of grateful dependence. Ideals of democratic equality and accountability go by the wayside in the process. Although some researchers claim to have noticed a shift in the acceptability of women occupying positions of authority since fall 2001 (O'Connor 2002), in the contemporary United States the position of protector and the position of those protected does not correspond to that of men and women. A few of the most security-minded leaders are women, and many of those who accept the promise of protection are men. What matters, I believe, is the gendered meaning of the positions and the association of familial caring they carry for people. It also matters that this relationship carries an implicit deal: forgo freedom, due process, and the right to hold leaders accountable, and in return we will make sure that you are safe.

IS IT A GOOD DEAL?

I discussed earlier how the logic of masculinist protection constitutes the "good" men who protect their women and children by relation to other "bad" men liable to attack. In this logic, virtuous masculinity depends on its constitutive relation to the presumption of evil others. Feminists have much analyzed a correlate dichotomy between the "good" woman and the "bad" woman. Simply put, a "good" woman stands under the male protection of a father or husband, submits to his judgment about what is necessary for her protection, and remains loyal to him. A "bad" woman is one who is unlucky enough not to have a man willing to protect her or who refuses such protection by claiming the right to run her own life. In either case, the woman without a male protector is fair game for any man to dominate. There is a bargain implicit in the masculinist protector role: either submit to my governance or all the bad men out there are liable to approach you, and I will not try to stop them.

I have argued so far that the position of citizens and residents under a security state entails a similar bargain. There are bad people out there who might want to attack us. The state pledges to protect us but tells us that we should submit to its rule and decisions without questioning, criticizing, or demanding independent review of the decisions. Some of the measures in place to protect us entail limitation of our freedom and, especially, limitation of the freedom of particular classes of people. The deal is this: you must trade some liberty and autonomy for the sake of the protection we offer. Is it a good deal?

Some years ago, Susan Rae Peterson likened the state's relation to women under a system of male domination to a protection racket. The gangland crowd offers protection from other gangs to individuals, their families, and businesses, for a fee. If some people decline their services, the gangsters teach them a brutal lesson and, by example, teach a lesson to others who might wish to go their own way. Thus, those who wish to break free of the racketeer's protection discover that they are most in danger from him. Insofar as state laws and policies assume or reinforce the view that a "good" woman should move under the guidance of a man, Peterson argued, the state functions as a protection racket. It threatens or allows men to threaten those women who wish to be independent of the individualized protection of husbands or boyfriends. Not only do the protectors withhold protection from the women who claim autonomy, but they may become attackers (Peterson 1977; cf. Card 1996).

The security state functions as a similar protection racket for those who live under it. As long as we accept the state's protection and pay the price it exacts not only in taxpayer dollars but also in reduction of our freedom and submission to possible surveillance, we are relatively safe. If we try to decline these services and seek freedom from the position of dependence and obedience in which they put us, we become suspect and thereby threatened by the very organization that claims to protect us.

Current forms of "homeland security" in the United States look like a protection racket. As long as we are quiet and obedient, we can breathe easy. If we should step out of the bounds of "good" citizens, however, we may find ourselves unprotected and even under attack by the protector state. If we publicly criticize the state's policies, especially the war or foreign policy, we may land on lists of unpatriotic people published to invite our neighbors or employers to sanction us. We may find that we are no longer allowed to assemble in some public places, even when we wish to demonstrate about issues other than war and the security regime, and that we are subject to arrest if we try. When we are able peaceably to protest, government officials nevertheless threaten us with horses and tear-gas canisters and cameras taking our pictures. Organizations we support may appear on lists of terrorist organizations at the discretion of bureaucrats, and we will not even know that they are monitoring our e-mail or tapping our phones.

Some citizens become defined as not good citizens simply because of their race or national origin. Although public opinion only recently claimed to disapprove of policy and security practices that use racial or ethnic profiling, many now accept the state's claim that effective protection requires such profiling. Residents who are not citizens, especially those from places defined as sources of danger, lose most of the protection they may have had from attack by neighbors or arbitrary and punitive treatment by state agents.

The United States is by no means unique in enacting such measures and justifying them by appeal to protective emergency, nor is this the first time in the past century when such logic has been apparent. This is not the first time, either, that citizens have applauded the threatening and surveillance activities of the security regime because they are anxious for protection and believe that such measures will only apply to others—the terrorists, the foreigners, and the disloyal citizens—and not to themselves. We endanger democratic practice, however, when we consent to this bargain. When we fail to question a legal distinction between the good citizen and the bad citizen that affords less legal protection to the latter, and when we allow the rhetoric of fear to label any foreigners enemies within, increasing numbers of us are liable to find that our attributes or activities put us on the wrong side of the line. If we allow our fear to cow us into submission, we assume the position of subordinates rather than democratic citizens equal to and not above our neighbors, equal to and not beneath our government.

There is little evidence that the way the United States has chosen to conduct its war on terrorism has in fact made us or others in the world any safer. Indeed, it may have put Americans at even greater risk. When U.S. planes began bombing Afghanistan in October 2001, officials publicly admitted that the action put Americans inside and outside the country at greater risk from retaliating attackers. It is plausible to suggest that the stances of increased belligerence between India and Pakistan that emerged in summer 2002 resulted in part from U.S. military actions, and it seems that the government of Israel was emboldened by the U.S. example to conduct its own brutal war on terrorism. The Bush administration has buried the Cold War doctrine of deterrence and announced its willingness to make preemptive strikes against what it decides are terrorist threats. The United States waged a war against Iraq that has made the region more disorderly. Even before the war, many Americans believed that the likelihood of terrorist attacks against Americans would increase if the United States went to war against Iraq (Longworth 2002). The claimed desire to protect by means of guns generates a spiral of danger and uncertainty (cf. Tickner 1992, 51–53).

The logic of masculinist protection positions leaders, along with some other officials such as soldiers and firefighters, as protectors and the rest of us in the subordinate position of dependent protected people. Justifications for the suspension of due process or partial abrogation of privacy rights and civil liberties, as well as condemnation of dissent, rest on an implicit deal: that these are necessary tradeoffs for effective protection. The legitimacy of this deal is questionable, however, not only because it may not be effective in protecting us, but also because it cheapens and endangers democracy. Subordinate citizenship is not compatible with democracy. The relation of leaders to citizens under democratic norms ought to be one of equality, not in the sense of equal power, but in the sense that citizens have an equal right and responsibility with leaders to make policy judgments, and thus that leaders entrusted with special powers should be held accountable to citizens. Institutions of due process, public procedure and record, organized opposition and criticism, and public review both enact and recognize such equal citizenship. Trading them for protection puts us at the mercy of the protectors.

WAR AND FEMINISM

The logic of masculinist protection, I have argued, helps account for the rationale leaders give for deepening a security state and its acceptance by those living under their rule. There are two faces to the security state: one facing outward to defend against enemies, and the other facing inward to keep those under protection under necessary control. So far I have concentrated on describing legislative and executive actions of the U.S. government in terms of the inward-looking face. Now I shall turn to the outward-looking face, the United States as war maker.

In fall 2001, the United States led a bombing campaign against Afghanistan. Even though that state had not taken aggressive action against the United States, the United States justified the war as a defensive reaction to the attacks of September 11. Perhaps because the claim that the state of Afghanistan actively supported al-Qaeda was weak, the United States quickly repackaged the war as a case of humanitarian intervention to liberate the Afghan people. The logic of masculinist protection appears in the claimed relationship of the United States to people outside the West, particularly in Islamic countries, ruled by brutal dictatorships. The United States will fight and sacrifice to save them. The Bush administration used the same discourse to justify war against Iraq. The United States defends not only itself in this scenario, but all the world's freedom for which the weapons Iraq might have are a threat. By saving ourselves we also save the Iraqi people from domination. So the United States is the protector of the world. Through this logic, the American people and others who choose to identify with the actions of the United States can put themselves into the role of the protector, even as the state restricts our freedom for our own good.

Packaging the war against Afghanistan as a humanitarian war to protect the Afghan people from domination was particularly effective because the Bush administration and journalists focused on women (cf. Tickner 2002). The women of Afghanistan constituted the ultimate victims, putting the United States in the position of ultimate protector. Use of the rhetoric of women's rights by the Bush administration during and after the war against Afghanistan should make feminists very uncomfortable. I wonder whether some seeds for such cynical appeals to the need to save women might not have been sown by some recent discourse and practice that positioned North American and European feminists as protectors of oppressed women in Asia and Africa.

On November 17, 2001, Laura Bush became the first wife to give the president's Saturday morning radio address, which was devoted to condemning what she called the Taliban's war on women and justifying the U.S. war as an effort to free Afghan women (Stout 2001). After the overthrow of the Taliban regime, the Bush administration repeatedly invoked women's liberation to justify the war. In his 2002 State of the Union address, for example, George W. Bush said, "The last time we met in this chamber, the mothers and daughters of Afghanistan were captives in their own homes, forbidden from working or going to school. Today women are free, and are part of Afghanistan's new government" (Bush 2002b). On International Women's Day, Laura Bush spoke to the U.N. Commission on the Status of Women, linking the terrorist attacks with the oppression of women and thus, by implication, the war on terrorism with the liberation of women:

> The terrorist attacks of September 11 galvanized the international community. Many of us have drawn valuable lessons from the tragedies. People around the world are looking closely at the roles women play in their societies. Afghanistan under the Taliban gave the world a sobering example of a country where women were denied their rights and their place in society. Today, the world is helping Afghan women return to the lives they once knew. Women were once important contributors to Afghan society, and they had the right to vote as early as the 1920s. . . . This is a time of rebuilding—of unprecedented opportunity—thanks to efforts led by the United Nations, the United States, the new Afghan government, and our allies around the world (Bush 2002).

Years before the attacks of September 2001, U.S. feminists mounted a campaign directed at saving the women of Afghanistan from the Taliban. Although they lobbied the Clinton administration to put pressure on the Taliban government regarding women's rights, neither Clinton nor Bush evinced any concern for the situation of women under the Taliban before the war. Appeal to women's rights was thus a cynical attempt to gain support for the war among the citizens of the United States and other liberal countries. Some feminists jumped onto the war bandwagon. Shortly after the war began, for example, Eleanor Smeal, leader of the Feminist Majority, chatted cordially with U.S. generals. " 'They went off about the role of women in this effort and how imperative it was that women were now in every level of the Air Force and Navy,' said Smeal, who found herself cheered by the idea of women flying F16s. 'It's a different kind of war' she says, echoing the President's assessment of Operation Enduring Freedom" (quoted in Lerner 2001).

Certainly, the Taliban should have been condemned for its policies, as should all the world's governments that perpetrate or allow systematic and discriminatory harms to and subordination of women. The Taliban stood with only a few other governments in the world in the degree of legally enforced restriction of women's freedom and horrible punishments. Even before the war, however, it seemed to me—and still seems to me—that feminists' focus on women under the Taliban constructed these women as exoticized others and paradigmatic victims in need of salvation by Western feminists, and it conveniently deflected attention from perhaps more intractable and mundane problems of gender-based violence, domination, and poverty in many other parts of the world, including the enlightened West. What is wrong with this stance, if it has existed, is that it fails to consider the women as equals, and it does not have principled ways of distancing itself from paternalist militarism.

The stance of the male protector, I have argued, is one of loving self-sacrifice, with those in the feminine position as the objects of love and guardianship. Chivalrous forms of masculinism express and enact concern for the well-being of women, but they do so within a structure of superiority and subordination. The male protector confronts evil aggressors in the name of the right and the good, while those under his protection submit to his order and serve as handmaids to his efforts. Colonialist ideologies have often expressed a similar logic. The knights of civilization aim to bring enlightened understanding to the farther regions of the world still living in cruel and irrational traditions that keep them from developing the economic and political structures that will bring them a good life. The suppression of women in these societies is a symptom of such backwardness. Troops will be needed to bring order and guard fledgling institutions, and foreign-aid workers will be needed to feed, cure, and educate, but all this is only a period of tutelage that will end when the subject people demonstrate their ability to gain their own livelihood and run their own affairs. Many people living in Asian, African, and Latin American societies believe that not only U.S. military hegemony but also international trade and financial institutions, as well as many Western-based nongovernmental development agencies, position them in this way as feminized or infantilized women and children under the protection and guidance of the wise and active father.

In its rhetoric and practice, according to some scholars, the British feminist movement of the late nineteenth century and early twentieth century aligned itself with the universal humanitarian civilizing mission invoked as the justification for the British empire. Feminists endorsed male imperial leaders' assessment of the status of women in other nations as a measure of their level of moral development. Such interest in the status of women was useful to feminists in pointing out the hypocrisy of denying women's rights in the center as one fought for them in the periphery. Providing services for Indian women and other oppressed women in the empire also offered opportunities for the employment of middle-class professional women (Burton 1994).

Some contemporary feminists have worried that Western feminism today has had some tendency to express and act in similar ways in relation to non-Western women. In a well-known essay, Chandra Mohanty, for example, claims that Western feminists too often use an objectified general category of third-world women, who are represented as passive and victimized by their unenlightened cultures and political regimes (Mohanty 1991). Uma Narayan claims that much feminist discussion of the situation of women in Asian and African societies, or women in Asian immigrant communities in Western societies, "replicates problematic aspects of Western representations of Third World nations and communities, aspects that have their roots in the history of colonization" (Narayan 1997, 43).

Assuming that these criticisms of some of the discourse, attitudes, and actions of Western feminists have some validity, the stance they identify helps account for the ease with which feminist rhetoric can be taken up by today's imperialist power and used for its own ends. It also helps account for the support of some feminists for the war against Afghanistan. Sometimes feminists may identify with the stance of the masculine protector in relation to vulnerable and victimized women. The protector–protected relation is no more egalitarian, however, when between women than between men and women.

According to some reports, the lives of women in Afghanistan have changed little since before the war, except that some of them have lost their homes, their relatives, and what little livelihood they had (Reilly 2002). The oppression of most of them remains embedded in social structure, custom, and a culture of warlord anarchism. I would not argue that humanitarian reasons can never justify going to war against a state. I think, however, that such protectionist grounds for military intervention must be limited to situations of genocide or impending genocide and where the war actually makes rescue possible (Young 2003a). Even if the U.S. government is sincere in its conviction that its military efforts are intended to save the world from evil, its political and military hegemony materially harms many poor and defenseless people of the world and positions most of the world in a position of subordination that nurtures resentment.

DEMOCRATIC GLOBAL CITIZENSHIP

The contemporary security state in the United States, like many security states, has two faces, one looking outward and the other inward. Each aspect reinforces the other. Both threaten democratic values in the institutions and practices of the United States, as well as globally. Citizens and residents who accept the security state because they fear attack allow themselves to be positioned as women and children in relation to paternal protector leaders. At the same time, to the extent that we identify with a rhetoric of war for the sake of saving the victims of tyranny, we put ourselves in a position superior to those we construct as in need of our aid. Whether looking outward or inward, adopting a more democratic ethos entails rejecting the inequality inherent in the protector–protected logic.

When leaders promulgate fear and promise to keep us safe, they conjure up childish fantasies and desires. We are vulnerable beings, and we want very much to be made safe by a being superior in power to all that might threaten us. Democratic citizens, however, should resist leaders' attempts to play father over us. We should insist that government do its job to promote security without issuing guarantees it cannot redeem or requiring subordination from the people it promises to protect.

Democratic citizenship should first involve admitting that no state can make any of us completely safe and that leaders who promise that are themselves suspect. The world is full of risks. Prudence dictates that we assess risks, get information about their sources, and try to minimize them, and we rightly expect our government to do much of this for us. In a democracy, citizens should not have to trade this public responsibility for submission to surveillance, arbitrary decisions, and the stifling of criticism.

In making this claim, I am extending recent feminist arguments against a model of citizenship that requires each citizen to be independent and self-sufficient in order to be equal and fully autonomous. Feminist theorists of care and welfare have argued that the rights and dignity of individuals should not be diminished just because they need help and support to carry out their chosen projects (Kittay 1999; Tronto 1993). People who need care or other forms of social support ought not to be forced into a position of subordination and obedience in relation to those who provide care and support; not only should they retain the rights of full citizens to choose their own way of life and hold authorities accountable, but they also ought to be able to criticize the way in which support comes to them (Hirschmann 2002, chap. 5; Sevenhuijsen 1998; Young 2003a). This feminist argument rejects the assumption behind a notion of self-sufficient citizenship that a need for social support or care is more exceptional than normal. On the contrary, the well-being of all people can be enhanced by the care and support of others, and in modern societies some of this generalized care and support ought to be organized and guaranteed through state institutions. The organization of reasonable measures to protect people from harm and to make people confident that they can move and act relatively safely is another form of social support. Citizens should not have to trade their liberty of movement or right to protest and hold leaders accountable in return for such security.

Democratic citizenship thus means ultimately rejecting the hierarchy of protector and protected. In the article I cited earlier, Stiehm (1982, 374) argues that rejection of this hierarchy implies installing a position of defender in place of both that of the protector and the protected. A society of defenders is "a society composed of citizens equally liable to experience violence and equally responsible for exercising society's violence." Modern democracies, including U.S. democracy, are founded partly on the principle that citizens should be able to defend themselves if they are also to defend the republic from tyranny. In the twenty-first century, in a world of organized and less organized military institutions and weapons capable of unimaginable destruction, it is hard to know what it might mean for world citizens to exercise collective self-defense. It certainly does not mean that every individual should amass his or her own weapons cache. Nor does it mean whole groups and nations engaging in arms races. The distinction between defender and protector invokes an ideal of equality in the work of defense, and today this may have at least as much to do with political processes that limit weapons and their use as with wielding arms.

The United States claims to use its arms to do this, much as a policeman does in domestic life. In a democratic relationship, however, the policeman protector comes under the collective authority of the people whose neighborhood he patrols. Democratic citizenship at a global level, then, would constitute a relationship of respect and political equality among the world's peoples where none of us think that we stand in the position of the paternal authority who knows what is good for the still developing others. To the extent that global law enforcement is necessary, it is only legitimate if the world's peoples together have formulated the rules and actions of such enforcement (cf. Archibugi and Young 2002).

NOTES

Earlier versions of this article were presented at conferences at Washington University in St. Louis and Lancaster University in England, and I have benefited from discussions on both occasions. I am grateful to David Alexander, Gopal Balakrishnan, Neta Crawford, Tom Dumm, Samantha Frost, Susan Gal, Sandra Harding, Anne Harrington, Aaron Hoffman, Jeffrey Isaac, Patchen Markell, John McCormick, Linda Nicholson, Sara Ruddick, Lora Viola, Laurel Weldon, Alexander Wendt, and an anonymous reviewer for Signs for comments on earlier versions. Thanks to Anne Harrington and Kathy McCabe for research assistance.

1. When the USA PATRIOT Act was considered for renewal in late 2005, it was subjected to protest and criticism. However, these were largely ineffectual, and the act was renewed in 2006 with only minor changes to protect individual rights.

wwwwwwwwwwwwwwwwwww
Timothy Kaufman-Osborn
wwwwwwwwwwwwwwwwwww

Gender Trouble at Abu Ghraib?

It's not a pretty picture," conceded Defense Secretary Donald Rumsfeld in assessing the photographs taken by U.S. military personnel at Baghdad's Abu Ghraib prison complex during the final three months of 2003 (Higham, White, and Davenport 2004, sec. A).[1] Shortly thereafter, en route to Iraq, Rumsfeld contended that "the real problem is not the photographs—the real problems are the actions taken to harm the detainees" (quoted in Brison 2004, 10). This claim is problematic insofar as it fails to appreciate the transformation of these images into so many free-floating weapons deployed to secure partisan advantage on various cultural and political battlegrounds within the United States. This was perhaps nowhere so evident as in their mobilization to rehash the struggle over the contemporary import of feminism, especially in light of the equality–difference debate that has vexed feminists and their opponents for decades. The initial purpose of this essay, accordingly, is to explain how the mass-media flap regarding the Abu Ghraib photographs indicates that gender, understood as a set of mobile disciplinary practices, can sometimes become unsettled, thereby provoking efforts to restabilize hetero-normative understandings of what it is to be masculine or feminine. Giving the defense secretary his due, however, I employ my discussion of the domestic reception of these photographs as a preface to asking how we might make better sense of the gendered import of the abuses committed at Abu Ghraib. To answer this question, in the second half of this essay, I argue that much of what appeared so shocking when these photographs were first released can be read as extensions of, but also threats to, the logic of masculinized militarism. The most convenient scapegoat for such "gender trouble," to appropriate the title of Judith Butler's best-known work (Butler 1990), is Lynndie England, a military file clerk who was captured by the camera's eye while restraining an Iraqi prisoner at the far end of a dog leash.

MISTAKING LYNNDIE ENGLAND

Like all photographic images, those taken at Abu Ghraib do not speak for themselves. Henry Giroux explains:

> Photographs such as those that revealed the horrors that took place at Abu Ghraib prison have no guaranteed meaning, but rather exist within a complex of shifting mediations that are material, historical, social, ideological, and psychological in nature. This is not to suggest that photographs do not capture some element of reality as much as to insist that what they capture can only be understood as part of a broader engagement over cultural politics and its intersection with various dynamics of power. . . . Representations privilege those who have some control over self-representation, and they are largely framed within dominant modes of intelligibility. (Giroux 2004, 8)

Giroux's point about the framing of photographic meaning in terms of "dominant modes of intelligibility" is well illustrated by the contest to determine what to make of the Abu Ghraib images that include Lynndie England. In addition to the now infamous dog leash photograph, another shows England standing next to a naked Hayder Sabbar Abd, a thirty-four-year-old Shiite taxi driver from Nasiriya, as a cigarette dangles from her lips, the thumb of her right hand gestures upward in triumph, and her left hand, with forefinger cocked, takes aim at Abd's genitalia as he is forced to simulate masturbation. Still another depicts England, arm-in-arm with Specialist Charles Graner, as both grin and offer a thumbs-up sign while perched behind a cluster of seven naked Iraqis piled awkwardly atop one another in a human pyramid.

The general tenor of the mainstream press's response to these photographs, which altogether displaced documented reports of the abuse of women prisoners at Abu Ghraib (Harding 2004), is indicated by the subtitle of an article written by *Newsweek*'s Evan Thomas (2004): "How did a wispy tomboy behave like a monster at Abu Ghraib?" It may well be, as Cynthia Enloe has suggested, that the media's horrified representation of England as a sub- or inhuman creature indicates America's visceral response to her violation of conventional norms regarding the conduct becoming to women (Enloe 2004b, 91), and, as M. S. Embser-Herbert (2004) has suggested, the fixation on these particular photographs may well indicate that Americans today are better prepared to see women come home from Iraq in body bags than to see them return as quasi-sexualized aggressors. There is some truth to both of these readings, and it is equally true that the media's preoccupation with the photographs portraying women involved in "abnormal" conduct facilitated the Bush administration's interest in representing what transpired at Abu Ghraib as the "disgraceful conduct by a few American troops who dishonored our country and disregarded our values" (Bush 2004c) and thus as an anomalous departure from established military doctrine. That noted, neither Enloe nor Embser-Herbert fully captures the ways in which these photographs were mobilized, especially during the months immediately following their release, in the service of larger domestic political and cultural agendas. This proved most strikingly so when the proponents of various right-wing agendas seized on Lynndie England to advance a reactionary backlash aimed at reversing whatever advances women have made in the military, under the banner of gender equality, since termination of the all-male draft in 1972.

Three examples, all published in May 2004, less than two weeks after the Abu Ghraib photographs initially aired on CBS's *Sixty Minutes II*, suffice to illustrate this appropriation. First, the president of the Center for Military Readiness, Elaine Donnelly, asserted that the photograph of England with leash in hand "is exactly what feminists have dreamed of for years." To explain, she represented England's conduct as an articulation of the dispositions displayed by those feminists "who like to buy man-hating greeting cards and have this kind of attitude that all men abused all women. It's a subculture of the feminist movement, but the driving force in it in many cases, certainly in academia" (quoted in Thibault 2004). On this basis, which figures feminists as so many would-be dominatrixes afflicted by a burning desire to transform men into obsequious lapdogs, Donnelly argued that the U.S. military should abandon its unofficial gender quotas aimed at enlisting more women and return to basic training segregated by sex. Arguing on behalf of the same counter-reforms, Peggy Noonan (2004), columnist and contributing editor of the *Wall Street Journal*, claimed that before basic training became co-educational, women "did not think they had to prove they were men, or men at their worst. I've never seen evidence to suggest the old-time WACs and WAVES had to delve down into some coarse and vulgar part of their nature to fit in, to show they were one of the guys, as tough as the guys, as ugly at their ugliest." In this reading, England is a young woman whose turn to the dark side can be explained by her desire to be embraced by her brutish counterparts, with the implication that she never would have acted as she did had she been excluded from their crass company. Finally, in a screwy twist on much the same narrative, the president of the Center for Equal Opportunity, Linda Chavez, suggested that England's participation in the abuse at Abu Ghraib can be explained by the mounting "sexual tension" that has accompanied "the new sex-integrated military." Because that stress produces hormone-crazed soldiers, which in turn undermines "discipline and unit cohesion" (Chavez 2004), we should not be unduly surprised when those in uniform occasionally release their pent-up passions by sexually abusing their captives.

What Donnelly, Noonan, and Chavez share is the conviction, expressly articulated by George Neumayr (2004), columnist for the *American Spectator*, that the conduct of Lynndie England "is a cultural outgrowth of a feminist culture which encourages female barbarians." Their concern that women are "losing their femininity" requires that an unambiguous masculine identity be refortified and that it be sharply distinguished from the equally unambiguous gender identity of women (e.g., by reconfining GI Janes to suitably ladylike roles on the sidelines of the military in accordance with their customary roles as civilizers of beastly men). Such claims presuppose an uncritical conception of gender—one that includes a dyadic conception of sexual identity, the naturalness (as well as the apparent irresistibility) of heterosexual desire, and stereotypical, if not essentialized, conceptions of masculine and feminine conduct. Lest there be any doubt on this latter score, also in May 2004, the president of the Eagle Forum, Phyllis

Schlafly, asserted that "the picture of the woman soldier with a noose around the Iraqi man's neck" demonstrates "that some women have become mighty mean, but feminists can't erase eternal differences" (Schlafly 2004).[2]

Unhappily, many readings of the Abu Ghraib affair advanced by mainstream liberal feminists have swallowed the bait proffered by the right wing. Embracing the construction of these photographs as a referendum on feminism and its commitment to the equality of women, these readings have demonstrated the stubborn persistence of conceptions of gender that, though not wedded to the reactionary political agendas advanced by Schlafly and her ilk, are nonetheless quite problematic. This sort of appropriation is best illustrated by Barbara Ehrenreich, whose 2004 commencement address at Barnard College, following its publication in the *Los Angeles Times*, became a subject of widespread discussion, especially on the Internet.

"As a feminist," Ehrenreich began, the Abu Ghraib photographs "broke my heart. I had no illusions about the U.S. mission in Iraq—whatever exactly it is—but it turns out that I did have some illusions about women." These illusions were based on the belief that women are "morally superior to men," whether because of "biology" or "conditioning" or "simply the experience of being a woman in a sexist culture," and it was on this basis that Ehrenreich "secretly" entertained the "hope that the presence of women would over time change the military, making it more respectful of other people and cultures, more capable of genuine peacekeeping." It is these illusions that were shattered when Ehrenreich first saw the image of Lynndie England, her Iraqi prisoner in tow: "a certain kind of feminism, or perhaps I should say a certain kind of feminist naivete, died in Abu Ghraib. It was a feminism that saw men as the perpetual perpetrators, women as the perpetual victims, and male sexual violence against women as the root of all injustice." But now, having witnessed "female sexual sadism in action," Ehrenreich rejects as "lazy and self indulgent" any form of feminism that is "based on an assumption of female moral superiority." "A uterus," in sum, "is not a substitute for a conscience" (Ehrenreich 2004a).

In retrospect, Ehrenreich confesses, she should not have been so shocked to learn that "women can do the unthinkable," for, unlike her right-wing opponents, "she never believed that women were innately gentler and less aggressive than men." But the very fact that she was so shocked by England's conduct, as well as the fact that this response was situated at the far edge of comprehensibility ("the unthinkable"), indicates the deep-seated tenacity with which, too often, we cling to a vision of the world that neatly distinguishes between powerful men and powerless women, between those who are guilty of acts of sexual violence and those who are their victims. This vision of the world presupposes the self-evident intelligibility of the category of "women," as well as their fundamental differences from the equally self-evident category of "men," and it presupposes problematic stereotypes about women, including, in Ehrenreich's case, the belief that because they "do most of the caring work in our culture," they are less inclined "toward cruelty and violence" (Ehrenreich 2004a). As such, and despite their very different political agendas, there are unsettling points of convergence between the conception of gender that Ehrenreich embraced before Abu Ghraib and the conception that Schlafly and her cohorts continue to promote after Abu Ghraib.

Ehrenreich is to be commended for the intellectual honesty that prompted her to question this conception of gender (although she does not advance any more adequate alternative). It remains true, however, that she accepts her opponents' construction of the Lynndie England affair as a referendum on feminism and its quest for gender equality. That, though, is a misguided enterprise. It is problematic when the revulsion provoked by these photographs is predicated on retrograde gender representations, and it is pernicious when it animates an antifeminist backlash that seeks to resituate women in a world where they are compelled to live out those odious stereotypes. Moreover, this construction encourages sterile repetition of unproductive and arguably unanswerable questions (e.g., are women really different from men?), and it plays into the hands of feminism's detractors by inviting them to assert that the ultimate import of the quest for gender equality is revealed in the conduct of Lynndie England. This is to suggest not that we discard the category of gender in thinking about what happened at Abu Ghraib but, rather, that we turn away from the conception that is presupposed whenever someone asks, "How could women do that?" (Hong 2004). Instead, I would urge that we think of gender as something constructed through engagement in a complex set of performative practices, including the abusive techniques deployed at Abu

Ghraib, and that we ask how those practices en-gender persons in ways that are not readily reducible to what Ehrenreich or her adversaries mean when they uncritically speak of "women" and "men."

TECHNOLOGIES OF EMASCULATION AT ABU GHRAIB

The official investigative reports issued in the wake of Abu Ghraib do not themselves offer a more nuanced account of its gendered import. Read in light of a more adequate understanding of gender, however, they provide clues toward such an account. The principal documents include the Taguba and Fay-Jones reports, both of which were commissioned by Lieutenant General Ricardo Sanchez, commander of Coalition Ground Forces in Iraq; the Mikolashek report, conducted by the Army's inspector general; and the Schlesinger report, issued by an independent panel chartered by the secretary of defense. Though conceding certain failures of leadership in higher (but not too high) ranks, all explain what happened at Abu Ghraib in terms of the pathological or criminal conduct of a handful of rogue soldiers.[3] The Schlesinger report, for example, concludes, "The events of October through December 2003 on the night shift of Tier 1 at Abu Ghraib prison were acts of brutality and purposeless sadism" (quoted in Greenberg and Dratel 2005, 909). In much the same vein, according to the "psychological assessment" appended to the Taguba report, the events at Abu Ghraib were the work of "immoral men and women" who engaged in "sadistic and psychopathic behavior," including "abuse with sexual themes" (quoted in Greenberg and Dratel 2005, 448–49). Finally, the Fay-Jones report determines that "the primary cause of the most egregious violent and sexual abuses was the individual criminal propensities of the particular perpetrators" (quoted in Greenberg and Dratel 2005, 1007).

These readings will not do. They decontextualize these deeds, rendering them so many transgressions enacted by a few unruly anomalies. Once Abu Ghraib is defined in these disingenuous terms, these soldiers, including Lynndie England, can all too easily be assigned the role of patsies whose service to the military now includes distracting attention from the institutional forces that breed and sanction such exploitation. These readings also will not do because they occlude the ways in which gender is in fact constitutive of what happened at Abu Ghraib. The representation of these events as "sexual abuse" does not adequately specify the particular form of degradation involved here. That degradation is trivialized when James Schlesinger, former secretary of defense and lead author of the report bearing his name, refers to Abu Ghraib as "Animal House on the night shift" (CNN 2004b). To compare what happened on Tier 1 to so much reprehensible behavior on the part of intoxicated undergraduates at a fraternity bash is to confound the distinction between sexual abuse, on the one hand, and acts of imperialist and racist violence that mimic sexual exploitation, on the other. It is, moreover, to fail to ask *why* so much of the abuse meted out at Abu Ghraib, as the reports make abundantly clear, trafficked in gendered stereotypes, as well as what that might teach us about how gender operates as a complex vector of power within the context of masculinized militarism.

The acts of principal concern to me in this section are a subset of the larger group that exhibited sexualized dimensions. Although the distinction is admittedly problematic, I will primarily confine my attention to those that traded on misogynistic understandings, as opposed to those that were patently homophobic as well as arguably homoerotic (e.g., forcing prisoners to masturbate while being photographed; compelling prisoners to engage in simulated fellatio; and sodomizing a prisoner with a phosphorous light stick; see Puar 2004). My chief concern is with incidents such as the following: compelling otherwise naked men to wear women's underwear, often red and often on their heads; having a servicewoman apply red ink to the face of a prisoner after she had placed her hand in her unbuttoned pants and informed him that she was menstruating; forcing men to remove their clothing and then stand before female service personnel; and, lest we forget Lynndie England, placing a leash around a naked prisoner's neck while posing with him for a snapshot.[4]

How are we to make sense of these incidents? Loosely following the lead of Judith Butler (1990, 1993),[5] I propose that we think not about men and women in the unreflective sense in which all of the authors discussed in the previous section employ these terms but, rather, about complex disciplinary practices that en-gender bodies by regulating, constraining, and constituting their conduct in ways that prove intelligible in light of the never entirely stable or coherent categories of masculine and feminine. "Men" and "women," in other words, are constantly being gendered as they participate in practices mandated by cultural norms of masculinity and femininity, which are themselves contingently related to anatomical equipment. "When the constructed status of gender is theorized as radically independent of sex," Butler argues, "gender itself becomes a free-floating artifice, with the consequence that *man* and *masculine* might just as easily signify a female body as a male one, and *woman* and *feminine* a male body as easily as a female one" (Butler 1990, 6). If this is so, then what we should be exploring at Abu Ghraib is the differential production of masculinity and femininity, as well as the ways in which specific performances sometimes unsettle foundational illusions about the dependence of gender on sex. This redirection of inquiry suggests that much, but certainly not all, of what happened at Abu Ghraib can be understood in terms of what I will call the "logic of emasculation," where the aim of disciplinary techniques is to strip prisoners of their masculine gender identity and turn them into caricatures of terrified and often infantilized femininity. What this implies for our reading of Lynndie England is the question taken up in this essay's conclusion.

In applying this performative account of gender to Abu Ghraib, it is useful to begin by doing precisely what the Fay-Jones report, which insists that "no policy, directive or doctrine directly or indirectly caused violent or sexual abuse" (quoted in Greenberg and Dratel 2005, 989), discourages us from doing: to relate the exploitation at Abu Ghraib to the U.S. military's approved techniques regarding the treatment of those detained during combat. For present purposes, the directive of principal concern is *Army Field Manual 34–52* (U.S. Department of the Army 1992), which officially governed the treatment of those imprisoned at Abu Ghraib.[6] It is my contention that many of the practices commended in this manual, whether employed in the context of formal interrogations or in conjunction with efforts to "soften up" prisoners as a preface to such interrogations,[7] trade on specific conceptions of masculinity and femininity. One of the principal virtues of the Abu Ghraib photographs is the way they render visible this implicit content.

"Unless this publication states otherwise," *Field Manual 34–52* affirms, "masculine nouns or pronouns do not refer exclusively to men" (U.S. Department of the Army 1992, v). Because *Field Manual 34–52* is formally neutral, revelation of its gendered content must be a matter of plausible inference. An intimation of that content is provided by the Central Intelligence Agency's 1963 manual titled *Counterintelligence Interrogation*, which, according to a correspondent for the *Atlantic Monthly*, "remains the most comprehensive and detailed explanation in print of coercive methods of questioning" (Bowden 2003, 57–58). Unearthed in 1997 via a Freedom of Information Act request, what came to be known as the KUBARK manual is refreshingly candid in specifying the summum bonum of disciplinary techniques applied to the incarcerated:

> It is a fundamental hypothesis of this handbook that these techniques . . . are in essence methods of inducing regression of the personality to whatever earlier and weaker level is required for the dissolution of resistance and the inculcation of dependence. . . . [T]he circumstances of detention are arranged to enhance within the subject his feelings of being cut off from the known and the reassuring, and of being plunged into the strange. . . . Control of the source's environment permits the interrogator to determine his diet, sleep pattern and other fundamentals. Manipulating these into irregularities, so that the subject becomes disorientated, is very likely to create feelings of fear and helplessness. (Central Intelligence Agency 1963, 41, 86–87)[8]

A 1983 revision of KUBARK, titled *Human Resource Exploitation Training Manual*, goes on to state:

> Throughout his detention, subject must be convinced that his "questioner" controls his ultimate destiny, and that his absolute cooperation is essential to survival. . . . This can be achieved by radically disrupting the familiar emotional and psychological associations of the subject. Once this disruption is achieved, the subject's resistance is seriously impaired. He experiences a kind of psychological shock, which may only last briefly, but during which he is far more open and far likelier to comply. . . . Frequently the subject will experience a feeling of guilt. If the "questioner" can intensify these guilt feelings, it will increase the subject's anxiety and his urge to cooperate as a means of escape. (Central Intelligence Agency 1983, F20, K–1, c–e)

For those familiar with feminist literature on battered women, it is difficult to read these passages without recalling accounts of abusive relationships in which men seek to secure the wholesale subordination of women by isolating and terrifying them either through violence or threats of violence. Such compliance is best secured when a woman, consumed by fear, determines that her situation is helpless and, still more perfectly, when she concludes that she is ultimately culpable and thus guilty for the abuse to which she is subjected. In this light, consider the claim, advanced in KUBARK, that well-designed interrogation techniques strip those undergoing questioning of all vestiges of autonomy, thereby transforming them into creatures who are "helplessly dependent on their captors for the satisfaction of their many basic needs, and experience the emotional and motivational reactions of intense fear and anxiety" (Central Intelligence Agency 1963, 83–84). If such techniques harbor tacit gendered baggage, as I believe they do, then arguably the effect of their application is to emasculate subjects by dismantling the qualities conventionally associated with masculinity and replacing them with a hyperbolic incarnation of the qualities stereotypically associated with femininity: obedience, passivity, depression, anxiety, and shame.

Although certain of the harshest techniques prescribed by KUBARK in 1963 were deleted from its 1983 revision, and are no longer present in either the original 1987 version of Army Field Manual 34–52 or its 1992 revision, there is little reason to believe that the basic logic of these disciplinary practices has changed in any significant way;[9] and there is every reason to believe that the latent gendered content of that logic announced itself at Abu Ghraib. Consider, for example, the tactics identified as "futility," which aims to demonstrate that resistance of any sort is hopeless, and "pride and ego down," which attacks "the source's sense of personal worth. Any source who shows any real or imagined inferiority or weakness about himself, loyalty to his organization, or captured under embarrassing circumstances, can be easily broken with this approach technique" (U.S. Department of the Army 1992, chap. 3, 18). How the general terms of these tactics were to be translated into practice at Abu Ghraib, as the Fay-Jones report acknowledges, left "certain issues for interpretation" (quoted in Greenberg and Dratel 2005, 1004). How those issues were resolved says much about the conceptions of masculinity and femininity that, by and large, remain predominant within the U.S. military, and although I will not deal with this issue with the care it deserves, it also says much about the possibilities of emasculating those who are already effectively infantilized, if not feminized, in virtue of their identity as colonized and racialized "others."

Consider, for example, the stripping of male prisoners, who were then forced to stand before American servicewomen. In addition to offending cultural sensitivities, especially those dictated by Islamic law regarding proper attire, this technique emasculates prisoners by exposing them in a way that is familiar from representations of women, including but by no means limited to those conventionally labeled "pornographic." What one sees here, in inverted form, is a sort of enforced vulnerability joined to a fantasy of absolute sexualized power. Much the same logic is apparent in the practice of smearing prisoners with red ink said to be menstrual blood; here, emasculation is a function of staining the male body with that which is taken to mark women's bodies as distinctively female and, as such, a source of degradation. Finally, with the requirement that some of those imprisoned at Abu Ghraib wear women's underwear on their heads for hours, days, and even weeks, the logic of emasculation achieves its consummation in drag. In each of these cases, misogyny is deployed as a tactic to humiliate prisoners, where the term "humiliation" can be translated as "treat like a woman." That this aim often succeeded is confirmed by Dhia al-Shweiri, who, several months following his release from Abu Ghraib, was quoted as saying, "They were trying to humiliate us, break our pride. We are men. It's OK if they beat me. Beatings don't hurt us, it's just a blow. But no one would want their manhood to be shattered. They wanted us to feel as though we were women, the way women feel and this is the worst insult, to feel like a woman" (quoted in Faramarzi 2004).

This process whereby the gendered import of formally gender-neutral disciplinary tactics becomes explicit achieved its official confirmation when, in mid-2005, the U.S. Army released the results of an investigation conducted by Lieutenant General Randall Schmidt of the Air Force into the treatment of those imprisoned at Guantánamo Bay (Schmidt 2005).[10] Making clear that many of the abuses now associated with Abu Ghraib were put into play in Cuba and later "migrated" to Iraq, Schmidt codified these techniques under the rubric of "gender coercion," which, in his account, includes authorizing servicewomen to "perform acts designed to take advantage of their gender in relation to Muslim males." Specifically, in late 2002 two "high-value" but resistant prisoners were subjected to the following actions in accordance with Field Manual 34–52's "pride and ego-down" as well as "futility" provisions: "the subject of the first Special Interrogation Plan [Mohamed Qahtani, the alleged twentieth hijacker in the attack of September 11, 2001] was forced to wear a woman's bra and had a thong placed on his head during the course of the interrogation"; had his face marked with alleged menstrual blood; had a leash clasped around his neck, after which he was led around the interrogation room "and forced to perform a series of dog tricks"; and, during a strip search, was "forced to stand naked for five minutes with females present." Concluding his investigation, Schmidt reported that "the creative, aggressive, and persistent" questioning of this prisoner, especially in light of his solitary confinement for 160 days, as well as his subjection to eighteen- to twenty-hour interrogations on forty-eight days in a fifty-four-day period, constituted "degrading and abusive treatment." However, because "every technique employed" by the interrogation team at Guantánamo Bay "was legally permissible under the existing guidance," Schmidt found no evidence "of torture or inhumane treatment at [the Joint Task Force–Guantánamo Bay]." Accordingly, when Schmidt recommended that the commander at Guantánamo Bay, Major General Geoffrey D. Miller, be "admonished" (Schmidt 2005, 7, 16, 19–20), he did so not because the specific techniques employed violated policy, but because Miller had failed to supervise the interrogation process adequately. That Miller was not in fact disciplined by General Bantz Craddock, head of the U.S. Southern Command, is telling, as is the fact that Miller was subsequently dispatched by the Pentagon to improve the quality of intelligence extracted from those imprisoned at Abu Ghraib.

The Schmidt report makes clear that interrogation taking the form of sexualized exploitation was conducted prior to the invasion of Iraq, and that the abuse perpetrated at Abu Ghraib was not an aberration. It is not implausible, therefore, to contend that the conduct of Lynndie England and Charles Graner, like that of Miller, was wholly within the parameters of the techniques specified in Field Manual 34–52. Indeed, Graner stated that when he ordered England to remove a prisoner from a cell using a leash, he was employing a legitimate cell-extraction technique (Zernike 2005), and England informed military investigators that forcing prisoners to crawl, while attached to dog leashes, was a "humiliation tactic" intended to facilitate formal interrogations (quoted in Jehl, and Schmidt 2004b). In this regard, Graner and England were not unusual, for many of the personnel at Abu Ghraib believed that their actions were entirely consistent with established military doctrine. As a warden in Tier 1 stated, "It was not uncommon to see people without clothing. I only saw males. I was told the 'whole nudity thing' was an interrogation procedure used by military intelligence, and never thought much of it."[11] That these scenes were so often photographed, absent any concerted effort to hide the evidence, may say more about the banality of officially sanctioned evil than it does about the "sadistic and psychopathic" impulses of England and her cohorts. "We thought it looked funny," England stated matter-of-factly, "so pictures were taken" (Zernike 2004).

Cynthia Enloe is quite correct to claim that we will not completely grasp what happened at Abu Ghraib until we fully explore the culture of masculinized militarism and, more particularly, "the masculinization of the military interrogators' organizational cultures, the masculinization of the CIA's field operatives and the workings of ideas about 'manliness' shaping the entire political system" (Enloe 2004, 100).[12] Obviously, it is beyond the scope of this essay to offer what Enloe rightly calls for. That said, because it offers insight into the specific form assumed by certain of the abuses at Abu Ghraib, I close this section by citing one factor that contributes to the culture of masculinized militarism in the United States.

Some have suggested that the exploitation at Abu Ghraib articulates American servicepeople's knowledge of Muslim culture, as well as its alleged taboos and phobias.[13] With Enloe, though, it seems equally plausible to ask whether

> American military police and their military and CIA intelligence colleagues might have been guided by their own masculinized fears of humiliation when they forced Iraqi men to go naked for days, to wear women's underwear and to masturbate in front of each other and American women guards. That is, belief in an allegedly "exotic," frail Iraqi masculinity, fraught with fears of nakedness and homosexuality, might not have been the chief motivator for the American police and intelligence personnel; it may have been their own home-grown American sense of masculinity's fragility . . . that prompted them to craft these prison humiliations. (Enloe 2004, 99)

But where and how might Graner and his cohorts have learned this fear of emasculation, which was then arguably incorporated into various techniques aimed at "softening up" his charges at Abu Ghraib? Though this is not a complete explanation,[14] the question can be answered in part by pointing to the hazing techniques that remain so prevalent in basic training. Consideration of these techniques requires that, albeit incompletely, I reconnect the misogynistic and homophobic elements of the exploitation at Abu Ghraib, which to this point I have separated for analytic purposes, although they are clearly joined in many of the incidents recounted in the investigative reports and depicted in many of the photographs.

In a striking recapitulation of the central premise of KUBARK (and, by extension, of Field Manual 34–52), a former head drill instructor explained that the key purpose of basic training is to "break [the recruit] down to his fundamental self, take away all that he possesses, and get him started out in a way that you want him to be. . . . Tell him he doesn't know a damn thing, that he's the sorriest thing you've ever seen, but with my help you're going to be worthwhile again" (quoted in Burke 1996, 214). Techniques employed to achieve this end, explains Carol Burke in a study of Australia's equivalent of West Point, include stripping recent recruits of their clothing; requiring them to run a gantlet while those in their second and third year slap them with towels, belts, and suspenders; forcing them to sit naked on a block of ice, which is sometimes electrified to produce a shock; handcuffing and hooding cadets before their pants are pulled down and a vacuum cleaner hose is applied to their genitals; and the performance of Reverse Vienna Oysters, in which one freshman is required to lie on his back while another, atop him, performs push-ups in a simulation of heterosexual intercourse (Burke 1996, 214–16).

That these are not Australian idiosyncrasies is made evident when Burke, anticipating one of the more infamous Abu Ghraib photographs, explains how, at the U.S. Naval Academy, once a year, a twenty-one-foot obelisk is greased with lard, and how all members of the outgoing freshman class, stripped to their underwear, "scramble to construct a human pyramid secure enough to raise a midshipman to the top more quickly than any preceding first year class." While the occasional woman cadet sometimes joins in this ritual, she "never get[s] far up the pyramid before her male counterparts toss her off, for no class wants to be the first to send a woman to the top of Herndon" (Burke 1996, 205). Furthermore, in her study of basic training at the Citadel, which erupted into mass-media frenzy when Shannon Faulkner became the first woman to be admitted, Susan Faludi found much the same logic at work. Specifically, one of Faludi's respondents explained how in basic training, under same-sex conditions, upperclassmen play the role of men while "knobs" play the role of women, "stripped and humiliated." "Virtually every taunt," Michael Lake confessed, "equated him with a woman. . . . They called you a 'pussy' all the time, or a 'fucking little girl.' " And when Lake showed fear, he was typically asked, "Are you menstruating?" "According to the Citadel creed of the cadet," Lake summarizes, "women are objects, they're things that you can do with whatever you want to" (quoted in Faludi 1994, 70).[15]

Obviously, unlike what happened at Abu Ghraib, where the aim was to emasculate in order to subjugate, the aim of hazing techniques employed in basic training is to destroy deficient forms of masculinity, but then to replace them with a construction built on what R. Claire Snyder (1999, 151) has aptly characterized as an "unstable masculine identity predicated on the denigration of femininity and homoeroticism." This combination is uneasy because it requires suppression not only of any "feminine" impulses soldiers may have harbored prior to enlistment, but also the very homoeroticism that is cultivated during basic training.[16] Coping with this tension requires that the well-disciplined serviceman perpetually reiterate what Snyder calls the ideal of "*armed masculinity*: He must constantly reestablish his masculinity by expressing his opposition to femininity and homoeroticism in himself and others. The anger, hostility, and aggressiveness produced in the process of constituting *armed masculinity* gets channeled into a desire for combat against [or, I would add, abuse of] the enemy" (Snyder 1999, 151). In short, the exploitation at Abu Ghraib is perhaps best understood as an externalized projection of the anxieties bred by a masculine identity that cannot help but subvert itself.

CONCLUSION

What about Private First Class Lynndie England? Is she or is she not a source of gender trouble? Given my representation of gender as a malleable signifier, and given my claim that women's bodies can act as vectors of patriarchal norms, whether as victims, as perpetrators, or as something more vexing than this binary categorization suggests, the answer to this question must be yes and no, depending on the contingencies of the context in which her deeds were first enacted, as well as the contexts into which those deeds subsequently entered via various cultural and media appropriations, domestic as well as foreign.

Within the context of Abu Ghraib, one might argue that England conducted herself in exemplary accordance with pathologized norms of feminine submissiveness. Located in the midst of an institutional culture predicated on the ideal of masculinized militarism, England found herself obliged to play by the rules of the game, which in this case included doing what she was ordered to do by her superior officers. "I was instructed by persons in higher ranks to stand there and hold this leash," she said. "To us, we were doing our jobs, which meant doing what we were told" (Johnson 2004). This reading is reinforced by the testimony of a psychologist who, during England's court-marital, argued that her "overly compliant" personality rendered her incapable of making an independent judgment about participating in the exploitation at Abu Ghraib, thereby justifying a defense on the grounds of "partial mental responsibility" (Cloud 2005a). This characterization would appear to be cemented by the fact that, according to one of her defense attorneys, England's love for Graner, who allegedly has a history of abusing women and who is the biological father of the child with whom England became pregnant while at Abu Ghraib, rendered her inordinately susceptible to bad influences: "she was an individual who was smitten with Corporal Graner, who just did whatever he asked her to do. Compounding all this is her depression, her anxiety, her fear" (Cloud 2005b).

Yet this reading becomes problematic when we recall that England at the same time was participating in abusive conduct aimed at emasculating Iraqi prisoners, who were thereby reduced to something akin to the sort of submissiveness she apparently displayed in her relationship with Graner. If, as Snyder's analysis implies (Snyder 1999), Graner must perpetually seek to bolster a troubled conception of masculinity by transforming the targets of his abuse into so many incarnations of a despised conception of femininity, then England's conduct surely complicates this task. That a woman who appears more master than slave is the means of propping up that identity, in other words, would appear to spell gender trouble for

Graner (which, although this is entirely speculative, may partly explain why he ultimately left England in favor of another, but less calumniated, of the women of Abu Ghraib). Graner's conundrum, moreover, may be ours as well. As Zillah Eisenstein (2004a) suggests, England and the other women pictured in the Abu Ghraib photographs are, in effect, "gender decoys" who "create confusion by participating in the very sexual humiliation that their gender is usually victim to."

I do not intend to choose between these rival readings of Lynndie England. Instead, I want to suggest that the apparent tension between them will begin to dissipate only when we abandon the conception of gender discussed in the first section of this essay and embrace that commended in its second section. In the latter account, what is significant about the Abu Ghraib photographs is not whether the perpetrators of such abuse are anatomically male or female or whether Lynndie England is a woman or some sort of gender-bending monster. Rather, what is significant are the multiple ways in which specifically gendered practices are deployed as elements within a more comprehensive network of technologies aimed at disciplining prisoners or, more bluntly, at confirming their status as abject subjects of U.S. military power. In the photographs of principal concern here, gender as a complex structure of asymmetrical power relations has been detached from human bodies and, once detached, deployed as something akin to so many weapons—weapons that can be employed by and against anyone, male or female. What we see here, in sum, are so many scripted practices of subordination that achieve their ends through the manipulation of gendered stereotypes, all of which work precisely because degradation, weakness, and humiliation remain very much identified with matters feminine. If Barbara Ehrenreich is shocked by Lynndie England, I would maintain, it is not because England is not a "true" woman, but because her conduct reveals the artificiality of normative constructions of gender, as well as the untenability of any essentialized account that insists on its rootedness in anatomical equipment. Whether Phyllis Schlafly and her kin can recapture England in a way that deflects her revelation of the way in which gender performances can sometimes simultaneously reinforce and trouble hetero-normative strictures remains to be seen.

What I have offered in this essay is a modest first step toward making better sense of certain of the Abu Ghraib photographs. This reading does not, however, capture much of the complexity of the gendered permutations at work in the Abu Ghraib photographs. It does not, for example, explore the irony implicit in the fact that the military continues to employ techniques saturated with misogynist stereotypes, even as the Bush administration highlights the alleged gains for women in Afghanistan and Iraq as a result of U.S. military intervention. Nor does this essay adequately consider the virulent homophobia among U.S. military personnel (although it does imply that when these assaults appear to assume the character of homosexual acts, what is salient is not the imputed sexual orientation of any of the participants but, rather, the fact that the abused are once again forced, at least in the minds of the perpetrators, to assume the position of those on the receiving end of sexualized violence). Nor, moreover, does this reading adequately grasp the complex interplay of race and gender in these photographs and the incidents they depict; we must not forget that the three U.S. women who appear in the Abu Ghraib photographs, Megan Ambuhl, Sabrina Harman, and Lynndie England, are all white women, and that those they abuse are all brown men. Nor, finally, does this essay adequately explicate the larger political logic—that of neocolonialism and imperialism—from which these practices derive much of their sense.

Mark Danner (2004, 47) was certainly correct when he contended that "officials of the Bush administration . . . counted on the fact that the public, and much of the press, could be persuaded to focus on the photographs—the garish signboards of the scandal and not the scandal itself." Saying so, he effectively indicated the strategic foolishness of Rumsfeld's contention that "the real problem is not the photographs—the real problems are the actions taken to harm the detainees." From the vantage point of the Bush administration, far better to encourage a single-minded fixation on these photographs since that, in a culture too saturated by obscene (which should be distinguished from pornographic) imagery, cannot help but depoliticize what happened at Abu Ghraib. To overcome such depoliticization, we ought to ask how these photographs expose the tangled strands of racism, misogyny, homophobia, national arrogance, and hypermasculinity, as well as how these strands inform the U.S. military's adventure in Iraq. What we ought not ask is whether or how these photographs should be read as a referendum on the feminist quest for gender equality.

NOTES

This essay has its origins in a round-table titled "Gender Relations in the Age of Neo-Liberalism," which was conducted in conjunction with the 2005 meeting of the Western Political Science Association. I thank the other participants in that roundtable, Jane Bayes, Mary Hawkesworth, and Judith Hicks Stiehm, as well as Paul Apostolidis, Renee Heberle, Jinee Lokaneeta, Jeannie Morefield, Aaron Perrine, Kari Tupper, and various anonymous reviewers for their comments on earlier drafts of the essay.

1. Additional Abu Ghraib photographs are reproduced in Danner 2004, 217–24, and still more can be found at http://salon.com/news/abu_ghraib/2006/03/14/intro duction.

2. It is perhaps no surprise that many other right-wing pundits, seeking to appropriate the Abu Ghraib images for partisan ends, did so by citing the alleged ubiquity of pornography, and especially gay porn, in American culture (see Rich 2004, 1). On this telling, England and her cohorts are marshaled in an effort to combat the excesses of a permissive culture whose primary causes, of course, include the rise of the women's liberation and gay liberation movements, both of which celebrate a promiscuous, if not depraved, conception of sexual freedom.

3. As of March 2006, ten soldiers have been prosecuted and convicted in the Abu Ghraib affair. Their punishments, for offenses that include dereliction of duty, maltreating prisoners, assault, battery, indecent acts, and conspiracy, range from demotion to ten years' imprisonment. Private First Class Lynndie England, following a botched plea bargain, was dishonorably discharged and sentenced to three years in prison (Schmitt 2006).

4. With the exception of that involving fake menstrual blood, which is related in Saar and Novak 2005, 225–29, these incidents, as well as others like them, are related in the Taguba and Fay-Jones reports reprinted in Greenberg and Dratel 2005, 416–17, 466–528, 1073–95.

5. For a more complete account of my reading of Butler on gender, see Kaufman-Osborn 1997, 120–36.

6. In response to the abuses reported at Abu Ghraib and elsewhere, a proposed new field manual governing "detainee treatment," including interrogation procedures, was prepared and then posted on the Pentagon's website, only to be withdrawn shortly thereafter. It is not without significance that the manual includes the following statement: "OSD [Office of the Secretary of Defense] is the sole release authority for photographs or videos of detainees" (Joint Chiefs of Staff 2005, II-25).

7. On "softening up" prisoners, as well as the way in which such practices blur the line between these efforts and formal interrogations, consider the following passage contained in a letter written by Sergeant Ivan Frederick, the senior enlisted officer convicted in the Abu Ghraib scandal: "military intelligence has encour-

aged and told us 'Great job.' They usually don't allow others to watch them interrogate, but since they like the way I run the prison, they've made an exception. We help getting them to talk with the way we handle them. We've had a very high rate with our style of getting them to break. They usually end up breaking within hours" (quoted in Brown 2005, 978).

8. The precise role of the CIA at Abu Ghraib remains unclear because, as the Schlesinger and Fay-Jones reports note, the agency "was allowed to conduct its interrogations separately"; it operated "outside the established local rules and procedures"; and its prisoners, "known locally as 'Ghost Detainees,' were not accounted for in the detention system" (quoted in Greenberg and Dratel 2005, 942, 1024).

9. The seventeen techniques in Field Manual 34–52 are listed as follows: direct questioning; incentive; emotional love; emotional hate; fear-up (harsh); fear-up (mild); fear-down; pride and ego-up; pride and ego-down; futility; we know all; file and dossier; establish your identity; repetition; rapid fire; silent; and change of scene (U.S. Department of the Army 1992, secs. 3–14–3–20). Exactly how Field Manual 34–52 functioned at Abu Ghraib is confused by the fact that its original version, produced in 1987, circulated throughout Iraq's detention facilities, even though it had been revised and superseded by the 1992 version. The later version deleted the 1987 version's very broad authorization to "control(s) all aspects of interrogations," including "lighting, heating, and configuration of the interrogation room, as well as food, shelter, and clothing given to the source" (U.S. Department of the Army 1987, chap. 3, sec. 2). That the earlier authorization to "control . . . all aspects of interrogations" received official endorsement is indicated by the fact that, on October 12, 2003, Lieutenant General Sanchez issued a "new [sic] interrogation and counterresistance policy," which included the very language that had been deleted from the 1992 version (Jehl and Schmitt 2004a).

10. For a table that charts the "evolution of interrogation techniques" at Guantánamo, including the temporary approval of "sleep adjustment," light and auditory deprivation, removal of clothing, hooding, isolation for up to thirty days, the use of stress positions, and the manipulation of prisoners' phobia (e.g., through the use of dogs), see the Schlesinger report in Greenberg and Dratel 2005, 966–67.

11. In much the same vein, the Fay-Jones report states that "the use of dogs to 'fear up' detainees was generally unquestioned and stems in part from the interrogation techniques and counterresistance policy distributed from CJTF [Combined Joint Task Force] 180, JTF [Joint Task Force] 170, and CJTF" (in Greenberg and Dratel 2005, 1084). See Zernike and Rohde 2004.

12. On the masculinization of the interrogators' culture, consider the following quotation from Sergeant First Class Anthony Novacek, an instructor in the approved techniques of Field Manual 34–52 at Fort Huachuca, Arizona. Teaching his new

students that, even on arrival, they already possess considerable intelligence-gathering skills, he offers the following example: "you're down at Jimbo's Beach Shack, approaching unknown females." Success, he continues, involves "assessing the target, speaking her language, learning her needs and appearing to be the only way she can satisfy them" (quoted in Bravin 2002).

13. See, for example, Schneider 2004.

14. Among other elements, a more complete explanation would require exploration of the masculinized culture of the American penal system. Several of the reservists at the center of the prisoner-abuse scandal were assigned to Abu Ghraib precisely because they had experience working in American prisons. Within these prisons, abuse not uncommonly assumes forms very similar to that meted out at Abu Ghraib. "In Pennsylvania and some other states, inmates are routinely stripped in front of other inmates before being moved to a new prison or a new unit within their prison. In Arizona, male inmates at the Maricopa County jail in Phoenix are made to wear women's pink underwear as a form of humiliation" (Butterfield 2004).

15. That this misogynistic abuse often assumes a racist character as well is indicated by the fact that new cadets at the Citadel were often warned by their older peers about "food contamination" from the germ-filled hands and the hair follicles of its all-black mess-hall staff (Faludi 1994, 70).

16. For an account of the combination of homophobia and homoeroticism in the U.S. Navy's basic training, see Zeeland 1995. Steven Zeeland describes "Navy initiation rituals involving cross-dressing, spanking, simulated oral and anal sex, simulated ejaculation, nipple piercing, and anal penetration with objects or fingers, such as the famous 'crossing the line ceremony'" (Zeeland 1995, 5).

Mary Hawkesworth

Feminists versus Feminization: Confronting the War Logics of the George W. Bush Administration

Extrapolating from an empirical claim that democracies do not go to war against each other, proponents of neoliberalism and globalization optimistically predict the gradual elimination of war as marketization produces democratization in nations around the globe. Yet the specter of war continues to haunt the global community. The confident forecasts of peace advanced by advocates of capitalism and free trade coexist uneasily with increasing national preoccupations with security, as "securitization" becomes the new vernacular of liberal democratic and social democratic states (Chang 2002; Waever et al. 1993). Rather than treating the expansion of the national security state as an aberration stemming from the trauma of the September 11, 2001, attacks on the World Trade Towers and the Pentagon, some scholars have begun to explore the intricate connections between the proliferation of security discourses and transformations in international laws governing military engagement as one more manifestation of "empire." As a blanket prohibition of military aggression has given way to toleration of military intervention for humanitarian purposes, the once inviolable boundaries of the nation-state have become permeable to transnational policing and international peacekeeping forces. Tallying some "two thousand sustained armed conflicts on the face of the earth at the beginning of the new millennium," Michael Hardt and Antonio Negri (2004, 31) suggest that, far from being an aberration, war has become the "general condition" of the world in the twenty-first century. Because lethal violence is present as a "constant potentiality," war "becomes the general matrix for all relations of power and techniques of domination, whether or not bloodshed is involved. War has become a regime of biopower, that is, a form of rule aimed not only at controlling the population but producing and reproducing all aspects of social life. This war brings death but also, paradoxically, must produce life" (Hardt and Negri, 2004, 13).

In this essay, I will explore the possibility that the strategic deployment of lethal force is also a mode of production and reproduction. In particular, I will investigate the discursive and material regimes (Mohanty 2003) that are being created, nurtured, and sustained, as well as those that are being expunged from the historical record, by the preemptive military operations launched by the George W. Bush administration. The focus of my analysis will be discursive changes aided and abetted by two Bush wars: the "war against terror/terrorism," a war that is not between states but pits a coalition of Western military forces operating under executive order against a non-state actor, the al-Qaeda network, which moves clandestinely within and across national boundaries of some sixty states; and the equally unconventional war against Iraq, in which the United States broke with international law and its own conventions for the deployment of military force and unilaterally launched a preemptive war against the regime of Saddam Hussein, which quickly morphed into an exercise in occupation, peace keeping, nation building, and insurrection quelling.

To suggest that war creates as well as destroys is not to claim that it creates ex nihilo. On the contrary, in the discursive realm, as in so many others, production and reproduction begin with the materials at hand, crafting new forms from contending possibilities and shoring up certain discursive formations while undercutting others. Thus, to trace how the Bush wars are shaping the dominant discursive regime, I will begin by presenting a tale of two temporalities, two simultaneous efforts to remake the world according to radically different visions of the future, contrasting global feminist activism with neoliberal activism in the last three decades of the twentieth century. While unevenly matched in every conceivable way, these alternative possibilities have engaged families, communities, non-governmental organizations (NGOs), governments, civil-society groups, nations, transnational mobilizations, and global formations for more than thirty years. While global feminism and neoliberal globalism (Steger 2002) have vied for popular allegiance and policy influence for more than thirty-five years, I will argue that one consequence of current war making is the occlusion of the feminist alternative. The space of social justice carved out in the public imagination by feminist activism has itself been "occupied," taken over by war logics that reinscribe traditional gender symbolisms to naturalize hierarchical relations and legitimate racist, neocolonial interventions.

ALTERNATIVE FUTURES: GLOBAL FEMINISM
AND NEOLIBERAL GLOBALISM

If we trace the emergence of neoliberalism as a transformative force to the "Washington Consensus" developed in the early 1970s, then there is a striking parallel between the decades of neoliberal and feminist ascendance. Neoliberalism was born as a top-down policy strategy, which relied on the policymaking power of nation-states and international financial institutions such as the World Bank and the International Monetary Fund for its materializations. Feminisms erupted both within international organizations and institutions and as bottom-up mobilizations of women engaged in grass-roots struggles in communities around the globe.[1] Both neoliberalism and feminism envision a future and combine activism, political interventions, and policy transformations to bring that future into being. One could also argue that neoliberal globalism and global feminism have devised similar multilevel formulae for success in achieving systemic changes, targeting transnational organizations, national governments, and individual consciousness as sites of transformation.[2] At a rudimentary level, the implementation of both transformative visions has required that activists pressing for change "from the outside" work with key government "insiders" to secure changes in law and policy. Both also have involved the development of appropriate state and international policy machinery to achieve desired policy outcomes. Both have relied on transnational covenants and conventions to leverage change within particular nations. Both neoliberalism and global feminism have also sought profound changes in consciousness, attitudes, mentalities, and expectations, not just of institutions and agencies of governance, but of individuals in their daily lives. Over the past three decades, both have wrought profound changes in the world.

What distinguishes neoliberal globalism and global feminism most starkly is the concrete vision of the future, which each seeks to produce. Global feminism in its various instantiations seeks to reduce, and ultimately eliminate, the complex inequities and inequalities characteristic of race- and gender-based oppression (Basu 1995; Hawkesworth 2006; Peterson and Runyan 1999). Toward that end, it envisions expanded state provision to create adequate health care, education, welfare, employment, personal security, and a range of equity policies that redress gender- and race-based injustices. Suspicious of the continuing depredations of male-dominant states, global feminism has sought to "en-gender" states and their policies, seeking gender parity and gender quotas in elective and appointive offices; constitutional guarantees of equal citizenship and equal protection of the law; policy changes to require gender mainstreaming; gender-impact analyses; gender-equitable budgets; and monitoring to ensure compliance with equality objectives across all policy domains. In the spheres of reproductive and domestic labor, feminist activists have sought to reduce the burden of women's triple shift, redistributing subsistence, child care, and community-building labor more equitably across genders. Global feminism envisions transformations in consciousness that would make visible, actionable, and intolerable gender- and race-based inequities that permeate interpersonal relations, social organizations, economic and political structures, and symbolic systems.

Neoliberal globalism seeks to cut back the very aspects of the state that feminist activists seek to build up. Structural-adjustment policies mandated by international financial institutions as a condition for loans necessitate severe funding cuts in state provision in the areas of health, education, and welfare, shifting responsibility for the private provision of these services largely onto women (Bakker and Gill 2003; Waring 1988). State strategies to produce marketization and privatization seek to winnow down the state, reducing expenditures on education and welfare, eliminating civil-service positions in social-welfare agencies that have been a route to economic security for many women, deregulating the corporate sector, devolving power in export-processing zones, and outsourcing a range of military-support and domestic-security operations. Embracing the economic determinism of modernization theory, neoliberal activists within international financial institutions seek to transform women into *homo economicus*, promoting the incorporation of women into the formal sector of the economy as the panacea for economic development, family well-being, and profit maximization (World Bank 2002a). Toward this end, World Bank policy papers identify transformation of consciousness as a goal and train field workers to cultivate "export mentality" and "market mentality" while whittling away "protest mentalities" among the poor in developing nations (Bedford 2005).

Although neoliberals describe their agenda as a means to foster individual rights as well as economic efficiency, feminist scholars have demonstrated important gendered and gendering effects of marketization. In addition to increasing inequalities within and across nations, globalization has been fostering various forms of "feminization." Indeed, feminization of the labor force in export-processing zones and feminization of migration have been hallmarks of globalization. There is more to feminization than a preponderance of women in any particular domain. Feminization of labor involves increasing numbers of women in the labor force, as well as deterioration of working conditions (casualization, flexibilization, violation of international labor standards, declining wages, diminishing status; Moghadam 2005). Feminization of migration involves not only the transnational movement of millions of women, but their loss of physical security, political rights, and rights of bodily integrity. Indeed, some feminist scholars have suggested that overseas domestic workers are emblematic of the "feminization of citizenship," the emergence of a mode of partial citizenship that requires payment of taxes yet affords no voting rights and tolerates diminished liberties pertaining to movement and conditions of labor, marriage, and reproduction (Barker 2005; Parrenas 2001a, 2001b; Rodriquez 2002). Since sending states lack power to protect their overseas nationals, "feminized citizens" face the abject vulnerability of the "nationless," a status masked by the neoliberal rhetoric of self-reliance and cosmopolitan citizenship (Parrenas 2001a, 54–55).

The feminization of poverty refers to more than the fact that 70 percent of the poor globally are women; the "poor" are constituted as a "feminized" category, as dependent, subrational, and in need of direction (Kingfisher 2002). The transnational marketization of the care economy provides that direction through "the return of the serving classes" (Sassen 2002, 259). The increase in low-wage work globally constitutes a "feminization of job supply," as poorly paid workers are expected to adopt the self-sacrificing demeanor of the subaltern (Sassen 2002, 259). Informalization and casualization constitute a "feminization of business opportunities," as microfinance subjects increasing numbers of women to the stern discipline of the market's "invisible hand" (Sassen 2002, 263). The World Bank promotes the "feminization of survival" as the solution to the problem of global poverty, and households, communities, and governments become increasingly dependent on women for their survival as the structural forces of globalization make the possibilities of poverty alleviation increasingly remote (World Bank 2002b).

The logic of "feminization" is complex and contradictory. Women are simultaneously hailed as resourceful providers, reliable micro-entrepreneurs, and cosmopolitan citizens and positioned as "disposable domestics," the exploited global workforce, and displaced, devalued, and disenfranchised diasporic citizens. In the early 1980s, Christine Delphy (1984) argued that what made "women's work" distinctive was not the particular tasks involved, but the requirement that those tasks be done in a relation of subservience. Feminization replicates this mandate for subservience. Regardless of the tasks involved, feminization entails menialization, requiring that tasks be performed with a measure of servility. Where patriarchy required women's generic subservience to men, feminization renders the "feminized" (men and women) subservient to market imperatives, profit maximization, and commodification.

Timothy Kaufman-Osborn (2005, 5) has suggested that feminization is a "strategy of power" involving "scripted practices of subordination designed to create helplessness and dependence," which work by cutting people off from the known and reassuring, casting them into the strange, and disorienting them to foster compliance. There is much about globalization that fits this description. Transnational migrants quite literally are cut off from all that is known and familiar, cast into strange homes in strange lands. Marketization in former socialist states superimposes the strange upon the remnants of a lost way of life. Deindustrialization and flexibilization of labor in emergent service economies disorients workers who can no longer rely on long-term employment at living wages. Structural-adjustment policies cut people in the global South off from livelihoods built on subsistence agriculture and subject them to the vicissitudes of export cropping, off-shore enterprises, urban and transnational migration, and radical restructuring of family and community life.

The dimensions of feminization contrast starkly with neoliberal claims concerning the beneficial effects of globalization. Rather than promoting freedom, equality, self-determination, maximization of self-interest, and individual flourishing, feminization produces marked inequalities, which workers rendered docile and subservient accept with resignation. Rather than conforming to the "developmental logic" of modernization discourses (Cruz-Malavé and Manalansan 2002), which suggests that the market obliterates "traditional" cultures and relations and establishes liberal individual freedoms in their place, feminization restores features of oppressive feudal relations, such as indentured servitude, servile relations, political disenfranchisement, and sexual slavery (Hawkesworth 2006).

ALTERNATIVE FATES

In the last three decades of the twentieth century, activists promoting both neoliberal and feminist visions for the future have been vying for popular allegiance, enacting systematic transformations and permeating the consciousness of supporters and detractors. The growth of neoliberalism has been carefully tracked in the press and in academic and policy circles—by proponents and opponents alike. Feminist activism, however, has received markedly different treatment.

Major media sources and mainstream academic publications provide no indication that feminism experienced unprecedented growth during the last decades of the twentieth century, although feminist scholars have documented an explosion of feminist activism. As Sonia Alvarez (1998, 4) has noted, "The sites where women, who declare themselves feminists, act or may act have multiplied. It is no longer only in the streets, in autonomous or consciousness-raising groups, in workshops for popular education, etc. Although feminists continue to be in those spaces today, they are also in a wide range of other cultural, social, and political arenas: the corridors of the [United Nations], the academy, state institutions, media, NGOs, among others." Through the far too invisible labor of feminist activists around the world, feminism has surfaced in manifold global struggles that seldom garner the attention of the press or of mainstream academics.

Within the official institutions of state in Africa, Asia, Australia, Europe, Latin America, and North America, feminist projects are ongoing through gender mainstreaming and the creation of "national machinery" for women, such as ministries for women, women's bureaus, gender equality commissions. The feminist arm of the United Nations, the U.N. Development Fund for Women (UNIFEM), is working with indigenous women's organizations on all continents to safeguard women's lives and livelihoods and to secure their economic, political, and civil rights. Several states, such as Sweden, Norway, and the Netherlands, have included gender-equity efforts among their major foreign-policy initiatives. Femocrats work within public agencies in all but one or two nations to structure policy initiatives that address women's needs, concerns, and interests, however contested these concepts may be. In the aftermath of four world conferences on women sponsored by the United Nations, 169 nations have ratified the Convention to Eliminate All Forms of Discrimination against Women (CEDAW), and women's rights activists in all those nations are working to pressure their governments to change constitutions, laws, and customary practices in accordance with CEDAW provisions. A nearly universal consensus among nations supports the Beijing Platform for Action, and feminist activists work locally as well as through the United Nations' monitoring processes to press for implementation of the Beijing Platform.

Feminist NGOs have proliferated, creating a vibrant feminist civil society. Tens of thousands of organizations around the globe created by women and for women seek to develop women's political agendas, conduct gender audits and gender-impact analyses of government policies, build progressive coalitions among women, deepen the meaning of democracy and democratization, deliver much needed services to women, and pressure public and private sectors to include more women and respond better to women's concerns. The substantive scope of such feminist work includes subsistence struggles; the politics of food, fuel, and firewood; women's health and reproductive freedom; education for women and girls;

employment opportunity, equal pay, and safe working conditions; protection against sexual harassment, rape, and domestic violence; sexual trafficking; women's rights as human rights; militarization; peace making; environmentalism; sustainable development; democratization; welfare rights; AIDS; parity in public office; women's e-news; feminist journals and presses; and curriculum revision, feminist pedagogy, and feminist scholarship.

In contrast to the sustained scholarly and media attention documenting and assessing the growth of neoliberalism, a markedly different phenomenon has accompanied the unprecedented growth of feminist activism around the globe: the recurrent pronouncement of feminism's "death." From the 1970s through the new millennium, journalists, academics, and even some feminist scholars have declared the demise of feminism and hailed the advent of the "postfeminist" age. Between 1989 and 2001, for example, during a period in which the number of feminist organizations grew exponentially, a LexisNexis search of English-language newspapers turned up eighty-six articles referring to the death of feminism and an additional seventy-four articles referring to the postfeminist era. How are we to make sense of such proclamations of the death of feminism? Given the vibrancy and the variety of proliferating forms of feminist theory and practice, why the premature burial of feminism?

Sarah Webster Goodwin and Elisabeth Bronfen (1993, 20) have characterized texts of death as forms of meaning making that are particularly ripe for analysis, for "every representation of death is a misrepresentation." In cases of literal death, words seek to make present that which death has made radically absent and thereby misrepresent their subject. But the death proclamations concerning feminism involve a very different kind of misrepresentation. These textual accounts of death serve as allegorical signs for something else, a means of identifying a perceived danger in need of elimination, a way for a community to define itself through those it symbolically chooses to kill. The premature burial of feminism, then, stands in need of further examination (Hawkesworth 2004).

Perhaps it is no accident that feminism's death notice was first published in the United States, a liberal democracy that professes to hold equality among its most cherished ideals.[3] For the purported death of feminism affirms the self-evidence of the truths proclaimed by the founders of the

American republic in the Declaration of Independence (1776): "that all men are created equal and . . . endowed by their creator with unalienable rights" (emphasis added). Now, as then, the ideal exists at great remove from the lived experiences of women and people of color. Yet when feminists try to realize the promise of equality, the project is deemed nonviable. The live burial of feminism serves at once to "de-realize" women's aspirations to equality and disempower women while affirming the wisdom of the status quo. Many who construct feminism temporally as a transitional moment between a pre-feminist and a postfeminist world instrumentalize the feminist project, casting it as a failed experiment in service to a larger truth: the truth of women's "natural role," the truth of "traditional masculinity and femininity." Feminism's function, then, is to demonstrate the impossibility of meaningful equality between men and women, a function served by the advent of postfeminism. In this sense, the invitation to imagine feminism dead is an invitation to repudiate sexual equality and gender justice, to accept asymmetrical power relations between men and women as the natural order of things, to accept an unbridgeable gap between our putative ideals and lived reality.

The emergence of feminism as a global phenomenon coincided with the end of the Cold War and the resurgence of capitalism under the sign of globalization. At the same time that the West was declaring victory over the Soviet system and equating democratization with neoliberal economic reforms and liberal democratic political reforms, feminists were documenting pervasive and growing inequality within capitalist states and between the North and South. The "feminization of poverty," which feminists have demonstrated to be a growing global phenomenon, bears potent witness to the limitations of neoliberal prescriptions for sustainable development. The vibrant activism of feminists in the global South against structural-adjustment policies and around the politics of subsistence makes a mockery of claims that capitalism remedies poverty. The ongoing struggle of feminists for gender balance in governance and for women's equal participation in public and private decision making constitutes a formidable challenge to liberal democratic regimes in which women are woefully underrepresented, holding less than 20 percent of the seats in national decision-making bodies.

Recurrent assertions of feminism's death remove feminist activism from the sensory perception of the living. Subtly transforming the active into the inert in the public mind, proclamations of feminism's death erase the activism of millions of women around the globe who are currently struggling for social justice. That erasure contains any threat that feminist activism poses to the prevailing system even as it helps sustain a myth of universal support for the neoliberal agenda. It underscores the hegemonic notion that the American way is the best way for the world. It relegates to the silence of the grave the voices of those who oppose U.S. efforts to remake the world in its own image. Removal of global feminism from the consciousness of the living by death proclamation fosters social amnesia, eliminating the threat to the values of the dominant regime with the mere application of a balm of forgetfulness.

In declaring themselves "women-identified," in crafting modes of gender analysis that place women at the center, in developing agendas for political action according to their context-specific articulations of women's needs and interests, in insisting that women's subordination is an intolerable injustice, feminists promote numerous causes deemed illegitimate by male-dominant national and international regimes. The premature burial of contemporary feminism might then be read as a particularly heinous fate, designed to inflict maximum pain on women who seek to enact their freedom. Burial is the ultimate privatization for feminist political strategies intended to public-ize hitherto private experiences of domesticity, intimacy, sexuality, consciousness. Feminism's live burial then coincides nicely with neoliberalism's curtailment of the political agenda, constricting public spaces, restoring the veil of privacy. In limiting feminists' sphere of action as well as public understanding of the politically actionable, neoliberalism's live immurement of feminism re-genders feminists as well as feminist projects, returning feminists to a coerced inertia while reasserting the sanctity of private relations beyond public scrutiny or political action.

The recurrent obituaries of feminist activism can also be interpreted as a redrawing of community boundaries designed to accomplish far more than the exile of feminism, designed, in fact, to annihilate it. Distantiation is a rhetorical device designed to separate an "us" from a "them." For mortals there is no greater distance than between the living and the dead. To declare feminism dead, then, is to characterize autonomous women's activism as altogether foreign to the living, to depict it as a mode of existence so alien that it cannot be tolerated within "our" communities. By ritually reinscribing the death of feminism with each invocation of post-feminism, those who would expel feminism from the contemporary world inflict damage while masking their own culpability. Jean-François Lyotard (1990, 5) has defined damage as a wrong accompanied by the loss of means to prove the injury. The premature burial of feminism constitutes just such damage. With no corpse, no proof of demise, just vague hints of self-inflicted wounds and natural causes, feminism's death by report erases the social-justice activism of women around the globe while covering the traces of the erasure. Proclamations of feminism's death invite the public to participate in this damage: to ritually bury those whose cause is race–gender–economic justice while placing injustice beyond remedy. Those who would expunge feminist activism from public perception and memory seek to construct fictive versions of the present and past that will become embedded in culture as shared memory. In so doing, they also shape the future by producing new generations who assent to these cultural fictions. The rhetoric of the Bush wars gains new salience when considered in the context of neoliberal efforts to bury feminism.

WAR AND THE NEGATIVE LOGIC OF FEMINIZATION

Feminist historians have identified several historical moments when war seriously derailed transnational feminist activism. World War One, for example, slowed the momentum of a bourgeoning international feminist movement and triggered an impressive counter-offensive by conservative forces to undermine and erase feminist transformative efforts. As women were forced out of the lucrative jobs to which they had been recruited as part of the war effort, pro-natalist legislation was passed to enlist women in a new effort to fight "the depopulation" caused by war. Family allowances and mothers' pensions were introduced in a number of European states as an incentive for women to bear more children. Abortion and birth control were criminalized to restrict the options for those uninspired by the pro-natalist incentives. Similarly, World War Two halted virtually all of the transnational feminist activity that had been re-created in the interwar years. And within the nations at war, feminist claims for social justice were made to seem petty and selfish, as women were once again urged to sacrifice for the sake of their nations and for their men at war (Anderson 2000; Bolt 2004; Offen 2000; Rupp 1997).

How is the heightened militarism of the twenty-first century affecting feminist projects? If the strategic deployment of lethal force is also a mode of production and reproduction, then what discursive and material regimes are being created, nurtured, and sustained by war? And which are being expunged from the historical record by the preemptive military operations launched by the George W. Bush administration?

Since September 11, there has been a profound shift in the discursive regime of the Anglo-American world. Gender symbolism is invoked in very old and familiar ways, anathema to feminist values and objectives. Discourses of women fighting for rights have been supplanted by discussions of feminizing processes that trade on a notion of the feminine as weak, vulnerable, and at risk, in need of rescue and protection. As Ann Orford (2005) has pointed out, the rhetoric of rescue cries out for "muscular interventions." Thus, it is little surprise that multiple modes of heroic masculinity have been resurrected. Whether in New York City or at the Pentagon, in Afghanistan or Iraq, in Madrid or London, working-class blokes rise to the challenge: firefighters, police, soldiers, security personnel respond to the call to protect and defend, and the media celebrate their valor—front page above the fold in the print media, and 24–7 on the airwaves.

Helen Kinsella (2005) has suggested that such gendered appeals to male protectors do far more than mobilize young men willing to come to the aid of women in distress. The mythos of the male protector, "defender of home and hearth," sustains the psyches of men who are compelled by their states to kill. Masking the harm that war does to women, warriors, and other living things, the mythos of the male protector affords soldiers an uplifting balm that instrumentalizes wartime atrocities, linking the abyss of death and destruction to the demands of "civilization," to chivalrous codes of conduct that undergird the rightness of their cause. Within this mythic frame, the definition of a war of self-defense can subtly expand to encompass pre-emptive military action, which "defends" against hypothetical future attacks.

In the immediate aftermath of September 11, gendered images and narratives migrated from embodied subjects to discursive constructions of the nation. The United States was stripped of its sense of invulnerability. The impregnable fortress was breeched. America joined the ranks of the violated, its borders penetrated by foreign terrorists. Security forces were mobilized and the military put on alert to prevent the further feminization of the U.S.A. Speaking for and to a grieving nation, the president promised retaliation in a place and at a time of his choosing. Echoing honor codes with ancient roots, the president characterized deployment of American military might as the appropriate means to redress the violation. An assertion of force would redress the nation's feminization. Demonstrating the depths of our potency, a show of American military might would performatively restore American virility.

In the months that elapsed between the terrorist attacks and the U.S. retaliation, perhaps because questions were raised concerning the efficacy of a violent response and the ethical propriety of punishing others for a crime they had not committed—and for which the terrorists had already paid with their lives—the president developed a second rationale for the deployment of the "coalition of the willing" in Afghanistan: to save Afghan women from the Taliban. In so doing, he not only invoked the mythos of the male protector, but he embraced the gendered logic of neocolonialism, which Gayatri Spivak (1985) has documented time and again: heroic white men set out to "rescue" brown women from "barbaric" brown men. At the very moment that Afghan spokeswomen argued forcefully against invasion, cataloging the disproportionate harms that would befall women and children by additional recourse to military force, the Bush administration "feminized" them, rejecting their articulate assessment of their own situation and subjecting them to a form of paternalist intervention premised on the assumption that the coalition of Western forces knew what was good for Afghan women better than they knew themselves.

Iris Young's essay in this volume suggests that the gendered logic of the national security state "feminizes" the American citizenry. Recirculating the patriarchal rationale first vindicated by Thomas Hobbes, which posits threat and fear as endemic and the need for protection as dire, the national security state promises protection of the "homeland." Within this discursive frame, the home is re-territorialized. Lifted from the private sphere and given geographic purchase, the home *qua* women's domain is refigured as "homeland" with borders in need of policing. The private becomes public, but not in the democratic sense envisioned by feminist campaigns for "the personal as political." At one level of public (mis)appropriations of the private, thousands of vigilantes converge on ranches spanning the Mexican border, pledging their guns and their lives to protect the United

States from the "security threats" lurking south of the border. At a second level, the state withdraws constitutional protections of the private sphere. The USA PATRIOT Act authorizes securitization measures that suspend the right of habeas corpus, as well as Fourth Amendment guarantees against unwarranted searches and seizures. According to the logic of the national security state, the provision of protection necessitates critical tradeoffs: civil liberties are eroded; racial and ethnic profiling are legitimated; surveillance is heightened; detention absent due process of law is routinized; foreign nationals passing through American airports are "rendered" to Egypt, Poland, Romania, or Syria for torture and confinement; and the citizenry is reduced to a subordinate position of dependence and obedience. Rather than enacting their democratic rights through protests against such constitutional violations, citizens of the national security state are expected to be grateful for the protection provided. Some preliminary evidence suggests that this fear-induced feminization of the citizenry is generating the desired effects. Indeed, so grateful are the docile citizens to the valor of their self-sacrificing protectors that they willingly overlook rape within the military and against women in occupied areas and exponential increases in domestic violence on military bases by soldiers returning from war zones. Inured to the demands of homeland security, the feminized citizenry grow increasingly insensitive to heightened control tactics that secure gendered subordination.

But citizens at home are not the only ones who experience feminization at the hands of the national security state. Paradoxically, feminization is part of the basic training of soldiers who must be transformed into a cohesive fighting force. Judith Stiehm (2005) suggests that tactics of feminization, such as insulting and humiliating recruits by calling them "girls," has been a standard practice in basic training as the military simultaneously seeks to "break down" individuality and produce order-obeying soldiers while turning "boys" into "men" (see also Burke 2004). Beyond basic training, the logic of feminization also structures military interrogation techniques. Kaufman-Osborn (2005, 5) has pointed out that the CIA's 1963 *Counterintelligence Interrogation Manual* endorses scripted practices of subordination with marked gendered associations as strategies to produce helplessness, dependence, and compliance among "resistant sources." Depicting feminization as a "strategy of power deployed by masculinized nationalism," Kaufman-Osborne suggests that the modes of torture enacted at Abu Ghraib, at Guantánamo, and in Afghanistan bear striking similarities to the logic of feminization incorporated in established military interrogation practices (Kaufman-Osborne 2005, 5).

Long ago, Edward Said (1978) pointed out that "Orientalism" has pronounced gendering effects. Under the Orientalist spell, Westerners construe the Middle East and the Far East as an eroticized, feminized Other and act in accordance with that racist construction. U.S. military personnel serving in Iraq have made manifest the behavioral implications of the Orientalist gaze. Perhaps no image captures Orientalism's feminizing effects more powerfully than the snapshots from Abu Ghraib, in which American soldiers coerce Iraqi detainees to feign homosexual relations. As Jonathan Goldberg (1992) has demonstrated, enacting torture in the form of sexual subordination in general, and allegations of sodomy in particular, is part of the arsenal of violent colonization. During the European conquest of the Americas, the conquistadors repeatedly sent home reports that the indigenous peoples "were all sodomites." In Goldberg's view, the colonizers used the accusation of sodomy to rationalize their slaughter of the accused. Applying a particular calculus of biblical culpability, the colonizers could reckon that those who have "perverted nature" "deserve" to be exterminated. The coerced simulation of sodomy among imprisoned Iraqis manifests the same self-vindicating rationale. By forcing prisoners to assume formations that represent homosexual acts, American soldiers—male and female—reap the surge of superiority and the psychic distance that enables them to perform the daily tasks of humiliating and torturing human beings under the ruse that such treatment is warranted. By circulating the images among troops, these perverse colonizing effects are generalized. The construction of the Iraqis as feminized men who enjoy penetration legitimates the U.S. presence, as the Christian civilizing mission once again transforms unlawful invasion into righteous occupation.

Underlying the logic of feminization in each of these instances is a vindictive construction of femininity. Those who are produced as "feminine" are weak, violated, silenced, docile, obedient, humiliated, and craven. The solution to their existential situation is invariably a masculine assertion of power for which the appropriate feminine response is gratitude. This is the discursive gender regime produced and reproduced by the Bush war machine.

Within this discursive formation, feminizing processes simultaneously produce and justify profound inequalities. Trading on forms of gender symbolism that naturalize hierarchies of dominance and subordination, the gendered discourses of war make scenarios of rescue, retaliation, and retribution appear matters of necessity. Fear and angst are cultivated to vindicate patriarchal values. Long-discredited norms of secrecy and paternalism are proffered as sound public policy within a security state in which access to "intelligence" is restricted, circulating only on a "need to know" basis. Struggles for sexual equality, for racial and gender justice, for fair and open democratic practices, seem hopelessly naive within the realpolitik of a state conducting a "war against terror."

CALCULATING THE COSTS OF THE NEW DISCURSIVE REGIME

The 2004 presidential election in the United States manifested the far-from-subtle effects of the shift in discursive regime. Myths of heroic men who serve, protect, and defend dominated campaign discourses. Military valor became the mark of character and leadership, as principled critics of war and militarization were ridiculed as "girlie men." Simulations of valor were sufficient to trump actual war records as Bush campaign ads celebrated the commander-in-chief in "top-gun" attire while the organization Swift Boat Veterans for Truth indulged in levels of historical revisionism only dreamed of by Stalin's propaganda machine. The decorum of political wives and daughters supplanted any discussion of women as running mates, as President Bush and Vice President Cheney entertained their hawkish following with jibes that the vice-presidential contender John Edwards was just "a pretty face" (Eisenstein 2004b).

Although the United States lags behind fifty-seven nations in the proportion of women in elected offices (Interparliamentary Union 2005), concern for women's political representation receded from the public political imagination at the very moment that women were losing ground in state legislatures. In the first study of the effects of the war on terrorism on voters' attitudes, Jennifer Lawless (2004) found that the sustained gender stereotyping in the post–September 11 era was providing clear electoral benefits for men. "Citizens prefer men's leadership traits and characteristics, deem men more competent at legislating around issues of national security and military crises, and contend that men are superior to women at addressing new obstacles generated by the events of September 11, 2001.

As a result of this stereotyping, levels of willingness to support a qualified woman presidential candidate are lower than they have been in decades" (Lawless 2004, 480).

"In war time, only men matter" (quoted in Offen 2000, 252). This astute observation was made during World War One by Mary Sargent Florence and C. K. Ogden, two British antiwar suffragists who noted that hostility to feminism was a deliberate, sustained, and central project of nations involved in that round of multilateral war making. Taking the argument one step further, the Irish feminist Francis Sheehy Skeffington insisted in 1914 that "war is necessarily bound up with the destruction of feminism" (quoted in Offen 2000, 252). If the form of life being created and nurtured by the Bush wars is governed by a negative logic of feminization that is at odds with and inherently destructive of feminism, then the collateral damage of this war making involves more than the 60,000 civilian and 3,500 combatant deaths (United States and allies) currently estimated in the Iraq body count. The casualties could also include the tens of thousands of organizations around the globe created by women and for women that seek to develop women's political agendas, build progressive coalitions among women, and extend the meaning of democracy to include women. In jeopardy are also the wide-ranging feminist projects going on around the globe, which include struggles for subsistence; for education and health and reproductive freedom; for employment opportunities, equal pay, and safe working conditions; for protection against sexual harassment, rape, and domestic violence; for women's rights as human rights; and for gender-equitable sustainable development. Also at risk are feminist struggles against violence, militarization, and war. For despite feminism's vibrant presence around the globe, the new discursive regime would "disappear" feminism and replace it with the realpolitik of evangelical masculinity, crusading against a "feminized" perversity of its own making, in order to protect paternalism at home and abroad.

FEMINISTS VERSUS FEMINIZATION

The paternalist future envisioned and the feminist future put at risk in the Bush wars starkly illuminate the challenges confronting contemporary transnational feminist activism. Despite invocations of freedom and democracy, the neoliberal agenda of the Bush administration is permeated by patriarchal policies that subordinate women to men, restrict women's reproductive freedom, undermine their bodily integrity, and preclude their achievement of meaningful equality. Consider, for example, the gulf between U.S. support for UN Security Council Resolution 1325, which requires that women and women's concerns play an integral role in every new security institution and in every decision-making stage in peacekeeping and national reconstruction in the aftermath of armed conflict, and the practices of the United States in the "national reconstruction" of Afghanistan and Iraq. Rather than use its power to promote equitable inclusion of women in transitional governments and commissions empowered to draft new constitutions, the United States has forged alliances with traditional male elites. In 2003, the Afghanistan constitution-drafting commission included twenty-eight men and seven women (Enloe 2004a, 287). Three women were appointed to the twenty-five member Iraqi Governing Council (one of whom, Alkila al-Hashimi, was assassinated on September 20, 2003). None of the women appointed to the Iraqi Governing Council had "access to the four bargaining chips crucial to effective political influence. . . . Each entered the Governing Council without her own political party, militia, treasury, and without direct lines of communication to Washington" (Enloe 2004a, 293). Despite major mobilization of women in Iraq to press for the establishment of a gender quota in the new system of governance, when the twenty-five-member committee was appointed to draft the constitution, all were men.

Despite such pronounced barriers to their participation, women in Afghanistan and Iraq have not resigned themselves to perpetual exclusion. On the contrary, the Afghan Women Lawyers Association, based in Kabul, mobilized to monitor the deliberations of the commission drafting the constitution and to lobby the commission for equitable provisions for women citizens. Indeed, after organizing a series of hearings on systemic violations of women's human rights, the Afghan Women Lawyers Association drafted proposed constitutional provisions to promote women's equality. To ensure Afghan women's participation in public life as fully autonomous and effective citizens, they recommended:

(1) mandatory education for girls through secondary school, (2) guaranteed freedom of speech for women, (3) insurance that every woman would be free to cast her own ballot and to run for elected

office, (4) insurance that women would have equal representation with men in the new government's legislature, (5) the appointment of an equal number of women and men to judgeships, (6) entitlement of women to pay rates equal to those of men, (7) guarantee that women would have the right to exert control over their own finances and to inherit property, (8) permission for women to bring criminal charges against men for domestic violence and sexual harassment, whether those violations occurred in a public place or at home, (9) a ban on the common practice of family members handing over girls and women to another family as compensation for crimes committed by the former against the latter, (10) raising the legal age of marriage from sixteen to eighteen years, (11) the right of women to marry and divorce "in accordance with Islam," and (12) a reduction of the amount of time that women would have to wait to remarry if their husbands abandoned them or disappeared. (Enloe 2004a, 288)

This lobbying effort produced a partial victory. The Afghan constitution includes a provision guaranteeing the equality of men and women—a provision that coexists in tension with another constitutional provision mandating that all laws be "informed by the principles of Islam," which conservatives claim precludes gender equality (Enloe 2004a, 289).

In Iraq, as in Afghanistan, women have mobilized, reinvigorating longstanding organizations, such as the Iraqi Women's League, and creating new organizations, such as the Organization of Women's Freedom in Iraq (OWFI), to protest the American occupation, to demonstrate against growing violence against women, to protest the re-masculinization of Iraqi politics and public life, and to demand equal constitutional and political rights (Ferguson 2005a).

The courageous struggle for inclusion, empowerment, and justice that Afghan and Iraqi women are waging at considerable personal cost is emblematic of feminist struggles that continue all around the globe. Despite the fact that "international and regional organizations such as the [United Nations], the [European Union], the Southern African Development Community, the Summit of the Americas, and the Association of Southeast Asian Nations, have declared that growth in women's leadership contributes to democratic consolidation and economic and social progress" (Htun 2004, 444), the obstacles to success that national and transnational feminist activists confront are monumental. Within the current global system, most governments are unwilling or unable to seek the fundamental transformation of existing economic and political systems necessary to improve women's lives (Stienstra 1994, 141). Increasing recognition of women as actors at the international level has not been accompanied by concomitant change in the number of women participating in decision making within national and international elites. Despite growing attention to women's issues at the global level, gender inequalities within and across nations, and inequalities among women within and across nations are greater now than they were in 1970.[4] Despite arduous efforts to transform the discursive politics of human rights, feminist strategies that foreground "equality" and "rights" tend to be curtailed by neoliberal presumptions, which limit their transformative agenda to the sphere of civil and political rights. Moreover, "difference" discourses are often co-opted by conservative forces and tied to long-standing gender stereotypes that reinscribe women's "double duty" and "triple shifts" while perpetuating women's marginal status.

In the face of such momentous obstacles, twenty-first-century transnational feminist activists, like their forebears in the nineteenth and twentieth centuries, remain resolute. Keenly aware of the challenges they face, and chafing against the limits of these constraints, feminist activists continue to push the boundaries of the possible, making some gains against the odds. Fueled by their commitment to social justice and buoyed by solidarity generated through collective struggle against injustice, feminist activists continue their transformative efforts.

In contrast to pessimists who advocate resignation to the growing inequities of globalization on the grounds that there is no alternative (Giddens 1998), transnational feminist activists continue to craft alternative possibilities. In the words of Peggy Antrobus, a veteran transnational feminist activist and co-founder of Development Alternatives with Women for a New Era: "Feminism offers the only politics that can transform the world into a more human place and deal with global issues like equality, development, peace, because it asks the right questions about power, about links between personal and political and because it cuts through race and class. Feminism implies consciousness of all the sources of oppression: race, class, gender, homophobia, and it resists them all. Feminism is a call to action" (quoted in Moghadam 2005, 88).

In contrast to optimists who dream of a revolution miraculously transforming all dimensions of social life (Hardt and Negri 2000, 2004), feminist activists construe their transformative praxis more along the lines of a slow boring of hard boards. Mobilizing in response to specific problems, crafting policies to mitigate pressing abuses, cracking open closed spaces to inject feminist content, envisioning and voicing concrete alternatives, transnational feminist activists practice a diplomacy from below when all other options remain closed to them. Starting from the terms dictated by global capitalism, male-dominant politics, militarization, and war making, they seek to transform the parameters of debate and the processes by which such parameters are set.

The amendments proposed by the Women's Caucus to the Copenhagen Declaration and Program of Action provide a powerful example of this engaged transnational feminist praxis, an example that maps the contours of an alternative to the global future prized by neoliberalism. The World Summit for Social Development, which took place in Copenhagen in March 1995, attracted the largest number of world leaders to date to deliberate on the issue of sustainable development. The Copenhagen Declaration pledged to make the conquest of poverty, the goal of full employment, and the fostering of social integration the overriding objectives of development. Despite these worthy objectives, the strategies endorsed in the Program of Action were largely neoliberal. Noting that neoliberalism was increasing rather than decreasing global poverty, transnational feminist activists proposed critical changes to neoliberal policy directions that would enable world leaders to achieve the goals they had agreed on in principle.

The proposed Women's Caucus Amendments were multiple and concrete. They urged that the program of action shift emphasis away from "promoting dynamic, open free markets" to an emphasis on "regulating markets in the public interest with a view to reducing inequality, preventing instability, expanding employment, and establishing a socially acceptable minimum wage." They urged that international trade equity be established though effective regulation of the trade and investment activities of transnational corporations. They recommended the creation of "a global fund for human security," funded by a tax on global finance that could compensate those subjected to social insecurity caused by the instability and recurrent crises of the international market. They endorsed the creation of an enforceable global "Code of Conduct" for transnational corporations, including provisions guaranteeing labor rights, safe working conditions, and community and environmental protection clauses. They proposed a cap of 1 percent of gross domestic product (GDP) on military spending and, until that cap became effective, annual reductions in military spending equivalent to 5 percent of GDP. The funds reclaimed from military uses should be dedicated to programs designed to meet pressing social needs. In keeping with existing international agreements, they recommended that gender equality be fully integrated into all relevant policy areas and budgetary decisions and that additional resources be devoted to women's empowerment in all spheres of social life. Finally, the Women's Caucus identified new mechanisms to generate financial resources to promote sustainable social and economic development, such as taxes on resource use and the commodification of common resources, taxes to discourage the production of toxic products, and taxes on international financial speculative transactions (Petchesky 2003, 55–56).

Generating a vision of an alternative, more equitable future—albeit one that continues to operate within the confines of global capitalism—remains at great remove from the realization of that vision. The "Millennium Objectives" devised by the United Nations in collaboration with the major international financial institutions fall far short of the recommendations by the Women's Caucus. Recognizing the gulf between rhetorical commitments to and achievable policies for gender and racial equality, social justice, and sustainable development, transnational feminist activists continue to produce trenchant critiques of the defects of national and international initiatives. At the Beijing + 5 meeting in 2000 and the Beijing + 10 meeting in 2005 at the United Nations, feminist activists produced detailed reports on every nation in the world, documenting their failure to fulfill their constitutional commitments and their commitments under international treaties to racial and gender equality. These documents are rich in policy proposals designed to address the specific needs of women in particular nations.

Despite pervasive efforts to bury feminism alive, prevailing global economic and political conditions committed to the perpetuation of male dominance, and the brutal enactment of war logics designed to feminize women, men, citizens, and certain states, feminist activists remain undeterred in their transformative projects. Echoing the words of freedom fighters in the African National Congress, Angola, Mozambique, and Guinea-Bissau, global feminists participating in the United Nations' NGO Caucus have issued recurrent statements under the title, "La Lutta Continua [The Struggle Continues]." Indicating their profound disappointment about the lack of progress on gender equality and the lack of political will on the part of the United Nations and its member states to make good on their commitments to promote social justice, these statements also assert transnational feminists' unswerving commitment to stay the course and to seize whatever opportunities present themselves to push for a more equitable and just world. The stakes in this struggle are high, for they involve the long-term prospects of the majority of the world population, encompassing questions concerning the nature of women's waged and unwaged work; the conditions of labor within the global economy; the scope of democratic practices within neoliberalism; gendered power relations within families, communities, nations, global institutions, and transnational arenas; and freedom from increasing militarization and war making.

NOTES

1. Feminism is a collective noun. At first glance, then, it appears that any reference to "feminisms" involves a grammatical mistake. But the concept of feminisms has a history and a politics tied directly to transnational feminist encounters. As Francesca Miller has pointed out, the pluralization of feminism was introduced in the late 1980s to indicate that feminism was not the sole preserve of any one group and "to signify the multiplicity of ways in which those who share a feminist critique may come together to address issues." As a strategic term introduced by transnational feminist activists to help negotiate a complex array of ideological differences and differences in national and regional policy priorities, "feminisms" was intended to "create discursive space in a fraught arena" by "resisting homogenization, generalization, nostalgia" (Miller 1999, 225). For further elaboration of this history, see Miller 1999.

2. Manfred Steger conceives globalism as the "dominant ideology of our time. It is an Anglo-American free-market doctrine that endows the relatively new concept of globalization with neoliberal norms, values, and meanings—all of which are produced and reproduced within the media and popular culture for public consumption." In a sense, then, the locution "neoliberal globalism" is redundant. Nonethe-

less, I have chosen to include the neoliberal referent to help keep the contours of this ideology clearly fixed in the public eye: see Steger 2002, x.

3. In November 1976, *Harper's* published as the cover story "Requiem for the Women's Movement," the first of many media pronouncements that "second-wave" feminism was dead. Nothing particular had happened in November 1976 to signal the death of feminism. There was no cataclysmic event, no tragic accident, no death thrall, no bedside drama—simply a messenger with the news, delivered at a moment when feminist activism was escalating in all parts of the world: see Geng 1976.

4. The small decreases in gender inequality that have occurred in some nations over the past thirty years are due to the worsening economic condition of men rather than the improvement of the economic condition of women. For a more complete discussion of this problem, see Bayes et al. 2006.

PART IV

Feminist Responses

wwwwwwwwwwwwwwww
Michaele L. Ferguson
wwwwwwwwwwwwwwww

Feminism and Security Rhetoric
in the Post–September 11 Bush Administration

The worldwide advancement of women's issues is not only in
keeping with the deeply held values of the American people; it is
strongly in our national interest as well.

—SECRETARY OF STATE COLIN POWELL (2002)

Since September 11, 2001, the Bush administration's rhetoric on national security has been sounding more and
more feminist. The invasion of Afghanistan in 2001 was justified not only in terms of the War on Terror but also in terms
of restoring the rights of women mistreated under Taliban
rule. The U.S. government has openly supported the codifi-
cation of women's equality and participation in both Afghan
and Iraqi interim governments and constitutions, on the
grounds that women's inclusion in these emerging democracies is essential to our national security. The U.S. Mission
to the United Nations sponsored Resolution 58/142, which
was passed by the General Assembly in December 2003 and
expresses a commitment to women's equal political and economic participation around the world based on its importance to international security. Arguing for these policies,
Bush administration officials sound almost indistinguishable
from feminist activists.

Feminists have responded to this new security rhetoric in two ways. Not surprisingly, many feminists are cynical. They have dismissed the rhetoric as mere rhetoric, noting that the Bush administration has a pattern of saying it supports women's rights while at the same time it is actively dismantling feminist political gains, especially in the areas of reproductive health, AIDS policy, and violence against women.[1] One commentator has referred to this as "stealth misogyny" (Goldstein 2003). This disjunction between rhetoric and reality has led numerous feminists and others to be deeply skeptical of the administration's increasing use of feminist rhetoric to support its policies abroad.[2] The concern is that the Bush administration is not actually committed to women's equality and rights but has cynically used this rhetoric to increase support for its foreign policy and to win reelection by appealing to women voters.[3]

What is surprising is that a coalition of feminist groups—the Center for Health and Gender Equity, the Feminist Majority, and the Women's Environment and Development Organization—has greeted the Bush administration's rhetoric on women and security with praise. In these groups' once periodically updated "Global Women's Issues Scorecard on the Bush Administration," they gave the administration grades for its rhetoric about women in Iraq and Afghanistan that rose from Bs and Cs in August 2003 to a peak of straight As in March 2004.[4] In their last report, the grades for rhetoric ranged from A (for "Women in Political Decision Making in Afghanistan and Iraq") down to C (for "Women's Security in Afghanistan and Iraq"). Yet even they have been deeply skeptical of the administration's willingness to act accordingly. The scorecard's grades for what they call the "reality" of the Bush record on women's issues in Afghanistan and Iraq are strikingly lower than those for the "rhetoric": the administration's grades there have been consistently Ds, Fs, and Is for "incomplete."[5]

It is my contention that neither of these responses is adequate to a feminist analysis of the Bush administration's feminized security rhetoric. Both reactions rest on a distinction between words and deeds that obscures the very political work that words do in framing how we see the world.[6] For example, when we dismiss the Bush administration's rhetoric as a cynical strategy to get votes, we overlook how it is an indication of the success that feminists have had in altering security rhetoric in recent years. The Bush administration's use of feminized security rhetoric is only possible now because feminist and other peace activists have been struggling for decades to reframe how political actors conceptualize security (Blanchard 2003; Grant and Newland 1991; Peterson 1992; Tickner 1992, 2001). Over the past decade, we have witnessed signs that their activism is beginning to have an impact. In 1998, the International Criminal Tribunals for the Former Yugoslavia set precedent that found rape to be a war crime. In 2000, the UN Security Council passed Resolution 1325 on "Women, Peace, and Security," which draws an explicit connection between women's rights and international security. Now the officials of the most powerful government in the world seem so conversant with this feminized security rhetoric that their words often appear to be indistinguishable from those of feminist activists. Even if we accept the claim that the Bush administration has been using this rhetoric only to get votes, we should still see this as a sign of the progress feminists have made: a neoconservative administration believes that feminized security rhetoric is viable enough to attract voters, which was unthinkable twenty or thirty years ago. If we dismiss the rhetoric as mere words, then we fail to appreciate the work feminists have done to make the connection between women and security sound reasonable and mainstream to our contemporary ears.

Similarly, when we praise the rhetoric of the Bush administration for being feminist, we risk missing the work that this rhetoric is doing to frame women's rights in a particular way. This is why I refer to it as feminized rather than feminist—to leave open the question of whether what sounds at first to be feminist rhetoric is indeed so. As the diversity and contention within feminist scholarship demonstrates, there are many different ways to argue for women's rights, each of which brings certain political issues to the foreground while others recede to the back. When we simply accept that this rhetoric is feminist, we stop asking critical questions: how is it feminist? How does it frame women's issues? How does it shape which issues appear salient and which do not? How does it constrain and limit possible discursive responses?

Neither of the responses that has emerged so far provides the analytical tools necessary to think about how rhetoric works, since each participates in the myth that words are not also deeds. Accordingly, we end up with a Manichaean set of alternative evaluations: either the language of the Bush administration is feminist (and therefore gets good grades) or it is a cynical co-optation of feminist ideas (and therefore must be rejected). How-ever, when we think about the framing work that rhetoric performs, it is impossible to read this as either an unqualified success or a complete fail-ure for feminism. By shifting our attention to framing, I hope to open up space to consider successes and failures where we did not think to look for them before. I want to appreciate how the Bush administration's rhetoric is a particular kind of response to the growing influence of feminist ideas about security—and, as such, represents both a failure and a success.

In the following section, I situate my argument within the interdisci-plinary literature on framing. I then analyze the Bush administration's feminized security rhetoric by showing how it draws not only on feminist ideas about women's rights but also on discourses of respect for women and democratic peace. I conclude by making some suggestions about how these two feminized frames have shifted the terms of discourse on women's rights in the United States and how feminists might effectively respond in this climate to the administration's policies on women at home and abroad.

FRAMING REALITY

We're an empire now, and when we act, we create our own reality. And while you're studying that reality—judiciously, as you will—we'll act again, creating other new realities, which you can study too, and that's how things will sort out. We're his-tory's actors . . . and you, all of you, will be left to just study what we do.
—SENIOR BUSH ADVISER IN 2002 (SUSKIND 2004)

I assume in this analysis that how issues of women's rights and equality are framed matters—and it matters even more when the framing is being done by the spokespeople for the world's most politically, economically, and militarily dominant state. Rhetoric is never merely rhetoric; it con-structs a particular (if incomplete) worldview that enables us to see cer-tain connections, yet occludes others. Like a picture frame, the rhetorical framing of political issues shapes and contextualizes the perspective of the audience.

This idea of "framing" has been theoretically elaborated in a number of disciplines, including sociology, psychology, and political science.[7] While scholars have not reached consensus about how precisely to define the term, they converge on the basic idea that frames are conceptual structures that enable us to make sense of information by selectively presenting it from a particular viewpoint. This concept primarily has been used to explain how journalists frame stories in mass communication (Iyengar 1991) and how surveys frame questions in social-science research (Kahneman and Tversky 1984), although the concept broadly understood has relevance to a variety of applications. For example, Robert Entman (1993, 52) describes framing as a feature of "a communicating text." This suggests that the analysis of framing may be helpful for understanding speeches, protest signs, literature, advertisements—in short, anything that we can characterize as a text.

The empirical literature on framing confirms my contention that frames do matter because they affect audience perceptions.[8] However, this does not mean that when issues are presented to us in a particular way, we simply adopt that perspective uncritically. Rather, as researchers have noted, we respond to frames based on our existing perspectives.[9] Accordingly, we should not expect that the Bush administration, or any other source of framing discourse, will succeed at imposing a single perspective on its audience. Different people will respond to the same framing rhetoric in different ways.[10] Drawing on this work, I characterize frames as constructions that *enable* a particular view of the world but do not guarantee that audience members will adopt it.

While to this extent I follow the general trends of the literature, I also add to it an account of an aspect of framing that has been largely undertheorized: its dialogicality.[11] Rhetorical frames are introduced into an existing discursive context in which other frames are already operative. Like interlocutors in a dialogue responding to what the other says and how she says it, agents attempting to frame an issue respond to the framing discourse that has preceded them. This response is neither identical with nor wholly unrelated to what came before. Rather, it makes use of and redeploys existing modes of discourse. Indeed, even where a frame is intended to construct an entirely new issue for an audience, it is intelligible as a frame only insofar as it builds on narratives and ideas already in currency.[12] We might think of this in terms of how William Sewell (1992, 18) has described human agency as "the capacity to transpose and extend schemas to new contexts." In political discourse, we use existing rhetorical frames, but we also transform them as we apply them to different situations.[13]

Furthermore, influential framing rhetoric does more than just respond to what came before. It also shapes the discursive context to which future actors will have to respond. Clever framing disarms opponents by making likely lines of attack seem illegitimate or morally questionable. Consider how opposition to Senator Eugene McCarthy's witch hunt was immobilized for a long time by the rhetorical threat of being named un-American. Or consider how opponents of abortion reframed their position as pro-life, a frame that has the effect of placing pro-choice activists on the moral defensive. Even the most hegemonic of discourses never completely forecloses alternatives, but it does help to shape the terrain for resistance. Accordingly, attention to dialogicality shows that framing rhetoric does work, not just by placing limits on how we view the world, but also by placing limits on how our interlocutors may respond to our worldview.

This dialogical understanding of frames can help us to analyze the Bush administration's feminized security rhetoric as a kind of political action that aims to shape how Americans think about women's rights. It accomplishes this by drawing on an existing feminist rhetoric of women's rights. However, I hypothesize that the Bush rhetoric on women is not a straightforward repetition of feminist discourse (whether cynical or sincere); rather, it represents a *different* way to frame women's issues. We should not presume that just because this rhetoric often sounds familiar, it is necessarily feminist. The Bush administration, as I argue here, makes use of existing discourses of respect, democratic peace, and feminism, yet it alters each of these discourses by combining them in novel ways and extending them to new contexts. Accordingly, we should not assume that the administration's use of the rhetoric of women's rights will look exactly like preexisting modes of feminist discourse. We should expect to find differences.

However, many political actors might attempt to reframe women's rights without achieving any results. What makes the Bush administration's rhetoric worthy of study is the likelihood that it has had and will have *significant* influence over how women's rights and equality are framed. This is likely since, at least within American public discourse, the Bush administration has enjoyed a kind of hegemonic authority to set the terms for discussion of women's rights and status—because of its access to media, political, and budgetary resources. While this authority is not unchallenged, we can expect that the executive branch has the opportunity to shape how many Americans think about women's rights and feminist issues.[14] In particular, as a right-wing administration with a reputation for social conservatism, it may have the capacity to influence citizens who would not give credence to arguments for women's rights coming from feminist organizations or leftist politicians. While there is no reason to suppose that the Bush administration's rhetoric will be uniformly influential on Americans, there is reason to suppose that it can have some effect on how many citizens view their world. The coalition behind the global scorecard, for instance, has seemingly accepted this rhetoric as feminist.

When we examine the Bush administration's words from the perspective of framing, then it is clear that these are not mere words but, rather, a form of political action—one that aims to change how we think about women's rights. Consequently, separating criticism of words from criticism of deeds, as many feminists have done, is an ineffective response. We need to reveal that these words *are* deeds—that the Bush administration is engaged in the very political act of shifting the discursive terrain for women's rights. As the official quoted at the beginning of this section states, "We create our own reality." Insofar as this is the reality in which feminists now find themselves, we need to analyze its logic as fully as possible. Accordingly, in the remainder of this essay I engage in interpretive analysis of the Bush administration's feminized security rhetoric to (1) reveal how it frames women's rights and frames them in a way that is different from what came before; and (2) contest it by identifying the kinds of responses it renders ineffectual and the kinds it enables.

A METHODOLOGICAL NOTE

Before turning to the analysis of the Bush administration's rhetoric, I should clarify the methodology I have used to identify it. First of all, with the term "Bush administration" I mean to refer to a collection of individuals in prominent positions in the executive branch under President George W. Bush. They include Bush himself, First Lady Laura Bush, cabinet members, and other top executive-branch officials and political advisers. I focus on the leadership because I assume that of all the people working in the administration, these few will have the greatest access to the media to convey their message, and they will be perceived as the most authoritative by their audience. In short, I expect the leadership of the administration to have the greatest influence on how citizens frame their world.

I take the statements of these officials as indicative of the position of the administration as a whole. I do not presume anything about the intentions of any particular individual, about whether he or she is a sincere or cynical advocate of women's rights.[15] I find it reasonable to suppose that most, if not all, public comments made by these people have been approved as representing the position of the administration. They are spokespeople for the administration and so can reasonably be expected to be expressing a somewhat coherent, consistent, and coordinated position on the issues—regardless of their individual motives or beliefs about the language they use. Indeed, the rhetorics used by these officials are consistent enough that it is either extraordinary chance that they are so coordinated or they really have intentionally coordinated with one another.

This feminized security rhetoric became commonplace in the administration after September 11, 2001—so much so that it is typical for an official who gives a speech about American actions in Iraq and Afghanistan or about the U.S. policy of promoting democracy around the world to draw the connection to the pursuit of women's rights. Accordingly, I have focused my attention on speeches and other texts that concentrate on women's issues or that announced new policies or initiatives regarding women. These include a variety of official and public documents produced throughout Bush's first term in office, from both before and after September 11, 2001. I have examined documents posted at www.whitehouse.gov, the official White House website (such as speeches by the president and the first lady, policy reports, and press briefings); op-eds and other opinion pieces written by members of the Bush administration; interviews and quotations reproduced in the media; and other policies and public speeches available from additional sources (such as former UN Ambassador John Negroponte's speeches before the Security Council).

The majority of these texts are attributed to President Bush, Laura Bush, or former Secretary of State Colin Powell. The most surprising absence from these texts is Condoleezza Rice, who served as national security adviser during Bush's first term in office. As a woman in charge of national security, we might suppose her to be an obvious choice to be a spokesperson for this rhetoric. However, when she has talked about the relation of women's rights to national security, it has been only as a passing reference in a speech focused on some other matter (e.g., Rice 2002). She is often mentioned in speeches as an example of the success of women's rights in the United States, but she was never the one who introduced any new policies or initiatives on women.[16] Rather, Laura Bush is the woman who most frequently represented the administration on women's issues. Rice's relative silence about women during the period studied may be due in part to her role as national security adviser. For example, at the G-8 Summit in 2004, she attended the meetings while Laura Bush hosted a separate event about women's issues for the other wives of world leaders.

However, having Laura Bush as the primary female spokesperson for women's rights may also be a strategic choice on the part of the administration.[17] Whereas Dr. Rice is a single, childless, and ambitious career woman, Mrs. Bush is a wife and mother who quit her job to raise her children. She has shown no career aspirations at odds with those of her husband. Through her role as first lady, acquired by virtue of her marriage to the president, she literally embodies the notion that a woman's primary identification should be with her family. Consequently, she seems comparatively unthreatening as an advocate of women's rights, since her personal choices to date seem to correspond with relatively traditional gender roles.

TWO RHETORICS OF WOMEN'S RIGHTS

When I began to examine how the Bush administration was framing women's rights issues in relation to national security, I realized that there is not one but multiple rhetorical strategies at work. This is because Bush and his spokespeople draw on different preexisting discourses to express a commitment to women's rights: first, a discourse of chivalrous respect for women, which reinforces the administration's contrast between the civilized world and the barbaric Taliban and Hussein regimes; and second, a discourse of democratic peace, which reflects the administration's policy of seeking to build democracy in Iraq and Afghanistan. I distinguish two different rhetorics that correspond to these discursive sources. While these rhetorics are often used separately, they are also frequently deployed in the same speech or statement. Consequently, I feel justified in treating them as if they are each different components of the same overall framing strategy.

These two rhetorics share one very important feature: they both position Americans as superior to some particular others in terms of their treatment of women. Accordingly, both rhetorics motivate and justify intervention in other countries in the name of women's rights. However, whereas the rhetoric of democracy clearly positions women's rights as a national security concern, the rhetoric of respect draws no similar connection. This is significant because it means that, in the current political climate in which national security is of prime importance, the rhetoric of democracy is much more rhetorically powerful in making women's rights a central (rather than a marginal) concern in U.S. foreign policy. I treat each of these rhetorics in turn.

THE RHETORIC OF RESPECT

Respect for women is a Bush administration foreign policy priority.
—"U.S. INTERNATIONAL WOMEN'S INITIATIVES FACT SHEET"
(U.S. MISSION TO THE UNITED NATIONS 2004)

There was little discussion of women's rights by the Bush administration before September 11.[18] Women's rights were generally mentioned only on ceremonial occasions celebrating women (e.g., Bush 2001b), they were usually mentioned by Laura Bush rather than by her husband, and they were mentioned as an achievement that had successfully occurred in the past.[19] The primary message of these early speeches is that women's rights have already been achieved in the United States; gender inequality no longer exists. Insofar as women's rights are today only imperfectly enjoyed, this is simply a function of a lack of enforcement of the existing laws.[20] No new laws, no new rights are necessary. Consequently, the women's movement is always referred to in the past tense—women struggled once upon a time for their rights, and inequality is a matter of the past (Bush 2001b; L. Bush 2001a). Suffrage is an achievement that we should all be proud of, but there is no continuing need for women to organize and struggle for rights—at least, in the United States. Indeed, reading through the statements by the president and the first lady during the first 233 days of the administration, one might never know that the women's movement is still quite active.

Immediately after September 11, this narrative of women's rights as already achieved in the United States appeared in Bush administration discourse in the context of a rhetoric of *respect for women*—that is, our respect for women at home should motivate us to care about the status of women abroad.[21] This rhetoric predates September 11, but it does not seem to have been explicitly connected with women's rights until afterward.[22] After September 11, the recognition of women's rights is figured as a sign of respect for women. Civilized nations and civilized peoples respect women and therefore treat them with dignity and recognize their rights. The United States clearly respects its women, since for almost a century now it has recognized women's rights. Afghanistan, by contrast, did not respect its women under Taliban rule. Accordingly, Afghanistan was uncivilized and needed to be brought under control and domesticated. This rhetorical strategy works, then, by redeploying an existing conservative narrative of chivalry: those who respect their women are civilized; those who do not are barbarians.[23]

Laura Bush delivered a key speech that connected this rhetoric of respect to U.S. national security policy on November 17, 2001, in the first Presidential Radio Address to the Nation delivered in full by a first lady.[24] In her brief speech, Bush catalogs the horrible acts committed or threatened by the Taliban against Afghan women: "Women have been denied access to doctors when they're sick. Life under the Taliban is so hard and repressive, even small displays of joy are outlawed—children aren't allowed to fly kites; their mothers face beatings for laughing out loud. Women cannot work outside the home, or even leave their homes by themselves" (L. Bush 2001b). Yet she is quick to tell us that this disrespect is a characteristic of the Taliban regime in particular, not of Islam in general, which we learn is a civilized religion that emphasizes respect for women. "Only the terrorists and the Taliban forbid education to women. Only the terrorists and the Taliban threaten to pull out women's fingernails for wearing nail polish. The plight of women and children in Afghanistan is a matter of deliberate human cruelty, carried out by those who seek to intimidate and control" (L. Bush 2001b). The Taliban have shown themselves to be uncivilized not only because they have harbored terrorist organizations but also because they lack respect for women.

Listening to her speech, we learn that we should therefore equate the struggle for women's rights with the war on terror: "The fight against terrorism is also a fight for the rights and dignity of women" (L. Bush 2001b). We are instructed by her model to feel a kind of instinctual, natural outrage at the Taliban. This is what her example of having one's fingernails pulled out does: it elicits a visceral revulsion, a kind of Rousseauean pity at the pain of another.[25] We should do more than just feel outrage, however. We should also speak out about it. We should speak out against the Taliban, which is to say that we should speak out in support of the U.S. military action against the Taliban. This is what civilized people do. Like chivalrous knights in shining armor, they rush to the aid of defenseless women and children everywhere. "Civilized people throughout the world are speaking out in horror—not only because our hearts break for the women and children in Afghanistan, but also because in Afghanistan we see the world the terrorists would like to impose on the rest of us. All of us have an obligation to speak out." (Bush 2001b). Here the language of respect enters the picture: "We respect our mothers, our sisters and daughters. Fighting brutality against women and children is not the expression of a specific culture; it is the acceptance of our common humanity—a commitment shared by people of good will on every continent" (L. Bush 2001b). Unlike the Taliban, *we* respect our mothers, sisters, and daughters. This is a sign that *we*, unlike they, are civilized people.

This rhetoric obviously was politically useful at the time. It helped to demonstrate that the Bush administration was not anti-Muslim, only anti-terror; it also helped to construct an image of a natural solidarity among "civilized peoples" who ought to support a United States–led War on Terror. This language does so not only by drawing a distinction between civilized and uncivilized people but also by calling for a vague course of action: respect for women. Laura Bush does not specify a catalog of rights that women do or should have; she simply calls for *respect*. This is a language that is not threatening to those U.S. allies who do not themselves fully recognize women's rights but who do claim to respect women.[26] In other words, this language of respect is only contingently connected to women's rights. There are lots of ways to respect women, only some of which include recognizing women as rights-bearing subjects.

However, this language of respect is also consistent with other ways of conceptualizing women. As I have been suggesting, Laura Bush invites us to imagine ourselves as the chivalrous masculine protectors who must defeat the misogynist enemy and show Afghan women the respect that the Taliban refuses them. Women are victims, vulnerable, in need of masculinist protection, here embodied in the figure of the United States, which is willing to intervene and protect them from the indignities suffered at the hands of the Taliban.[27] Women are identified with the family: they are mothers, sisters, and daughters—rather than citizens.[28] They are conduits of civilization and culture. The Taliban *men* are uncivilized, but there is no corresponding concern that the Afghan women are also uncivilized. Rather than being a radical rhetoric in unconditional support of women's rights, the rhetoric of respect is only contingently related to rights and reinscribes traditional gender roles of chivalrous male protectors rescuing female damsels-in-distress.

Not only is this rhetoric contingently connected to rights, it is also only contingently connected to national security. In other words, in an era immediately following September 11 in which security concerns dominated and legitimated all kinds of political programs, women's rights were being framed in terms having little or nothing to do with security. We can see this by looking at the National Security Council's September 2002 "National Security Strategy"—the document that outlines the Bush doctrine of preemptive war. It contains only three passing references to gender in thirty-five pages of text.[29] The most important of these is found in a list of eight "nonnegotiable demands of human dignity" that the United States must "champion": the rather ambiguous demand of "respect for women" (National Security Council 2002, 3). Although respect for women is not negotiable, it makes no other appearance in the document. The message is that national security is not really related to respect for women—or to women's rights—in any significant way.[30] The failure of the Taliban to respect women simply demonstrates how uncivilized they are; the Taliban do not pose any particular threat to the United States on account of disrespecting women. The fight against terrorism may also be a fight for the rights and dignity of women, but according to the logic of this rhetoric, it is simply unclear whether supporting women's rights would be an effective way to fight terrorism.

THE RHETORIC OF DEMOCRACY

Ensuring women's rights benefits individuals and their families, strengthens democracy, bolsters prosperity, enhances human rights and advances religious tolerance. It is at the core of building a civil, law-abiding society, which is an indispensable prerequisite for true democracy. The advancement of issues of concern to women has been a long-standing American goal. This administration has intensified that pursuit.

—UNDER SECRETARY FOR GLOBAL AFFAIRS PAULA J. DOBRIANSKY (U.S. DEPARTMENT OF STATE, OFFICE OF INTERNATIONAL WOMEN'S ISSUES 2004)

The connection between supporting women's rights and achieving national security is made explicit in the second rhetoric: a rhetoric that relates women's issues to the creation of stable democracies around the world. The framing logic of this rhetoric differs from that of respect in several important ways. First of all, whereas the rhetoric of respect was only contingently connected to women's rights and a conception of women as rights-bearing citizens, the rhetoric of democracy is unmistakably a rhetoric of women's rights. Second, this rhetoric ties women's rights directly to U.S. national security. This has the effect of making women's rights an issue that (rhetorically, at least) is central to U.S. foreign policy. This is the kind of language that has earned the Bush administration's rhetoric on Iraq and Afghanistan good grades from feminist groups: it is a rhetoric that takes women's rights seriously.

As an example of this rhetoric, consider an op-ed titled, "Women in the New Iraq." The article was written by Deputy Secretary of Defense Paul Wolfowitz and appeared in the *Washington Post* on February 1, 2004. Wolfowitz begins by discussing a new women's center in Iraq dedicated to women's rights. Soon, however, he gets to his main point: democracy. The women he met on his recent visit to Iraq want to protect their rights. Yet, by his account, these women want their rights not so much for themselves as because they understand that women's rights are necessary to create and maintain democracy in Iraq, and to make the world as a whole safer. While in Iraq, Wolfowitz met with a delegation of women leaders who "told us that *if Iraq is to become a democracy*, women must have an equal role, and more women should be included in Iraqi governing bodies and ministries" (Wolfowitz 2004; emphasis added). These women have numerous concerns, among them that "if women are not involved [in drafting a new constitution for Iraq], women will not be guaranteed equality under the law," but this concern is hardly the most important one for Wolfowitz. As he notes, "They also pointed out that we are now engaged with Iraqis in seeking *a far greater prize*: a chance for lasting change in the region that will help make our country and the world safer" (Wolfowitz 2004; emphasis added).

Wolfowitz clearly agrees with the logic of this delegation as he reports it. Women's rights are not to be protected *qua* rights but, rather, because they are an important indicator of the democratization of a state: "A government that does not respect the rights of half its citizens," Wolfowitz writes in language that evokes feminists all the way back to Mary Wollstonecraft, "cannot be trusted to safeguard the rights of any." It is because we need to be able to trust other governments to be democratic (that is, to respect the rights of all of its citizens) that we need to make certain that they recognize women's rights. This, he tells us, is the rationale for U.S. policy and funding to support women's rights in Iraq. President Bush himself, Wolfowitz reminds us, made the connection between women's rights and Iraq policy clear in his State of the Union address in January 2004 when he said, "Our aim is 'a peace founded upon the dignity and rights of every man and woman'" (Wolfowitz 2004, quoting Bush 2004a).

We can now trace out the reasoning that leads Wolfowitz to support women's rights in Iraq. First, it is essential to our national security that other countries democratize. The peace that Bush refers to in the State of the Union address is, as he himself notes, a democratic peace (Bush 2004a). In other words, the Bush administration is appealing to a long-standing view whose roots can be traced back to Immanuel Kant (1991 [1795]) that democracies will not go to war against one another. The presumption made by Wolfowitz and others is that only if countries like Iraq are democratic can we expect that their leaders will not seek to go to war with the United States and will not harbor terrorists. Accordingly, the security of the United States requires the creation of democracies to replace failed and dictatorial regimes around the world. Second, Wolfowitz's argument rests on certain assumptions about what counts as a democracy. Most important, a democracy is a form of government that respects the rights of *all* of its citizens—whether male or female. Therefore, it is in the interests of U.S. national security to support women's rights in Iraq to make sure that the new Iraqi government is indeed a democratic one.

Women's rights are then best understood as an instrumental good, according to the logic of this rhetoric. They are instrumental first in securing democracy: a state that recognizes women's rights is a democratic state. In turn, women's rights are instrumental in securing U.S. national security. Yet the rhetoric often sounds more idealistic, as if Americans ought to be committed to ensuring women's rights as a good in and of themselves. We can see this when we look at the larger context of the quotation Wolfowitz takes from the State of the Union Address. Bush stated, "America is a nation with a mission, and that mission comes from our most basic beliefs. We have no desire to dominate, no ambitions of empire. Our aim is a *democratic peace*—a peace founded upon the dignity and rights of every man and woman. America acts in this cause with friends and allies at our side, yet we understand our special calling: This great republic will lead the cause of freedom" (Bush 2004a; emphasis added).[31] Here, Bush speaks idealistically of freedom and rights as if they are ends in themselves. Yet he simultaneously reaffirms the realist premise that if rights are important, it is because international peace *requires* the recognition of rights. Even as Americans lead the cause of freedom, they do so with the aim of creating a democratic peace.

In fact, it is characteristic of this rhetoric connecting women's rights to democracy that it conflates idealist and realist positions on rights. Consider Laura Bush's remarks on "Efforts to Globally Promote Women's Human Rights" on March 12, 2004: "For a stable world, we must dedicate ourselves to protecting women's rights in all countries. Farahnaz Nazir, founder of the Afghanistan Women's Association, said, 'Society is like a bird. It has two wings. And a bird cannot fly if one wing is broken.' Without women, the goals of democracy and peace cannot be achieved. Women's rights are human rights, and the work of advancing human rights is the responsibility of all humanity" (Bush and Bush 2004).[32] Women's rights are human rights—but, we must dedicate ourselves to protecting them *for a stable world*.

The argument epitomized by Wolfowitz's op-ed is only one version of the rhetoric of democracy. I have identified three different arguments that connect women's rights to democratic peace, and it is in these arguments that we can see the tremendous influence of feminist activism on the Bush administration. All three are present in the quotation with which I began this section: "Ensuring women's rights benefits individuals and their families, strengthens democracy, bolsters prosperity, enhances human rights and advances religious tolerance." The first argument is the Wolfowitz argument: where women's political rights to vote and participate in self-government are recognized, there we can be assured is a democratic government. This claim is as old as the movement for women's suffrage.

The second line of argument takes the recognition of women's rights—political, social, and economic—to be necessary for sustainable prosperity. As George W. Bush notes, "The economic empowerment of women is one effective way to improve lives and to protect rights. Each year for the past five years, the United States government has provided an average of $155 million in small loans, micro-loans. About 70 percent of those benefit women. It turns out the world is learning what we know in America: The best entrepreneurs in the country are women. In America, most new small businesses are started by women. With the right help, that will be the case around the world, as well" (Bush and Bush 2004).[33] Entrepreneurial women, in turn, are the sign of a free-market economy, which is itself taken as a stand-in for a democratic government. The connection between women's enjoyment of their rights and general prosperity—while it is not always linked to free-market economics as it is here—has been well established.[34] Indeed, the feminist Katha Pollitt makes a very similar argument in her criticisms of Bush's policies.[35]

The third line of argument is a bit more subtle. It connects the recognition of women's rights to a secular society—which in the context of Afghanistan and Iraq means a society governed by secular rather than *sharia* law. Dobriansky suggests, for example, that ensuring women's rights also ensures religious tolerance. The institutionalization of women's rights is in direct contradiction with the imposition of *sharia* law; therefore, the support of women's rights and political participation is a way to support secular government, government that tolerates a variety of religions. This, again, is a claim made by feminist activists, Muslim and non-Muslim alike.

In all three of these logics, women's rights are taken to represent democracy—whether these rights signal women's political participation, women's social and economic participation, or the absence of *sharia* law. Indeed, the Bush administration goes so far to connect women's rights and democracy that they are often treated in speech as if they were synonymous: the one stands for the other. Speaking on "Global Women's Human Rights," George W. Bush tells us that "the advance of women's rights and the advance of liberty are ultimately inseparable" (Bush and Bush 2004). And so, in his remarks, Bush slides back and forth between talking about women's rights and talking about democracy as if he is always talking about the same thing. I quote from his speech at length to show how he constantly shifts from women to democracy and vice versa as if they really were the same:

> By radio and television, we're broadcasting the message of tolerance and truth in Arabic and Persian to tens of millions of people. And our Middle East Partnership Initiative supports economic and political and educational reform throughout the region. We're building women's centers in Afghanistan and Iraq that will offer job training and provide loans for small businesses and teach women about their rights as citizens and human beings. We're active. We're strong in the pursuit of freedom. We just don't talk a good game in America, we act.
>
> In Afghanistan, the U.S.–Afghan Women's Council is developing projects to improve the education of women, and to train the leaders of tomorrow. You heard Laura talk about her deep desire to help train women to become teachers, not only in the cities, but in the rural parts of Afghanistan. We'll succeed. We'll follow through on that initiative. We're pursuing a forward strategy of freedom—that's how I like to describe it, a forward strategy of freedom in the Middle East. And I believe there's no doubt that if America stays the course and we call upon others to stay the course, liberty will arrive and the world will be better off.
>
> The momentum of freedom in the Middle East is beginning to benefit women. That's what's important for this conference. A free society is a society in which women will benefit. (Bush and Bush 2004)

What are the rhetorical effects of equating democracy with women's rights in this way? To begin with, this way of framing women's rights has the effect of occluding the fraught relationship between real democracies and women's rights. Even a cursory look at the history of democracy shows that there is no necessary connection between democracy and women's rights. Most democracies have not recognized women's rights—or, at least, have only partially done so. Furthermore, the elision of women's rights with democracies makes it difficult to see any tension within contemporary states between the realization of democracy and the realization of women's rights.

Bush's words are also very reassuring to Americans. His equation of women's rights with democracy means that if the United States has already successfully achieved women's rights, then it must be a democracy, and if the United States is a democracy, then it must already recognize women's rights. He accomplishes this in his speech through a variety of techniques. First, he begins by showing his audience that women are present in the highest levels of U.S. government. He makes a point of introducing all of the female cabinet members, as well as other women serving in the administration who are present at the meeting. (Three of the women he mentions are his sister, Dick Cheney's daughter, and Donald Rumsfeld's wife, all of whom hold their positions arguably because of patronage and nepotism — but he shows no trace of irony in referring to these women as examples of women's rights and democracy at work.) He demonstrates that women have arrived in the United States: just look at how many of them he can show us! We are reassured that women can rise to the top and that, therefore, we must live in a democratic society.

Next, just as Laura Bush listed the train of Taliban abuses against women in her radio address, George W. Bush reminds us of what women suffered under the Taliban and Saddam Hussein — and that they no longer suffer because of U.S. military intervention. By contrast, his list of abuses reminds us that women in America really do seem to enjoy their rights after all. In the United States, we know that women and girls can become educated. In the United States, women can already receive the training to become teachers. In the United States, we do not have rape chambers or torture chambers. In the United States, women are not forced to wear the burqa or to stay in at night. The United States seems to be an egalitarian paradise in comparison with these oppressive regimes: what could women have to be concerned about here? Therefore, his narrative reassures us that women in the United States have their full rights — there is no additional work necessary to achieve them — and consequently, the United States must be a democracy.

Correspondingly, this narrative motivates us to be concerned about women's rights and democracy *abroad*. We are liberators, agents of civilization, progress, and democracy; because we have already achieved these things for ourselves, we must now bring them to others. In a new way, this rhetoric lands us in the same place as does the respect rhetoric: we need to act as masculinist protectors of women's rights around the world. We can see this in a story that Bush recounts of being hailed by an Iraqi woman (and member of the Iraqi Governing Council) as "My liberator" just before she burst into tears. Her tears provoke laughter from Bush's audience—a gentle laughter. Yet when he admits that he himself cried in response, he is greeted with enthusiastic applause.[36] This is the appropriate response to the rhetoric of democracy. We must feel compassion for those around the world who do not have rights or democracy, and we must be motivated to bring it to them—for the sake of national security.

SHIFTING THE FRAME

Now that we have taken a closer look at the logic of the Bush administration's feminized security rhetoric, we can turn to analyzing what this way of framing women's rights *does*. Recall that frames are sources of meaning; they help us to structure and make sense of our world. Consequently, the successful reframing of an issue alters how many people perceive it. It creates, as the Bush official suggested to Ron Suskind, a "new reality." How we perceive "reality" in turn affects our priorities, our allegiances, and our decisions. So what kind of a reality is created by this rhetoric?

I suggest that it can be captured by two narratives.[37] The first of these is a narrative of masculinist protection. We are superior to you (because we are civilized or because we have a democracy) and therefore we must take on the role of your protector. We will go to war against those who would hurt you, and we will bring you civilization and democracy. As J. Ann Tickner (2001, 57) suggests, a variant of this narrative has long been used to motivate military forces: men must fight wars to protect innocent women and children. Here, the feminization of the victims of the Taliban and of Saddam Hussein serves to masculinize and justify U.S. military actions. The second narrative is that of international women's liberation. Women's rights were achieved for Americans long ago, so there is no need for feminists to agitate for them at home. The work to be done is to be done abroad. Even if there are still problems that American women face—for example, sexual harassment, domestic violence—these are nothing compared with the atrocities that women suffered under the Taliban and in the rape camps of Saddam Hussein. So our attention is best directed toward liberating women in other countries.

Both of these narratives are problematic from a feminist perspective. The first is troubling because it trades on notions of men as protectors and women as victims that feminists have long criticized. In particular, by casting the United States as a protector, it obscures the many ways that our military actions increase the insecurity of women in the countries where we wage war and try to install democracy.[38] The second is disturbing because it undercuts the motivation for domestic activism. Feminists clamoring for rights at home are more likely than not to be seen as privileged whiners who cannot appreciate how good they have it in comparison with the brave women of Iraq and Afghanistan who struggle against true adversity.

Yet even as the Bush administration's rhetoric frames women's rights in these objectionable ways, I do not believe that we should simply condemn it, for there are also reasons to celebrate this feminization of security. I celebrate this rhetoric not because it is feminist (as the global-scorecard coalition seems to think) but, rather, for the perverse reason that it represents the co-optation of feminism. The Bush administration's repeated insistence on its record of standing up for women's rights demonstrates how feminists have successfully reshaped the worldviews of many Americans over the years. Appeals to women's rights are no longer treated as completely marginal; nor are they voiced primarily by members of the Democratic Party. Rather, Bush—a very socially conservative Republican—ran for re-election in 2004 in part on his record of pursuing women's rights in Afghanistan and Iraq.[39] As uncomfortable as some of his policies may make feminists, we have to allow ourselves to recognize the gains we have made in framing women's rights as an important political issue for the left and the right.

We should also be heartened by the Bush administration's ability to co-opt feminist concerns, because this suggests that we, in turn, might co-opt its concerns for feminist ends. Rhetorical frames, as I have argued, are transposable. Our worldviews are not fixed once and for all, but may be shifted. Just as the Bush administration has lifted elements of feminist rhetoric to suit its own agenda, we in turn can lift pieces of its rhetoric and redeploy them in new contexts for feminist ends. This, I expect, is a difficult process, especially since feminist groups have considerably less influence and power than the Office of the President. Nonetheless, I believe that we need to embrace the struggle to frame women's rights in a feminist way as an important political activity. This is an activity in which many feminists are already engaged, but it is an activity that is devalued and undermined when feminists themselves insist on drawing a stark division between words and deeds.

What my analysis suggests is that the more effective strategies of resistance will be those that respond to and directly contest the shift in the rhetoric of women's rights effected by the Bush administration. For example, if we are told that women's rights are instrumentally valuable for national security, then feminists might do well to reframe their demands in terms of security. In other words, the Bush rhetoric gives women's groups in Iraq, Afghanistan, and the United States a powerful lever to use against Washington's foreign policy. Insofar as women's rights are seen as instrumental to national security, they have a kind of centrality and rhetorical purchase in the War on Terror that they have not had in the past—especially with a conservative administration. If feminists can frame their concerns as concerns about security, they may be able to expand their domestic audiences. The feminist scholarship in international relations on the concept of security provides an example of what this might look like. It aims to replace a notion of state security with one of personal security for women—that is, security from war, from domestic violence, and from rape (e.g., Tickner 1992, 2001).[40] To demonstrate that many women in the United States lack this personal security is to undermine the Bush logic that women at home no longer have anything to complain about, for it reveals the continuity between our grievances and those of the women of Afghanistan and Iraq.[41] Yet mainstream feminist activists in America have been surprisingly reluctant to take advantage of the power of security discourse. Insofar as they have made use of it, they do not seem to make any attempt to resignify or challenge the dominant understanding of security.[42]

Another approach might be to resist the Bush administration's framing of women's rights by redeploying the rhetoric of democracy. Recall that part of the logic of this rhetoric is that the recognition of women's rights and the realization of democracy are equivalent. Why not take this equation seriously and use it to critically examine democracy in the United States? If a democracy is a government that recognizes women's rights, then can we say that the United States is truly democratic? After all, if we restrict our notion of equal rights to political rights, American women are significantly behind women from other countries. Consider that Iraq and Afghanistan have equal-rights provisions written into their constitutions, and they have quotas for female representatives that far exceed the current percentage of women in Congress.[43] The administration has supported these attempts to institutionalize women's rights—abroad. Why not leverage the administration's record of supporting women's rights in new democracies to pressure it to support similar provisions at home: an equal rights amendment and legislative quotas?[44]

Furthermore, we could use the rhetoric of democracy to critically assess Bush's domestic policies regarding women. Insofar as his domestic policies undermine women's rights, the logic of his own rhetoric would suggest that they simultaneously undermine democracy in the United States. So, for example, we might argue that the administration's under-funding of the Violence Against Women Act encourages the violation of women's rights. Since American women's security in their own persons is denied by a government that does not actively seek to eradicate gendered violence, women cannot be expected to enjoy citizenship equally with men. Accordingly, the United States under Bush's rule, while it aspires to be democratic, is actually wide of the mark.

Both of the rhetorical strategies I have only briefly outlined here refuse to accept the Bush administration's premise that feminism at home is irrelevant. Yet they do so in ways that importantly acknowledge the power of words to shape our way of seeing the world. They contest and redeploy the dominant framing rhetoric by transforming it anew into a rhetoric that is feminist.

My analysis does not point to a wholly new strategy or course of action for feminists. Indeed, it confirms the value of some of the actions that many feminists are already taking. It helps us to understand better why we should be engaged in rhetorical struggles over the framing of women's rights in relation to national security. This struggle is difficult—but we should be heartened by the power and influence feminism has had in framing public discourse, given that Bush clearly thinks he needs to talk about women's rights to woo women voters. We should also be heartened by the example that the Bush administration gives us of how the terms of discourse can be shifted through co-optation and transposition. Understanding that the Bush administration's rhetoric neither wholly embraces feminism nor completely rejects its accomplishments gives us reason to be optimistic—*cautiously* optimistic—that we, too, can again have a significant impact on how women's rights are framed, at home and abroad.

NOTES

I thank Karen Zivi, Jill Locke, Alison Jaggar, and Iris Young, the editors and anonymous reviewers from *Politics & Gender*, as well as fellow panelists and audience members at the Midwest Political Science Association, the Association for Political Theory, and the Center for Values and Social Policy at the University of Colorado at Boulder for their comments. I also thank Steve Chan for his encouragement. This project was funded, in part, by the University of Colorado at Boulder, Graduate School Council on Research and Creative Work Small Grant.

1. For a sampling of feminist views on Bush, see the collected essays in Flanders, ed., 2004.

2. For example, "Even though Bush used Afghan women's rights to drum up support for his war, this did not lead to a sustained commitment to Afghan women" (Bunch 2002).

3. "Bush has feebly attempted to use feminism to justify invasion [of Iraq], fantasizing that a 'democratic' Iraq would show 'that honest government, and respect for women, and the great Islamic tradition of learning can triumph in the Middle East and beyond.' But feminists aren't buying it; few see reason to hope war will relieve the miserable condition of the Iraqi people, women included" (Featherstone 2003). Liza Featherstone is quoting here from Bush 2002g. Laura Flanders (2004a) examines the cynical use of women within the Bush administration.

4. The grades fell for the first time to a mix of an A, a B, and a C in June 2004, the last date for which there was a report (Center for Health and Gender Equity, Feminist Majority, and Women's Environment and Development Organization 2004a). The web page was designed to mimic a child's report card. This site also reported on the Bush administration's performance in other policy areas, in which notably it scored less well. Most significant of these are issues having to do with population control and women's reproductive health, as well as the Convention on the Elimination of All Forms of Discrimination against Women. In these areas, the Bush administration earned grades of C, D, and Incomplete for its rhetoric. The website is no longer operative.

5. Center for Health and Gender Equity, Feminist Majority, and Women's Environ-

ment and Development Organization 2004c. In August 2003 and again in March 2004, the Iraq reality received an I for "Incomplete." When Iraq has been grouped together with Afghanistan, the reality has always received D and F grades.

6. It may be that these feminists are not actually committed to the idea that words are not deeds but are simply using this idea for political purposes. Even in this case, I would argue that this is politically problematic for feminists because this rhetoric aims to shape how others should understand the Bush administration in terms of words versus deeds. Regardless, then, of the assumptions these feminists make about the ontological status of words, their own rhetoric performs a separation of words from deeds that I consider to be problematic for reasons I discuss here.

7. Two interesting attempts to survey and synthesize the insights of these different fields are Entman 1993 and Pan and Kosicki 1993.

8. The clearest examples of the impact of frames on audiences are found in research on surveys. Numerous studies have shown that how a survey question is asked—that is, how the problem is framed—can significantly affect responses: see Kahneman and Tversky 1984; McClendon and O'Brien 1988; Schuman and Presser 1982.

9. For example, Zhongdang Pan and Gerald Kosicki (1993, 4) write that frames "will interact with individual agents' memory for meaning construction"; see also Entman 1993, 53.

10. One surprising finding is that "political knowledge and sophistication, whether narrow or broad, do not insulate one from the effects of framing . . . but rather seem to promote framing effects" (Nelson et al. 1997, 235).

11. I should note that I do not expect that my theoretical addition of dialogicality would be controversial to many scholars of framing. Indeed, some research seems to presuppose certain elements of dialogicality as I present it here: that framing rhetoric takes place in an existing context and that it shapes options for the future. Nonetheless, to my knowledge these aspects of framing have not been explicitly theorized until now.

12. This idea does find articulation in the literature on framing in the idea of "cultural resonance." This is the notion that frames must resonate with "words and images highly salient in the culture, which is to say *noticeable, understandable, memorable, and emotionally charged*" (Entman 2003, 417; emphasis in original).

13. In this way, frames that aim at opposing worldviews may not be mutually exclusive: One frame may transform and thereby co-opt the discourse of another, blurring distinctions between them. This is an important feature of framing discourse that is often occluded by the neatly oppositional examples used in the literature, which give the impression that there are always only two possible ways to frame an issue. The classic case of this is Kahneman and Tversky 1984. Thomas Nelson, Zoe Oxley, and Rosalee Clawson (1997, 222) also give an example of this while

discussing different ways of framing the conflict in the former Yugoslavia. This dyadic thinking sometimes seems to be a feature of our thinking about framing. Competition over how to frame an issue or a situation is often described as if there are only two competitors. For example, Robert Entman writes, "Successful political communication requires the framing of events, issues, and actors in ways that promote perceptions and interpretations that *benefit one side while hindering the other*" (Entman 2003, 417; emphasis added). I can see no reason to presume that such competition will always be restricted to only two parties.

14. Entman 2003 makes a similar argument about the influence of the administration in framing September 11 and the War on Terror.

15. I find it entirely plausible to believe that some (if not all) among the Bush administration do believe in the importance of women's rights in and of themselves rather than simply as a rhetorical tool to achieve policy and electoral goals. The question, then, is—regardless of their intentions—what is the *effect* of the particular way in which they frame women's rights and its relation to national security?

16. This was a part of Laura Bush's stump speech on the 2004 campaign trail. As a sample, see L. Bush 2004b.

17. This conjecture is supported by the fact that none of the other women in Bush's cabinet during his first term acted as spokespeople for women's rights.

18. The Bush campaign in 2000 used the slogan "W Is for Women" to capture Bush's support for women's rights. This support does not seem to have translated into any meaningful discourse about women's rights until after September 11: see Flanders 2004b. The slogan "W Stands for Women" was used in the 2004 campaign.

19. Laura Bush on one occasion said, "For our girls, women's suffrage is ancient history. They've never known the inequalities that women had to endure and overcome a couple of generations ago. That's why it's so important for us to be vigilant in our remembrance, and vocal in our celebration of women's history—because we owe the great women in our past for the opportunities that we enjoy today" (L. Bush 2001a).

20. Bush notes that "my 2002 budget requests increased funding for Federal initiatives to combat violence against women and to *continue* the guarantees of basic civil rights and liberties for women" (Bush 2001e; emphasis added). He also notes that women's equality is not yet achieved, but he does so with such a positive spin that there does not seem to be any need for activism or radical change. The tone is one of reassurance: we are already on the right track, even if we have not reached complete equality between the sexes. "More than 150 years later, we are closer than ever to realizing Margaret Fuller's dream. Women account for nearly half of all workers. Today, women are 'captains' of their own destinies, and they will continue to help shape our Nation's future. Women hold 74 seats in the United States

Congress, more than at any time in our country's history, and women own more than 9 million businesses employing more than 27.5 million workers. Through their tireless service on a daily basis, the women of our Nation have woven the fabric of families and communities. They contribute immeasurably through faith-based and community organizations" (Bush 2001e).

21. This logic of American superiority justifying foreign intervention is at work, for example, in a speech given by Lynne Cheney that expresses the idea of respect in the language of desert. She stated, "The United States is a land where women are free, and we are defending the freedom of our daughters as well as our sons against a foe that has decided that women do not even deserve to go to school" (Cheney 2001).

22. The rhetoric of respect is tied to the Bush administration's faith-based initiatives. Before September 11, it emerged in discussions of faith-based groups that are teaching boys to have respect for women. See, e.g., Bush (2001c, 2001d).

23. The connection between respect and civilization has often been made without specific reference to respecting women. Consider one of Bush's major speeches in the months following September 11: "This new enemy seeks to destroy our freedom and impose its views. We value life; the terrorists ruthlessly destroy it. We value education; the terrorists do not believe women should be educated or should have health care, or should leave their homes. We value the right to speak our minds; for the terrorists, free expression can be grounds for execution. We respect people of all faiths and welcome the free practice of religion; our enemy wants to dictate how to think and how to worship even to their fellow Muslims. . . . We wage a war to save civilization, itself. We did not seek it, but we must fight it—and we will prevail" (Bush 2001g).

24. She had on previous occasions joined her husband in giving the address. While much has been made about the historic nature of this event, it really was not a new role for Laura Bush. Certainly, the fact that she was the sole speaker performatively underscores the content of her speech: that Americans and the U.S. government, and the Bush administration in particular, already respect women. Indeed, George W. Bush respects women to such a degree that he will allow his wife to perform a (relatively symbolic) presidential task in his stead.

25. It also suggests that one of the rights we should be fighting for is the right of women to wear nail polish without fear of persecution. While I do not mean to trivialize the violence women have faced for a variety of "crimes" having to do with their personal appearance, I think it is worth noting that the crime in question here is that of conforming to a particular standard of female beauty associated with feminine weakness and vulnerability. This example, then, reinforces the notion that women should have the right to beautiful nails—a symbol that resonates at least in the West with the fragile femininity that requires a chivalrous, male protector.

26. Karen Hughes, at the time a counselor to the president, gave remarks in a press briefing that are typical of the Bush administration's rhetoric on Muslim countries in this period. In response to a question about the treatment of women in countries like Egypt and Saudi Arabia, she said, "Well, first of all, I would encourage you not to make a comparison. No other countries, for example, don't allow nine-year-old girls to be educated or to learn to read. And in many other Muslim countries, women are, in fact, greatly respected. And women in most of those other countries have the opportunity to work outside the home and to be—certainly, none of those other countries forbid women or little daughters at 9 and 10 years old from literally learning to read" (Hughes et al. 2001).

27. I take this language of "masculinist protection" from Young 2003b, which is reprinted in this volume.

28. This is, of course, reinforced by the fact that it is the president's *wife* who delivers the message—rather than the president himself, or the secretary of state or defense, or even (if it had to be a woman) a female cabinet member.

29. These include references to the importance of educating children—male *and* female, and to fathers *and* mothers who "want their children to be educated and to live free from poverty and violence"—the first in Bush's introductory remarks and the second on page 3 (National Security Council 2002).

30. Indeed, protecting women's rights is not mentioned at all in the four action points suggested in response to these eight demands.

31. Many commentators suggested after Bush's second inaugural speech that he was unveiling a new direction for his second term in office: encouraging the spread of democracy around the world. However, it is clear from this, as well as from much earlier speeches by Bush and other members of the administration, that this doctrine of democratic peace was well established long before January 2005.

32. She continues, "President Bush is firmly committed to the empowerment in education and health of women around the world. The President knows that women are vital to democracy and important for the development of all countries. And he has three very strong women at home who won't let him forget it." Her words fill the function of reassuring the listener that George W. Bush is committed to women's rights both politically and personally—a part of the rhetorical strategy that I discuss later in the essay. Her comments also paradoxically signal that the president needs three women at home to keep reminding him of the importance of women's rights. As with the rhetoric of respect, Laura Bush's remarks serve to remind us of the familial role of women even as she is speaking of women's rights.

33. Similar evidence is also cited in the UN Resolution on Women and Political Participation. Three of the clauses read,

Affirming that the empowerment and autonomy of women and the improvement of their political, social and economic status are essential to the achievement of representative, transparent and accountable government, democratic institutions and sustainable development in all areas of life,

Affirming also that the active participation of women, on equal terms with men, at all levels of decision-making is essential to the achievement of equality, sustainable development, peace and democracy. . . .

Recognizing also that women's full and equal participation in the political process and decision-making will provide a balance that more accurately reflects the composition of society, is needed to strengthen democracy and promote its proper functioning, plays a pivotal role in furthering women's equal status, and contributes to redefining political priorities and providing new perspectives on political issues" (United Nations General Assembly 2003).

34. The literature on gender and development shows this connection quite clearly. For an example of arguments linking gender to various aspects of development, see World Bank Gender and Development Group 2003.

35. Katha Pollitt's articles in *The Nation*, which are critical of the Bush administration's policies toward women, draw on the same kind of data. Pollitt writes, for example, that "where women are healthy and well educated and self-determined, you can bet that men are too, but the situation of women is not only a barometer of a society's general level of equality and decency—improving women's status is key to solving many of the world's most serious problems" (Pollitt 2002). She takes her argument perhaps a bit further than the Bush administration would by arguing that aiding women also would alter the gender inequality of the family: "Recognizing and maximizing women's key economic role would have a host of benefits—it would lessen hunger, improve women's and children's well-being, improve women's status in the family, lower fertility."

36. A transcript of this speech is available on the White House's official website, at www.whitehouse.gov/news/releases/2004/03/20040312-5.html. A webcast is also available from this page.

37. I take my understanding of narrative from Patterson and Monroe 1998. They describe narratives as the stories we tell ourselves to make sense of the world. Narratives differ from frames in that frames do not require a narrator. In other words, narratives are stories that reflect my self-understanding.

38. Tickner 2001 describes many ways that militarization and military action increase women's insecurity in the stated interest of national security.

39. See the campaign's official 2004 "W Stands for Women" page at www.georgewbush.com/women. The Republican National Convention in 2004 also featured a special 'W Stands for Women' event, at which various female family members of Bush and Cheney spoke of their record. According to one report, the event focused on "boasting of the President Bush's character, his appointments of women to high positions and his decisions to wage war in Afghanistan and Iraq" (Enda 2004). Furthermore, in the presidential and vice-presidential debates, both Bush

and Cheney mentioned the administration's achievements for women's rights in Afghanistan. For transcripts, see Commission on Presidential Debates (2004a, 2004b).

40. She also includes economic and environmental security in her resignification.

41. In fact, one of the organizations that has deployed this kind of rhetorical strategy to great effect is the Organization for Women's Freedom in Iraq. For more on how this organization is contesting the Bush administration's rhetoric of women and security, see Ferguson 2005a.

42. The global scorecard is a good example of this failure to interrogate the meaning of security. The commentary on the F that the Bush administration received for the reality of the security situation for women and girls in Afghanistan and Iraq distinguishes between "personal security" and "security," with the latter referring to a conventional understanding of security as the exercise of sovereign authority and of the state's monopoly over violence: see Center for Health and Gender Equity, Feminist Majority, and Women's Environment and Development Organization 2004b.

43. Both countries' constitutions include equal-rights statements, as well as quotas for women in the legislatures as high as 25 percent: See the Global Database of Quotas for Women, at www.quotaproject.org.

44. Barbara Ehrenreich (2004b) makes a related argument in an editorial calling on John Kerry to counter Bush's efforts at machismo on the campaign trail with a greater commitment to feminism.

wwwwwwwww
Lori J. Marso
wwwwwwwww

Feminism and the Complications of
Freeing the Women of Afghanistan and Iraq

Since September 11, 2001, President George W. Bush and members of his administration have noticed the lack of rights and freedoms of foreign women. The liberation of these women has frequently been cited as compelling justification for the removal of the Taliban in Afghanistan and of Saddam Hussein in Iraq. First Lady Laura Bush argues, for example, that "prosperity cannot follow peace without educated women and children" (L. Bush 2002) and that "empowered women are vital to democracy" (L. Bush 2004a). According to President Bush, the "central goal of the terrorists is the brutal oppression of women—and not only the women of Afghanistan," adding that "the terrorists who help rule Afghanistan are found in dozens and dozens of countries around the world" (Bush 2001i).

This essay introduces the complexities of freedom in feminist politics by exploring the implications of the Bush administration's appropriation of feminist language for its bombing campaign in Afghanistan and its invasion and occupation of Iraq. Though feminists in the United States might applaud attempts to empower, educate, and free Afghan and Iraqi women whose countries have been bombed, invaded, and occupied by military forces led by the United States, as feminists we must be critical of rhetoric and policies that position women as supplicants and that limit freedom solely to Western practices.[1] By way of examining what the Bush administration means by freedom for women and how this is situated within a colonial discourse, I will discuss the multiple meanings of freedom within feminist politics. How feminists position themselves in regard to Bush administration rhetoric of freeing oppressed women is of vital importance for feminist efforts to both appreciate difference and, at the same time, act in solidarity. I will argue that feminists should be suspicious of rhetoric that places feminism on the side of the West, that positions non-Western women as supplicants, and that fails to understand the possibility of difference. Appreciating and acknowledging difference, however, does not mean that feminists cannot make judgments about oppression. I will return to these questions later in this chapter.

First, I turn to a play by Tony Kushner, used in this essay as a heuristic device, in which Laura Bush meets children from the first Gulf War who have died to make freedom possible. I offer a brief reading of this play to emphasize that having meaningful choices available is a central aspect of exercising freedom, as well as to demonstrate how rigid ideological positions disallow any neutral evaluation of the lives of foreign others. Kushner's play positions Laura Bush as an ideological advocate of an abstract idea of freedom that completely obscures her vision. Kushner's play serves as a starting point for a discussion of how feminists might respond to this language of freedom, within which women in Afghanistan and Iraq are represented as foreign and backward others to be pitied, protected, advised, supported, and counseled and offered the "choice" of Western freedom or fundamentalist or totalitarian oppression.

FREEDOM'S LIMITS

In his short play first printed in *The Nation* just before the 2003 "shock and awe" bombings began in Iraq, Tony Kushner reveals the severe shortcomings in the administration's understanding of freedom by representing a "Laura Bush" character who promotes the "education" and "freedom" of Iraqi children. Titled "Only We Who Guard the Mystery Shall Be Unhappy," the play has only three main characters: an angel, Laura Bush, and a silent group of pajama-clad dead Iraqi children. The children sit in a circle around the first lady; the angel stays behind the group, politely and kindly attempting to make Laura aware that the children are dead and that they were killed by the actions of the United States. Each time the angel presents the first lady with a difficult truth pertaining to the former lives of the children, Laura responds in a way that only serves to obscure that truth and reinforce her own vision of reality. Laura wonders why the children are in pajamas and not uniforms and is informed that dead children wear pajamas. Laura responds:

> So you are the first Iraqi children I've met and you look real sweet in your PJs. And I'm sorry you're dead, but all children love books. All children can learn to love books if you read to them. That's why I've come—to read to you, to share one of my favorite books with you, because when a parent reads to a child, or any adult reads to a child, even if that child is dead, the child will learn to love books, and that is so, so important. (Kushner 2003, 11)

Soon after, Mrs. Bush learns that one of the children at her feet died a horrible death caused by diarrhea, intestinal parasites, and dehydration, all due to the bombing of a power station near his village by an American plane in 1999. The angel tells the first lady, "He died of dehydration, shitting water, then blood, then water again, so much! Then a trickle, everyone was sad, there was no food, he shook so hard the screws holding his bed together were loosened. It took three days to die" (Kushner 2003, 12). Laura's response? "Saddam Hussein is a terrible man." And then she elaborates:

> What can I say to you? Oh how can I say this? It isn't right that you should have had to die because your country is run by an evil man who is accumulating weapons of mass destruction. But he is, you see, he really is, everyone knows this and he will kill many, many other children all over the world if he isn't stopped. So, so it was, um, *necessary* for you to die, sweetie, oh how *awful* to say that, but it was, precious. (Kushner 2003, 12)

The inability of the Laura Bush character to acknowledge the United States' role in creating the conditions of the children's suffering and deaths mirrors the real-life rhetoric that accompanied Operation Enduring Freedom in Afghanistan as well as the 2003 invasion and continuing war in

Iraq. Accompanying the silence surrounding the historical role the United States has played within both countries are the evocative symbols of fully veiled women, uneducated children, Taliban evil, Islamic fundamentalism, and Saddam Hussein's tyranny. Within this "imaginative geography of West versus East, us versus Muslims," first ladies such as Laura Bush "give speeches" and educate and free women and children while in Afghanistan "women shuffle around silently in burqas" (Abu-Lughod 2002, 784).

Kushner's play culminates in a discussion of the reading the first lady has chosen for the children: Dostoyevsky's *Grand Inquisitor*. Laura chooses this reading precisely because it is about freedom, and though she intends to teach the dead Iraqi children that their sacrifice is worthy in freedom's name, Laura becomes confused. It is as if, in Kushner's world, she suddenly realizes the presumptions made in assuming that these children would prefer freedom (and hence, death) to something else. In an outburst, she cries:

> People want bread! They don't want God or freedom, they want bread! And they want to be free of free will! And they want everything to be uniform, universal everywhere, everyone just alike! This is what the Grand Inquisitor says. Jesus wanted people to be free, the Grand Inquisitor tells Jesus, but people can't manage freedom so the Church, and not just the Church but totalitarians of all sorts throughout history are here to enslave them, feed them, dictate to them. That's what the Grand Inquisitor offers, freedom from freedom! . . . . [But] my eyes start to blur sometimes when I am reading this passage and I forget who is the villain and who is the hero and I think, you know, "Right ON Grand Inquisitor FOR GOD'S SAKE WOULD IT BE SO GODDAM TERRIBLE TO FEED PEOPLE, AND IS IT REALLY WORTH IT STARVING KIDS SO THEY CAN WEAR PJS IN HEAVEN?" (Kushner 2003, 14)

In Kushner's dramatic rendering, the Laura Bush character struggles, for a moment, with the problems inherent in the rhetoric of freeing Iraqi children. As Lila Abu-Lughod reminds us, this language and these projects, rooted in colonial discourse, reinforce a sense of superiority of Westerners and a "form of arrogance that deserves to be challenged" (Abu-Lughod 2002, 789). In Kushner's play, it is the angel who challenges Laura

Bush's rhetoric, offering compelling details of the daily difficulties in the situation of the Iraqi children. Surely freedom can only be exercised meaningfully within a context where safety and health have already been ensured. Yet rather than see safety and health as minimal requirements for a context in which freedom might flourish, the first lady envisions these as stark alternatives. In her worldview, the choices are reduced to two: an extremely abstract version of "freedom" versus "survival" under totalitarian rule. Nevertheless, near the end of the play, she becomes confused seeing the dead Iraqi children, thinking about the words of the Grand Inquisitor, and she wonders aloud: "A year from now, in what pit of hell will I awake? I was a Democrat when I was a girl! This is what great literature can do!" She confesses that she gets "rattled till my screws come loose, I am rattled like, like . . . the way, when I am in a mood, I attack and scour a sooty pot" (Kushner 2003,14–15).

Maybe the First Lady can forget her role in the death of thousands by vigorously cleaning the house? The children do not know how to respond to this; neither does the angel. Laura's outburst is so baffling that it leaves everyone in silence. Finally, Laura asks if she can kiss the children. After kissing each one on the head, "she closes the book. She looks troubled. She smiles at the children. They smile at her." Then she says, "The kiss glows in my heart. But, I adhere to my ideas" (Kushner 2003,15).

This is the end of the play. There are two registers in which this play vividly illustrates that the idea of freedom, as currently construed by the Bush presidency, is both severely limited and inherently ideological. First, the choice for the Iraqi children is outlined as that solely between freedom and totalitarianism, in spite of the fact that the "liberators" are revealed to have killed the children. Second, in spite of the angel's interventions toward documenting the reality of the children's short lives, and although Mrs. Bush becomes confused and may even see some of the reasons that her version of "freedom" is insufficient, she still "adheres to her ideas."

FREEDOM'S CONTEXT

Though the histories and contexts of Afghanistan and Iraq are remarkably different, in the cultural imaginary painted by the Bush administration, they collapse into the same landscape, particularly when discussed rhetorically as areas of the world that must be democratized and liberated.

The promise of liberation for non-Western others was, and continues to be, a primary justification for the economic sanctions against Saddam Hussein's regime that culminated in the U.S. bombings referred to in the Kushner play, the ongoing war presence in Afghanistan, and the ongoing war against Iraq. As Kushner reveals in his work, this notion of freedom is both severely limited and inherently ideological. Not even minimal conditions of safety and health must be in place for this version of freedom to operate within an ideological universe that fails to notice that United States–led forces deliver so-called freedom through violence and war. Contrary to administration rhetoric claiming that non-Western women are offered more freedom through U.S. interventions in their countries, such interventions and war consistently have tended to make conditions less free for those without power, most frequently children (as in Kushner's play) and women (those whom we are said to be freeing). First of all, interventions have led to chaos making life less secure and more dangerous, particularly for women. Second, the insecurity, chaos, and humiliation that are the aftereffects of these interventions have allowed warring patriarchal factions to gain a foothold, such as in Afghanistan, or have led to an enhancement of sentiment and strength for nationalist and fundamentalist counter-movements, such as in Iraq.

I will elaborate these points by briefly comparing the promises of the administration with what women within Afghanistan and Iraq say about their experience with U.S. intervention. One week after the Afghan elections of October 2004, the real Laura Bush referred to a long list of offenses against the women of Afghanistan under the Taliban and took special care to emphasize the progress that women have made and continue to make within a newly democratic Afghanistan (L. Bush 2004a). Laura Bush traveled to Afghanistan in March 2005, spending six hours in the country, to announce that she felt great pride "as courageous women across the country have taken on leadership roles as students, teachers, judges, doctors, business and community leaders, ministers and governor" (quoted in Gall 2005). The rhetoric against the Taliban's abuse of women prior to the bombing campaign made the Feminist Majority's Eleanor Smeal and the Bush administration into strange bedfellows.[2] The image of fully veiled Afghan women served as visceral justification for the devastating war, and the much proliferated images that came later, those of women casting their veils aside, were used to show their liberation. In contrast, before the war, feminist groups in Afghanistan—namely the Revolutionary Association of the Women of Afghanistan (RAWA), though risking their lives for years working against the Taliban, spoke very strongly against U.S. military action. RAWA specifically warned against the tremendous suffering and potential loss of life such a war could entail for Afghanistan's women. As Charles Hirschkind and Saba Mahmood put it, "The twin figures of the Islamic fundamentalist and his female victim helped consolidate and popularize the view that such hardship and sacrifice were for Afghanistan's own good" (Hirschkind and Mahmood 2002, 341).

Yet recent reports document that, although there have been limited improvements for women in Kabul, conditions for women throughout the country remain grim. Competing warlords vying for power and control, sectarian and tribal rule, disintegration of national authority, and the mobility and strength of criminal gangs have made conditions far less secure for Afghanistan's women. Amnesty International, for example, reports that "women and girls are being subject to rapes, beatings, kidnappings and other forms of intimidation that are preventing them from going to their jobs or schools, registering to vote or just going about their daily business" (S. Frank 2004). Echoing the voice of the angel in Kushner's play, Hirschkind and Mahmood ask, "Why were conditions of war, militarization, and starvation considered to be less injurious to women than the lack of education, employment, and most notably, in the media campaign, Western dress styles?" (Hirschkind and Mahmood 2002, 345).

Likewise, the claim that United States–led sanctions, and then a U.S. invasion and occupation, have enhanced the quality of life for women and children in Iraq is very difficult to support. The UNIFEM gender profile documents that under the early rule of Saddam Hussein, women's literacy and health improved; restrictions on women outside the home were lifted; women won the right to vote and could hold political office; women could drive, work outside the home, and hold jobs traditionally held by men; women's literacy rates were the highest in the region; and Iraqi women were considered to be the most educated and professional women in the Arab world (UN Development Fund for Women 2006). Cynthia Enloe (2004a, 296) notes that "women's education, women's paid work, women's votes, all were encouraged by the Baathist-run government, not for the sake of democratization but for the sake of economic growth, to earn Iraq the status of being a 'modern' nation and to maximize the regime's wartime mobilization."

However, economic sanctions after the invasion of Kuwait severely affected women in all areas of their life. In addition, the 1990s had witnessed a more conservative model of "femininity" being demanded by Saddam Hussein's regime after the defeats in Iran and Kuwait. Thus, the 2003 war and occupation by U.S. troops has severely exacerbated the already precarious position of women. In a 2004 interview with the program *Democracy Now*, Yanar Mohammed, a leading secular activist and director of the Organization of Women's Freedom in Iraq (OWFI), a group that works to stop atrocities against Iraqi women, argues that U.S. troops must leave Iraq as a prerequisite for any change toward peace. She says:

> Now, our cities, our neighborhoods have turned into daily battlefields between the U.S. troops and the military resistance. Women cannot leave their homes for work, for studying, for even the streets have turned into unsafe places because of the inhumane practices against women by the rising Islamism. And it's not safe anymore. (Mohammed 2004)

The English version of *Aljazeera* reports that "the U.S. occupation forces have been arresting the wives of suspected resistance fighters in an attempt to force their husbands to turn themselves in" (Janabi 2004); Yanar Mohammed adds that the U.S. occupation has turned the streets of Iraq into a "no-woman zone" (Agence France-Presse 2003) and that in regions controlled by extremists, women are being forced to veil. Writing under the pseudonym "Nadia Ahmed," as the author of "An Iraqi Woman's Journal," published in the Paris newspaper *Le Monde* on February 4, 2005, one Iraqi woman describes the fear, insecurity, and day-to-day frustration and danger that has changed her life since the "accursed night of March 20, 2003, and the beginning of the Americans' war against my country." Of the first round of elections, she adds, "You've probably guessed: I didn't participate. For security reasons above all, and then, out of principle. Many political tendencies and cities were, in my opinion, excluded; which makes this a lame election whose results were predetermined" (article online at http://www.mindfully.org/Reform/2005/Iraqi-Womans-Journal7feb05.htm).

Allowing a Shiite-dominated coalition to hold power in the new Iraqi government could have an additional, profoundly negative effect on women's freedoms—of movement, for the potential to work, for reproductive choice, to name only a few issues. Article 2 of the final version of the Iraqi constitution cites Islam as the basic source of legislation as well as the official religion of the state and says that no law can be passed that contradicts its "undisputed" rulings (Coleman 2006, 30). But as documented earlier, *sharia* law and its potential impact on women's lives is not even the most troubling aspect of daily life in the current Iraqi state. Isobel Coleman confirms in *Foreign Affairs* that it is religious vigilantes who are having the greatest impact on women by "forcing their own fundamentalist views on Iraq's besieged population" (Coleman 2006, 35). She continues:

> Over the past two years, various towns in both Shiite and Sunni areas have fallen into the hands of extremists who are imposing stringent restrictions there, such as requiring women to wear full-length veils, forbidding music and dancing, and enforcing strict segregation of the sexes in public. Many of these vigilantes are unemployed, undereducated followers of demagogues such as Muqtada al-Sadr. But at least some are reportedly also members of the police force in several southern cities (notably Basra). As their activities suggest, the greatest danger to Iraqi women stems not from any legal restrictions, but from lawlessness. (Coleman 2006, 35–36)

Yet the Bush administration continues to claim that freedom is being delivered to the women of Afghanistan and Iraq in spite of all this mounting evidence to the contrary. The Bush administration's rhetoric concerning "freedom" for women has never matched its actions, and this is no surprise to feminists.[3] While it is risky (as well as patronizing and patriarchal) to align oneself on the side of those who claim to save women within the colonial framework, I do think it possible for feminists to argue convincingly, with the Bush administration, that women's lives around the globe should be taken seriously. While recognizing, all the while, how shallow the administration's rhetoric has turned out to be, feminists can nevertheless utilize this rhetoric to put women's lives on the political agenda.

FREEDOM'S COMPLEXITIES

Because the Bush presidency has usurped feminist language within the chivalrous gesture of offering freedom to supplicant others, when feminists speak of freedom for women in Afghanistan and Iraq we take the risk of replicating what Young, in this volume, has called the "logic of masculinist protection" toward non-Western women. It is precisely this logic and its implications that feminists must avoid. According to Kushner's play, it seems that no matter how we respond, members of the Bush administration will "adhere to their ideas." I will demonstrate, however, that the options are not as limiting as we might think. We might even probe deeper into Kushner's play and discover other possibilities. Evaluating the angel's role in Kushner's play, for example, could aid feminists in our efforts to strategically intervene within these treacherous debates. Recall that in response to Laura Bush's empty promises, the angel repeatedly points to the context in which the Iraqi children live their lives and the limited choices available to them. To begin to examine some of the complexities of freedom and develop a specifically feminist sense of freedom that can be usefully employed in response to the Bush administration rhetoric, I return first to the work of Simone de Beauvoir in *The Second Sex* (1989 [1953]). In this early feminist text, Beauvoir describes how any person's freedom is always bound by context, or what she calls "situation." Situation involves material forces as well as subjective response. One's situation is never preconditioned solely by objective circumstances because how one reacts to these forces is also part of one's situation.

Offering an account of the subject and her freedom as embodied, Beauvoir's subject of freedom is always already within a situation as well as always within a body. The subject's relationship to the world is constituted by certain material realities such as sexuality, race or ethnicity, age, physical prowess, and so forth. Being a woman is but one factor with which the individual woman must contend. As a Beauvoir scholar elaborates, "If I have to negotiate the world in a crippled body or sick body I am not going to have the same experience of the world or of myself as if I had a healthy or particularly athletic body . . . nor will the world react to me in the way it would if I had a different body" (Moi 1991, 68). One's body and how it is perceived in the world, combined with material circumstances, all contribute to our unique experience as individuals. Moreover, the body itself is "not a thing" but, rather, a "situation" (Beauvoir 1989 [1953], 34). Depending on the factors mentioned earlier, the body "is the instrument of our grasp upon the world, a limiting factor for our projects" (Beauvoir 1989 [1953], 34). This sense of freedom as always within a situation allows us to think about varieties of contexts where both external and internal factors (economic, social, and cultural context interacting with desire, will, and preference) are all at play in enhancing or restricting (constructing) one's freedom.

Clearly, freedom for the subject is never unlimited and never a phenomenon of consciousness alone. Unlike Kushner's Laura Bush, who thinks that the Iraqi children might still benefit from her reading to them even though their bodies are dead, Beauvoir's articulation of freedom within a situation reveals just how disembodied this articulation of freedom is. To be meaningful, we must understand freedom as constituted within bodily, national, class, historical, and cultural situations. Beauvoir, therefore, combines the subjective and the objective in her articulation of the subject's relationship to her world. She helpfully theorizes a subject who is both self-constituting as well as constituted by structures not of her making. The individual subject experiences desires and may be capable of achieving freedom, but only within a body and a world not of her choosing. Finally, Beauvoir adds that freedom is realized in association with others. Freedom is a "reaching out to the world" that is accomplished through collective projects rather than solely an individual consciousness achieved alone.

Following Beauvoir's lead, to explore women's situation in Afghanistan or Iraq we must understand the material, political, social, and economic conditions in which these women live and the various ways in which Afghan and Iraqi women *themselves* respond and react to these conditions. In attempting to spread a specifically American message throughout the Muslim world, this is precisely what the Bush administration and its representatives have failed to do. When Karen Hughes, for example, spoke to a group of handpicked elite Saudi women in September 2005, she was surprised to find that even these women, known as some of the most liberal in the country, questioned her message. According to the *New York Times*, "Ms. Hughes, the under secretary of state for public diplomacy, [was] on her first trip to the Middle East. She seemed clearly taken aback as the women told her that just because they were not allowed to vote or drive that did not mean they were treated unfairly or imprisoned in their own homes" (Weisman 2005).

Like Beauvoir, Nancy Hirschmann has emphasized the role of social, political, and economic context in formulating the desire to make choices and limiting the choices themselves (Hirschmann 2002). Building on this more complex notion of freedom, I will argue that feminists need to adopt and advance a notion of freedom as embedded in context, taking seriously the possibility of difference while making judgments about oppression. As I will explain, freedom defined as within a situation allows feminists to praise and encourage the enhancement of mobility and choice for women across the globe while articulating the historical, cultural, colonial, political, economic, and social context in which women's daily lives are embedded.

Clearly, the "Western feminist" or the "Western woman," never herself outside the colonial framework, should not form a judgment based on criteria that remain detached from the Afghan or Iraqi conditions that are themselves constructed through colonial, international, and global relationships, historically and in the present. One common conflict feminists identify within their national contexts arises from being asked to "choose between their feminism and their ethnicity or culture" (Lazreg 2001, 286). Uma Narayan explains the difficulty of embracing the identity "third world feminist," since charges of "Westernization" and "inauthenticity" are frequently leveled at these political positions and coalitions. Within the colonial and postcolonial context, Narayan explains, male-dominated third world elites choose certain practices as "authentic" to their culture, and within this context feminism is seen as culturally "inauthentic." "The nationalist cultural pride that was predicated upon a return to 'traditional values' and the rejection of 'Westernization' that began under colonial rule thus re-emerges today in a variety of postcolonial 'fundamentalist' movements, where returning women to their 'traditional roles' continues to be defined as central to preserving national identity and cultural pride" (Narayan 1997, 20).

Feminists within the context of colonialism and postcolonialism thus often reject the false choice between "Western" values and fundamentalist traditions. RAWA describes the "freeing" of Afghan women, as accomplished by the U.S. military, as that of "a captive, bleeding, devastated, hungry, pauperized, drought-stricken and ill-starred Afghanistan" being "bombed into oblivion by the most advanced and sophisticated weaponry ever created in human history" (Revolutionary Association of the Women of Afghanistan 2002). Yanar Mohammed, director of the OWFI, depicts the limited "choice" for Iraqi women as that between "the American occupation that is willing to do genocide, or . . . political Islam, that will make us live in a completely inhuman and unliberated way of life. The two alternatives do not look good" (Mohammed 2004).

Much of the work of feminist organizations in Afghanistan and Iraq has been to articulate why the choice between Western freedom and traditionalist fundamentalism is completely unacceptable for women within their situations. Yet, as Enloe (2004a) painfully reminds us, the imperial context in which these debates play themselves out often serves to create fissures and divisions within and between various feminist and women's groups within any given national context. Speaking of a conversation that she had with a female Afghan deputy minister in the post-Taliban state in early 2003, Enloe writes that this particular woman (whose identity remains confidential) voiced serious distrust of the women in RAWA. The Afghan woman argued that the women in RAWA had been "too sympathetic to Kabul's 1980s Soviet-backed secular regime" (Enloe 2004a, 278). Enloe elaborates:

Creating a sense of national identity in countries such as Afghanistan has meant for many women advocates crafting comparative judgments about both past and present foreign rulers and about rival male-led local parties, each claiming to represent the nation, each claiming to know what is best for the nation's women. One activist local woman's savvy use of openings created by the latest occupying power looks to another activist local woman like collaboration with the enemy, betrayal of the nation. Neither woman controls the masculinized political contest. Having to make such choices, often in the midst of war, displacement, and confusion, does not breed trust among women. (Enloe 2004a, 277)

In her work on women in Iraq, Coleman also shows that there are strong disagreements among women about how to best make political gains within their limiting context. While OWFI completely condemns Islam's having a role within the political sphere, other "Islamic feminists" seek to "search for Islamic answers to the questions of modern life" (Coleman 2006, 26). Coleman refers to an organization known as Women Living under Muslim Laws (WLUML) as a "transnational example of how women are pushing for change from within Islam" that provides "women's groups around the world with powerful Islamic justifications for gender equality" (Coleman 2006, 33).

What is important to notice is that within these disputes among local activist women in Afghanistan and Iraq, there are abundant examples of women using their own agency to make life better for themselves and their daughters. When we refuse to label women helpless "others" who need to be "saved," we can illuminate the contexts in which women demonstrate their agency. Speaking of sites of "scattered resistance" to the rise of global capital, Manisha Desai writes:

> When one shifts the focus to women's agency in the global political economy, we see a complex set of relations that are built on preexisting patriarchal, racial, and ethnic practices. One also sees women creating new sites for action at the local, national, and transnational levels in which to enact new political, economic, and cultural practices. In this way, women activists offer alternatives to the seemingly inevitable course of global capital. (Desai 2002, 16)

This more complex sense of freedom I have been developing allows us to see not only how a context limits one's real choices, but also how a context might shape a person's desires. Many feminists reject Western notions of freedom, not for fear of being labeled "Western" or "inauthentic" but, rather, subsequent to thoughtful examination of what "Western feminism" stands for. Haleh Afshar writes that "many highly educated and articulate Muslim women regard Western feminism as a poor example and have no wish to follow it. Not only do they dismiss Western feminism for being one of the many instruments of colonialism, but also they despise the kind of freedom that is offered to women under the Western patriarchy" (Afshar 2001, 350). Hirschmann (2003, 10) has emphasized the important role that the shaping of desires plays in the ability to exercise freedom by articulating how the "social construction of the choosing subject of liberty" must also be examined within any evaluation of freedom.

Saba Mahmood's study of Egyptian women in the piety movement is a compelling account of how desires are shaped within a context such that through the "repeated performance of virtuous practices" the "subject's will, desire, intellect, and body come to acquire a particular form" (Mahmood 2005, 162). Mahmood's ethnography of women's active and grassroots participation in mosques in Cairo challenges any simple assumption that feminists may have about what constitutes any particular woman's own sense of her freedom. Studying these women and the contexts of their lives, Mahmood concludes, "I came to reckon that if the old feminist practice of 'solidarity' had any valence whatsoever, it could not be grounded in the ur-languages of feminism, progressivism, liberalism, or Islamism, but could only ensue within the uncertain, at times opaque, conditions of intimate and uncomfortable encounters in all their eventuality" (Mahmood 2005, 199). These "intimate and uncomfortable encounters" lead to Mahmood's warnings against the conventional Western assumption that the liberal subject of freedom is the agent in every context. In fact, her work convincingly shows that there are conditions in which "submission to certain forms of (external) authority is a condition for achieving the subject's potentiality" (Mahmood 2005, 31).

When we look at individuals within their contexts, then, we can more clearly see that social, economic, cultural, religious, and historical structures, in relation to women's subjective response to them, constitute the conditions of freedom. This is the reality of freedom in restraint, of choice and of consciousness as intimately linked to the situation in which one finds oneself at any given moment in time. Such an articulation of freedom forces us to think through the complexity that belies any simplistic ideological notion that Western women (assumed as a coherent group uniformly "free") can "rescue" non-Western women (also a group, assumed to be uniformly oppressed). Clearly, feminists should be wary of any call to become rescuers. Using privilege responsibly would entail facilitating recognition and encouragement of women's own agency, as they enact it, to improve their living conditions within their own political and national contexts.

FREEDOM'S PROMISE

How, then, might feminists recognize the complexity of the meaning of freedom, combat the limited and rhetorical use of the term by the Bush administration, and still claim use of freedom's empowering impulse? Recall that, although Beauvoir recognizes constraints on one's freedom, she consistently values its exercise. Writing from the position of "existentialist ethics" (Beauvoir 1989 [1953], xxxiv), Beauvoir consistently claims the exercise of freedom as the highest good, defined as "a continual reaching out towards other liberties" into "an indefinitely open future" (Beauvoir 1989 [1953], xxxiv–xxxv). To authentically claim one's freedom is to take risks, to make a mark on the world, to act, to transcend. Indeed, situations that unduly limit our freedom are said to be problematic:

> Every time transcendence falls back into immanence, stagnation, there is a degradation of existence into the "*en-soi*"—the brutish life of subjection to given conditions—and of liberty into constraint and contingence. This downfall represents a moral fault if the subject consents to it; if it is inflicted upon him, it spells frustration and oppression. In both cases it is an absolute evil. (Beauvoir 1989 [1953], xxxv)

But at the same time, Beauvoir reminds us that to assume authentic freedom is not to act selfishly. To act freely in accordance with existentialist ethics, one must always remain cognizant of the effect of one's actions on others in the world. Our freedom can only be truly exercised in recognition of the human and political condition of plurality. As Beauvoir describes it, "So here is my situation facing others: men are free, and I am thrown into the world among these foreign freedoms" (Beauvoir 2004, 135). She continues, "I am dealing not with one freedom but with *several* freedoms. And precisely because they are free, they do not agree among themselves" (Beauvoir 2004, 131). Moreover, we cannot make others agree with us, adopt our ways, or conform to our notion of what freedom means or of what the good life might consist. Rather, we must respect the freedom of others in all their complexities, not only because this is our ethical responsibility, but also because it is the only condition under which our own freedom can be achieved. Again, as Beauvoir articulates, "Respect for the other's freedom is not an abstract rule. It is the first condition of my successful effort. I can only appeal to the other's freedom, not constrain it. I can invent the most urgent appeals, try my best to charm it, but it will remain free to respond to those appeals or not, no matter what I do" (Beauvoir 2004, 136).

One way to avoid the patronizing gesture that offers freedom to helpless others, yet still retain freedom's promise of being able to recognize conditions of oppression and value the expansion of choices for women, is to steer clear of any claims of knowing what women want. How, then, might Western feminists act in solidarity with non-Western women without presuming what they want or need—in other words, while recognizing that they, too, are free subjects with diverse goals and desires? Just as context and situation are defining factors for the exercise of freedom, the appreciation of different desires that are enhanced and nourished within other contexts enables us to complicate the limited Western frame. In her encounter with the Saudi women in late 2005, Karen Hughes emphasized the empowering effects of driving. A Saudi woman responded, "I don't want to drive a car. I worked hard for my medical degree. Why do I need a driver's license?" (quoted in Weisman 2005). The failure of communication between Hughes and the elite Saudi woman speaks volumes about the American fetishization of certain practices, such as veiling or driving, to indicate an exercise of freedom. Because she is an elite Saudi woman and a doctor, the woman would probably hire a driver to take her to work. Or if she were not of the elite class, she might choose to take public transportation, if it is available. The idea that driving equals freedom just does not translate in many parts of the world. In a *New York Times* article, Steven Weisman elaborates that "many in this region say they resent the American assumption that given the chance, everyone would live like Americans" (Weisman 2005).

Mahmood's anthropological topography of women's participation in the piety movement in Egypt deepens and extends the lessons of the exchange. Mahmood's account of women's active support of certain practices in Islam that sustain some aspects of women's subordination should lead us to question our own knowledge about desire, freedom, and the formation of the subject. Mahmood introduces us to women who find meaning in the embrace of certain customs, traditions, and what they see as virtuous practices. She is interested in understanding how social norms, some of which are inherently patriarchal (and possibly oppressive), are the necessary ground through which a subject is formed and her agency is realized. This encounter with "otherness" is valuable not only for what we learn about the other but also for what we might learn about ourselves.

This sense of women's agency is one that forces us to think deeply about our own assumptions concerning women's desires, something that we rarely do. Mahmood says, for example, that when she lectures in an academic setting, she is often surprised by her audience's "lack of curiosity about what else the veil might perform in the world beyond its violation of women" (Mahmood 2005, 195). Even feminists who argue that donning the veil is an act against Western norms are still confined to the framework of embracing or rejecting Western values. Hirschmann (2002, 180) notes that the "veil itself does not make women free or unfree; rather, the patriarchal use of the veil to control women sets the limits to women's agency." Mahmood argues, in contrast, that for the women in the piety movement, agency itself is defined in terms of a set of embodied practices rooted within cultural traditions, regardless of their patriarchal implications.

This disagreement aside, when we begin to ask questions about how context frames the exercise of freedom and shapes the possibility of subjectivity, we are a long way from a simplistic definition of freedom that fails to acknowledge even minimal necessities for freedom such as safety and health.

To ask an entirely different set of questions about the practices that may appear to inhibit women's freedom, as Mahmood does, allows us to see that women do not all want the same kinds of things. It also allows us to speak politically about women's conditions of life across cultures and demands that we interact politically in new kinds of ways. The method of political interaction demanded by the recognition and interplay of differences is one that draws on intense negotiation. We must listen, judge, and act while remaining attentive to the working of power. It stands in stark contrast to a technical, bureaucratic, or ideologically driven method of politics that disallows the kinds of intricate and often messy interactions in which differences must be understood and negotiated.

This is the kind of political interaction central to feminist practice that refuses the dominance of the Western model as enacted prominently within the Bush presidency wherein women's "freedom" is deployed in an instrumental and ideological fashion. In contrast, feminists should defend women's freedom non-instrumentally, as an end in itself. When women's freedom is promised as a justification for or as part and parcel of the betterment of society or to achieve certain social goals, women are identified in functional terms where we must articulate knowledge of their essential identity. Moreover, to speak in terms that claim knowledge of what women want or who women are leads away from active engagement and solidarity to endless discussion concerning how to mark out our identities and act politically solely in light of these social categories. Linda Zerilli (2005) distinguishes social claims that presume people's social function and their desires from political claims that are inherently plural and open to contestation. Political claims allow us to "test the limits and nature of agreement," discover "what happens when agreements break down or never materialize in the way we thought in the first place" (Zerilli 2005, 172). These kinds of claims open up the possibility of creating communities of women, across and within borders, that are not based in any essential identity or knowledge about what women want or desire. In this version of freedom as political action, freedom is not an attribute of the subject's will, but an accessory of doing and acting that is only achieved when acting in community. This sense of freedom and politics is part and parcel of engaging with others in the world, acting in concert and inherently tied to responsibility. As in Beauvoir's analysis, freedom must be understood as embodied, embedded in situation, and always already part of a community.

The reality of freedom as exercised within conditions of situation and plurality forces us to recognize that freedom is both political and collective. Because we always experience freedom in relationship to others, rather than singularly and alone, any free action in which we engage has an effect on others in the world. Almost as if speaking back to the Laura Bush character in Kushner's play, noting that Europeans find "something childish in [America]," Beauvoir adds that "in an adult, innocence cannot but mean some voluntary blindness" (Beauvoir 2004, 313). Taking our cues again from the angel in Kushner's play, feminists must reject this version of "innocence" that manifests itself as wanting to believe that we can offer freedom, untouched by power and situation, to non-Western women of the world.

Most important, however, we must note that acknowledging difference and plurality does not preclude feminists from forming judgments concerning contexts that enhance or inhibit women's ability to make meaningful choices about their lives. Parting ways with Mahmood on this particular issue, I find it absolutely necessary to retain a positive emphasis on freedom that, while complex, rooted within situation, and cognizant of differences, still allows us to make judgments concerning ways to alleviate conditions of oppression.[4] As feminists, we must retain our focus on the need to simultaneously condemn Bush's rhetoric and actions while condemning fundamentalist Islamists, or anyone else who is willing to decide what is right for women or who sees women's freedom in instrumentalist or ideological ways. We must be cognizant of opening up the space necessary for women to recognize and voice their desires and have the power necessary to make decisions about their day-to-day lives.

Indeed, our own location within the colonial and neocolonial situation demands that we face up to this greater responsibility that judgment entails. As Western feminists responsible to non-Western feminists whose countries our governments have invaded and occupied, we should applaud real efforts to enhance freedom for women in the United States as well as around the globe. We can express our support for women in Afghanistan and Iraq to vote to elect new leaders, for example. Yet in the same breath, it is our responsibility to ask detailed questions about women's lived experiences and their situations and make clear that these specific conditions are intimately linked to freedom. There are too many examples from around the world where women's rights legislation has been approved and passed, but the laws remain ineffectual in having any real impact on women's daily lives.[5] Enhancing the scope of freedom, in the complex sense I have articulated, also demands that we recognize conditions of oppression.

One of the clearest ways for women to gain some power over their own contexts, without a specification of what to do with that freedom and power, is to be participants in the political process. Here we can congratulate the Bush administration for emphasizing that women should have a political voice while demanding that this voice must have substance and be effective in women's daily lives. When progressive women in Iraq saw that they would lose the battle over Islam, for example, they focused on holding on to their quota in Parliament (Coleman 2006, 34) and were able to retain a 25 percent quota. Coleman suggests that following the lead of progressive women in Iraq, the United States should abandon support of the secular but marginalized Iraqi leaders popular in Washington and play a more constructive role in "identifying and cultivating Islamic feminists within Iraq's mainstream religious parties" (Coleman 2006, 36). While there is never any guarantee that the women filling the quota will not be female conservatives, to realize the role Islam is playing in the new constitution and support Islamic feminists goes farther in promoting the possibility that these women will seek to promote women's rights within an Islamic framework.

Another example of how feminists might act in solidarity with oppressed women without dictating their desires is offered by Judith Ezekiel in her analysis of debates over the wearing of the veil by French schoolgirls. Ezekiel documents that the February 2004 French law banning "conspicuous signs of religion in public schools" (Ezekiel 2005, 1) targeted the hijab and sought to resuscitate a national and universalist French identity seen to be under threat from "immigrant" communities and values. The response from French feminists has been divided and difficult for much the same reason that American feminists have felt divided over "saving" the women of Afghanistan and Iraq. Ezekiel notes that, "although the hijab story has mostly been told in gender-blind terms, women's oppression and emancipation have also been an on-going thread" (Ezekiel 2005, 11). Much of the talk about women's oppression has come from figures "who have never distinguished themselves for their feminism," and yet they depict the French Republic as the "defender of a supposedly established gender equality" (Ezekiel 2005, 11). Ezekiel calls this feminism "National Feminism, akin to Laura Bush and Lynn Cheney's sudden concern with Afghan and Iraqi women" (Ezekiel 2005, 11). Yet she notes that many long-time, committed feminists and activists also support the ban, on the side of women "oppressed and murdered in the Muslim world for not covering themselves," while others, such as Christine Delphy, oppose the ban in what Ezekiel calls an "antiracist zeal" (Ezekiel 2005, 12).

Within the debate over the headscarves in French public schools, as well as over what Western women might offer to non-Western women, we must keep in mind that freedom always has a context and is laden with internal contradictions. Ezekiel documents, for example, the feminist and activist work of new groupings of women emerging among the daughters of Maghrebi immigrants and some from sub-Saharan African and Caribbean backgrounds that she calls "women of color" feminism. These feminists demand "women's freedom from machismo from the men in the housing estates" (Ezekiel 2005, 12) yet are completely outside the purview as well as the ideological frame of "National Feminism." These emerging feminists are "denouncing the multiple sources of their oppression that include racism, economic injustice, and sexism and violence—from within and without the ghettos" and are "speaking for themselves, in different voices from those heard in the current [2004] hijab story" (Ezekiel 2005, 13).

Recognizing that freedom is always embedded within community thus points us in the direction of a definition of freedom and new versions of political action that take account of difference while continuing to value the enlargement of the scope of meaningful choices. Individuals exist within social contexts, make choices and exercise freedom within these contexts, such that freedom is never exercised alone or without any effect on others. Certainly, an emphasis on freedom within situation demands that feminists reject the patronizing (and patriarchal) rhetoric of rescue, yet it also provides a framework for critical engagements that allow comparisons about freedom's contexts. As feminists, and particularly as feminists in response to the Bush administration, it is imperative to reject Western "superiority" in favor of plurality and to reject language of rescue in favor of solidarity. For Western feminists to demand meaningful details concerning women's situation and women's lived realities from women in non-Western countries distances us from the Bush administration's rhetoric while still allowing for a positive emphasis on freedom as a good in itself. We can congratulate any gains toward enhancement of the scope of meaningful choices while demanding knowledge of the situation in which women live out their daily lives. Acknowledging plurality, particularly in terms of individual and collective desires, while positing and actively encouraging solidarity for women across cultures enables us to speak of freedom in more realistic, as well as more responsible, ways.

NOTES

For helpful comments on earlier versions of this essay, I thank Michaele Ferguson, Tom Lobe, Patricia Moynagh, Laurie Naranch, and Joan Tronto.

1. Throughout this essay, I refer to "Western" and "non-Western" women when discussing the relationship between feminists in the United States and the women of Afghanistan and Iraq whose countries have been invaded, bombed, and occupied by U.S. led forces. Though employing the terms "Western" and "non-Western" or "Western" and "Third World" does retain explanatory value, these terms can also

obscure other important historical and economic relationships and conditions. Chandra Talpade Mohanty argues, for example, that "the increasing proliferation of Third and Fourth Worlds within the national borders of ["Western" nations], as well as the rising visibility and struggles for sovereignty by First Nations/indigenous peoples around the world" (2003, 226) makes the terms "One-Third/Two-Thirds Worlds" a more useful description in certain instances. In addition, "non-Western" women often live in "Western" countries, and the conditions of life for women need to be analyzed within as well as across borders. I use the terms "Western" and "non-Western" with these complications in mind, and in light of Uma Narayan's insight that to speak about "Western" and "non-Western" societies and cultures is to "invoke '*idealized*' constructions, far from being faithful descriptions of the values that *actually pervaded* their institutional practices and social life. Thus, 'Western culture' could see itself as staunchly committed to values like liberty and equality, a commitment that was often upheld as its distinguishing feature, a mark of its 'superiority'" (Narayan 1997, 15).

2. Lila Abu-Lughod argues that we should certainly harbor suspicion about such bedfellows, reminding feminists to "look closely at what we are supporting (and what we are not) and to think carefully about why": see Abu-Lughod 2002, 787.

3. For a comprehensive discussion of the mismatch between rhetoric and reality on numerous policies affecting women, nationally and internationally, see Flanders, ed., 2004.

4. Mahmood argues that, "in order to grasp these modes of action indebted to other reasons and histories, I will suggest that it is crucial to detach the notion of agency from the goals of progressive politics" (Mahmood 2005, 14).

5. See, e.g., LaFraniere 2005, for a telling example of how, in spite of laws in the South African Parliament banning virginity testing for young girls, it remains a common practice. Also see Zerilli 2005, 119–23, for a discussion concerning how rights can deteriorate into legal artifacts if they lose their connection to practices of freedom. Practicing freedom politically is made possible, in the interpretation I offer in this chapter, only when acknowledging plurality and solidarity between differently situated women to alleviate conditions of oppression.

wwwwwwwww
References
wwwwwwwww

Abramowitz, Rachel. 2004. "Gibson Talks about Film, Furor and Faith." *Los Angeles Times*, February 15, A1.

Abramson, Paul R., John H. Aldrich, and David W. Rohde. 2005. "The 2004 Presidential Election: The Emergence of a Permanent Majority?" *Political Science Quarterly* 120, no. 1: 33–57.

Abu-Lughod, Lila. 2002. "Do Muslim Women Really Need Saving? Anthropological Reflections on Cultural Relativism and Its Others." *American Anthropologist* 104, no. 3: 783–90.

Afshar, Haleh. 2001. "Women and the Politics of Fundamentalism." Pp. 348–65 in *Feminism and Race*, ed. Kum-Kum Bhavnani. Oxford: Oxford University Press.

Agence France-Presse. 2003. "Over 400 Women Kidnapped, Raped in Postwar Iraq." August 24. Available online at www.ccmep.org/2003_articles/Iraq/082403_over_400_women_kidnapped.htm (accessed May 26, 2006).

Alford, C. Fred. 1993. "Greek Tragedy and Civilization: The Cultivation of Pity." *Political Research Quarterly* 46 (June): 259–80.

Altman, Lawrence. 2004. "Infant Drugs for HIV Put Mothers at Risk." *New York Times*, February 10, A22.

———. 2005. "U.S. Blamed for Condom Shortage in Fighting AIDS in Uganda." *New York Times*, August 30, A4.

Alvarez, Sonia. 1998. "Feminismos latinamericanos: Reflexiones teóricas y perspectivas comparativas." Pp. 4–22 in *Reflexiones teóricas y comparativas sobre los feminismos en Chile y America Latina*, ed. Marcela Rios. Santiago, Chile: Nostas del Conversatorio, 1998.

Ambrose, Stephen. 1997. *Citizen Soldiers: The U.S. Army from the Normandy Beaches to the Bulge to the Surrender of Germany*. New York: Simon and Schuster.

Anderson, Bonnie. 2000. *Joyous Greetings: The First International Women's Movement, 1830–1860*. New York: Oxford University Press.

Apostolidis, Paul. 2000. *Stations of the Cross: Adorno and Christian Right Radio*. Durham: Duke University Press.

Appadurai, Arjun. 1996. *Modernity at Large*. Minneapolis: University of Minnesota Press.

Archibugi, Daniele, and Iris Marion Young. 2002. "Envisioning a Global Rule of Law." *Dissent* 49 (Spring): 27–37.

Arendt, Hannah. 1965. *On Revolution*. New York: Penguin Books.

Arlia, Eva. 2004. " 'Train Up a Child'—How?" October 18. Available online at www
.beverlylahayeinstitute.org/articledisplay.asp?id=6552&department=BLI&cate
goryid=reports (accessed April 21, 2006).

Ashe, Marie. 1993. " 'Bad Mothers,' 'Good Lawyers,' and 'Legal Ethics.' " *Georgetown Law Journal* 81 (August): 2533–66.

Associated Press. 2005. "What Do You Know about George Bush?" January 17.

Axtmen, Kris. 2004. "Bush Reins in His Base with an 'Average Joe' Aura." March 10. Available online at www.csmonitor.com/2004/0310/p02s01-uspo.html (accessed March 26, 2006).

Bakker, Isabella, and Stephen Gill. 2003. *Power, Production, and Social Reproduction: Human In/security in the Global Political Economy*. Basingstoke: Palgrave Macmillan.

Balbus, Isaac. 2003. "Against the Idealism of the Affects." *Political Theory* 31 (December): 859–70.

Barker, Isabelle V. 2005. "Citizenship in an Era of Transnational Labor Migration and Inequality: The Status of Non-Citizen Women Workers in the Long-Term Care Industry in the United States." In *Feminists Contest Politics and Philosophy*, ed. L. Gurley, C. Leeb, and A. Moser. New York: Peter Lang.

Basu, Amrita, ed. 1995. *The Challenge of Local Feminisms: Women's Movements in Global Perspective*. Boulder, Colo.: Westview Press.

Bayes, Jane, Patricia Begné, Laura Gonzalez, Lois Harder, Mary Hawkesworth, and Laura MacDonald. 2006. *Women, Democracy, and Globalization in North America: A Comparative Study*. New York: Palgrave.

Beauvoir, Simone de. 1989 (1953). *The Second Sex*, repr. ed., trans. and ed. H. M. Parshley. New York: Vintage.

———. 2004. *Simone de Beauvoir: Philosophical Writings*, ed. Margaret A. Simons. Urbana: University of Illinois Press.

Bedford, Katherine. 2005. "The World Bank's Employment Programs in Ecuador and Beyond: Empowering Women, Domesticating Men, and Resolving the Social Reproduction Dilemma." Ph.D. diss., Rutgers University, New Brunswick, N.J.

Bellant, Russ. 1995. "Promise Keepers: Christian Soldiers for Theocracy." Pp. 81–85 in *Eyes Right! Challenging the Right Wing Backlash*, ed. Chip Berlet. Boston: South End Press.

Benjamin, Jessica. 1988. *Bonds of Love: Psychoanalysis, Feminism, and the Problem of Domination*. New York: Pantheon Books.

Berkowitz, Peter. 1999. *Virtue and the Making of Modern Liberalism*. Princeton: Princeton University Press.

———. 2003. "The Liberal Spirit in America." August. Available online at www.policyreview.org/aug03/berkowitz.html (accessed January 12, 2006).

———. 2005. "The Court, the Constitution, and the Culture of Freedom." August. Available online at www.policyreview.org/aug05/berkowitz.html (accessed January 12, 2006).

Berlant, Lauren. 1997. *The Queen of America Goes to Washington City: Essays on Sex and Citizenship*. Durham: Duke University Press.

Berlet, Chip, and Margaret Quigley. 1995. "Overview: Theocracy and White Supremacy." Pp. 15–43 in *Eyes Right! Challenging the Right Wing Backlash*, ed. Chip Berlet. Boston: South End Press.

Bissinger, H. G. 2000. *Friday Night Lights*. Cambridge, Mass.: Da Capo Press.

Black, Earl, and Merle Black. 2002. *The Rise of Southern Republicans*. Cambridge, Mass.: Harvard University Press.

Blanchard, Eric M. 2003. "Gender, International Relations, and the Development of Feminist Security Theory." *Signs* 28, no. 4: 1289–312.

Blankenhorn, David. 1995. *Fatherless America: Confronting Our Most Urgent Social Problem*. New York: Basic Books.

Bloom, Allan. 1979. "Introduction." Pp. 3–28 in Jean-Jacques Rousseau, *Emile or On Education*. New York: Basic Books.

Bolt, Christine. 2004. *Sisterhood Questioned? Race, Class and Internationalism in the American and British Women's Movements, c. 1880s–1970s*. New York: Routledge.

Bowden, Mark. 2003. "The Dark Art of Interrogation." *Atlantic Monthly*. October.

Boyer, Paul. 1992. *When Time Shall Be No More: Prophecy Belief in Modern American Culture*. Cambridge, Mass.: Harvard University Press.

Brannan, David W., Philip F. Esler, and N. T. Anders Strindberg. 2001. "Talking to 'Terrorists': Towards an Independent Analytical Framework for the Study of Violent Substate Activism." *Studies in Conflict and Terrorism* 24: 3–24.

Bravin, Jess. 2002. "Interrogation School Tells Army Recruits How Grilling Works — Thirty Techniques in Sixteen Weeks." *Wall Street Journal*, April 26.

Bremner, Ian. 1998. "Saving Private Ryan." *History Today* 48, no. 11:50–51.

Brison, Susan. 2004. "Torture, or 'Good Old American Pornography.'" *Chronicle of Higher Education* 50, no. 4 (June):B10.

Brod, Harry, and Michael Kaufman, eds. 1994. *Theorizing Masculinities*. London: Sage.

Brown, Michelle. 2005. "'Setting the Conditions' for Abu Ghraib: The Prison Nation Abroad." *American Quarterly* 57, no. 3: 973–97.

Bunch, Charlotte. 2002. "Whose Security?" *The Nation*, September 23. Available online at www.thenation.com/doc.mhtml?i=20020923&s=bunch&c=1 (accessed July 1, 2005).

Bunch, Charlotte, and Susana Fried. 1996. "Beijing '95: Moving Women's Human Rights from Margin to Center." *Signs* 22 (Fall): 200–204.

Bunch, Charlotte, and Samantha Frost. 2000. "Women's Human Rights: An Introduction." Pp. 1078–83 in *Routledge International Encyclopedia of Women: Global Women's Issues and Knowledge*, ed. Cheris Kramarae and Dale Spender. New York: Routledge.

Bureau of Labor Statistics. 2004a. "Annual Social and Economic Supplement, Table 24: Contribution of Wives' Earnings to Family Income, 1970–2003." Available online at www.bls.gov/cps/wlf-databook2005.htm (accessed April 26, 2006).

———. 2004b. "Annual Social and Economic Supplement, Table 25: Wives Who Earn More Than Their Husbands, 1987–2003." Available online at www.bls.gov/cps/wlf-databook2005.htm (accessed April 26, 2006).

Burke, Carol. 1996. "Pernicious Cohesion." Pp. 205–19 in *It's Our Military, Too! Women and the U.S. Military*, ed. Judith Hicks Stiehm. Philadelphia: Temple University Press.

———. 2004. *Camp All-American, Hanoi Jane, and the High and the Tight: Gender, Folklore, and Changing Military Culture*. Boston: Beacon Press.

Burton, Antoinette. 1994. *Burdens of History: British Feminists, Indian Women, and Imperial Culture, 1865–1915*. Chapel Hill: University of North Carolina Press.

Bush, George W. 2000. "Republican Nomination Acceptance Speech." August 3, 2000. Available online at www.2000gop.com/convention/speech/speechbush.html.

———. 2001a. "First Inaugural Address." January 20. Available online at www.white house.gov/news/inaugural-address.html (accessed May 26, 2006).

———. 2001b. "Women's History Month, 2001: A Proclamation." March 2. Available online at www.whitehouse.gov/news/releases/2001/03/20010302-2.html (accessed May 26, 2006).

———. 2001c. "Remarks by the President in Character Education Event." April 10. Available online at www.whitehouse.gov/news/releases/2001/04/20010410-2.html (accessed May 26, 2006).

———. 2001d. "Remarks by the President to National Organization of Black Law Enforcement Executives, Washington, D.C." July 30. Available online at www.white house.gov/news/releases/2001/07/20010730-5.html (accessed May 26, 2006).

———. 2001e. "Women's Equality Day, 2001, a Proclamation." August 24. Available online at www.whitehouse.gov/news/releases/2001/08/20010824-1.html (accessed May 26, 2006).

———. 2001f. "Guard and Reserves 'Define Spirit of America.'" September 17. Available online at www.whitehouse.gov/news/releases/2001/09/20010917-3.html (accessed March 26, 2006).

———. 2001g. "President Discusses War on Terrorism: In Address to the Nation, World Congress Center." November 8. Available online at www.whitehouse.gov/news/releases/2001/11/20011108-13.html (accessed November 8, 2005).

———. 2001h. "Address to United Nations." November 10. Available online at www.whitehouse.gov/news/releases/2001/11/20011110-3.html (accessed May 26, 2006).

———. 2001i. "Remarks by the President at Signing Ceremony for Afghan Women and Children Relief Act of 2001." December 12. Available online at www.white house.gov/news/releases/2001/12/20011212-9.html (accessed May 26, 2006).

———. 2002a. "State of the Union Address." January 29. Available online at www .whitehouse.gov/news/releases/2002/01/20020129-11.html (accessed May 26, 2006).

———. 2002b. "The State of the Union: President Bush's State of the Union Address to Congress and the Nation." *New York Times*, January 30, A22.

———. 2002c. "President Calls for Quick Passage of Defense Bill: Remarks by the President in Fayetteville, North Carolina." March 15. Available online at www .whitehouse.gov/news/releases/2002/03/20020315.html (accessed Nov. 7, 2006).

———. 2002d. "President's Remarks at Victory 2002 Event: Remarks by the President to the Republican Party of Texas." March 29. Available online at www.white house.gov/news/releases/2002/03/20020328.html (accessed May 26, 2006).

———. 2002e. "Fact Sheet on Compassionate Conservatism." April 30. Available online at www.whitehouse.gov/news/releases/2002/04/20020430.html (accessed May 26, 2006).

———. 2002f. "President Promotes New Mother and Child HIV Prevention Initiative." June 19. Available online at www.whitehouse.gov/news/releases/2002/06/20020619-3.html (accessed May 26, 2006).

———. 2002g. "President's Remarks at the United Nations General Assembly." September 12. Available online at www.whitehouse.gov/news/releases/2002/09/20020912-1.html (accessed May 26, 2006).

———. 2002h. "President Bush Outlines Iraqi Threat." October 22. Available online at www.whitehouse.gov/news/releases/2002/10/20021007-8.html (accessed April 26, 2006).

———. 2003a. "State of the Union Address." January 28. Available online at www .whitehouse.gov/news/releases/2003/01/20030128-19.html (accessed May 26, 2006).

———. 2003b. "Fact Sheet: The President's Emergency Plan for AIDS Relief," January 29. Available online at www.whitehouse.gov/news/releases/2003/01/20030129-1.html (accessed May 26, 2006).

———. 2003c. "Address to Nation." May 1. Available online at www.whitehouse.gov/news/releases/2003/03/20030319-17.html (accessed May 26, 2006).

———. 2004a. "State of the Union Address." January 20. Available online at www .whitehouse.gov/news/releases/2004/01/20040120-7.html (accessed Nov. 7, 2006).

———. 2004b. "President Calls for Constitutional Amendment Protecting Marriage." February 24. Available online at www.whitehouse.gov/news/releases/2004/02/20040224-2.html (accessed May 26, 2006).

———. 2004c. "President Outlines Steps to Help Iraq Achieve Democracy and Freedom." May 24. Available online at www.whitehouse.gov/news/releases/2004/05/20040524-10.html (accessed May 26, 2006).

———. 2004d. "President Bush Discusses HIV/AIDS Initiatives in Philadelphia." June 23. Available online at www.whitehouse.gov/news/releases/2004/06/20040623-4.html (accessed May 26, 2006).

———. 2005a. "President Commemorates Veterans Day, Discusses War on Terror." November 11. Available online at www.whitehouse.gov/news/releases/2005/11/20051111-1.html (accessed March 25, 2006).

———. 2005b. "President Outlines Strategy for Victory in Iraq." November 30. Available online at www.whitehouse.gov/news/releases/2005/11/20051130-2.html (accessed March 26, 2006).

———. 2005c. "President and Mrs. Bush Discuss HIV/AIDS Initiatives on World AIDS Day." December 1. Available online at www.whitehouse.gov/news/releases/2005/12/20051201.html (accessed May 26, 2006).

———. 2006. "State of the Union Address." January 31. Available online at www.whitehouse.gov/stateoftheunion/2006/index.html (accessed May 26, 2006).

Bush, George W., and Laura Bush. 2004. "President and Mrs. Bush Mark Progress in Global Women's Human Rights." March 12. Available online at www.whitehouse.gov/news/releases/2004/03/20040312-5.html (accessed May 26, 2006).

Bush, Laura. 2001a. "Remarks by Mrs. Bush to Women CEOs." March 20. Available online at www.whitehouse.gov/news/releases/2001/03/20010320-15.html (accessed May 26, 2006).

———. 2001b. "Radio Address by Laura Bush to the Nation." November 17. Available online at www.whitehouse.gov/news/releases/2001/11/print/20011117.html (accessed May 26, 2006).

———. 2002. "Mrs. Bush Discusses Status of Afghan Women at U.N.: Remarks by Mrs. Laura Bush." March 8. Available online at www.whitehouse.gov/news/releases/2002/03/20020308-2.html (accessed May 26, 2006).

———. 2004a. "Remarks by First Lady Laura Bush to the International Lion of Judah Conference." October 18. Available online at www.whitehouse.gov/news/releases/2004/10/20041018-13.html (accessed May 26, 2006).

———. 2004b. "Remarks by First Lady Laura Bush at Bush–Cheney '04 Event in West Allis, Wisconsin." October 22. Available online at www.whitehouse.gov/news/releases/2004/10/20041022-8.html (accessed May 26, 2006).

Butler, Judith. 1990. *Gender Trouble.* New York: Routledge.

———. 1993. *Bodies That Matter: On the Discursive Limits of "Sex."* New York: Routledge.

———. 2004. *Precarious Life: The Power of Mourning and Violence.* New York: Verso.

Butler, Linda. 2002. "Suicide Bombers: Dignity, Despair, and the Need for Hope." *Journal of Palestine Studies* 31, no. 4 (Summer): 71–76.

Butterfield, Fox. 2004. "Mistreatment of Prisoners Is Called Routine in U.S." *New York Times,* May 8.

Campbell, Nancy. 2000. *Using Women: Gender, Drug Policy, and Social Justice.* New York: Routledge.

Card, Claudia. 1996. *The Unnatural Lottery: Character and Moral Luck.* Philadelphia: Temple University Press.

Center for American Women and Politics. 2004. "Gender Gap Persists in the 2004 Election." Eagleton Institute, Rutgers University, November 5. Available online at www.cawp.rutgers.edu/Facts/Elections/GG2004Facts.pdf (accessed March 26, 2006).

Center for Health and Gender Equity, Feminist Majority, and Women's Environment and Development Organization. 2004a. "Global Women's Issues Scorecard on the Bush Administration." From http://www.wglobalscorecard.org (accessed June 29, 2005; no longer posted).

———. 2004b. "Global Women's Issues Scorecard on the Bush Administration, June 2004: Women's Security in Afghanistan and Iraq." From http://wglobalscorecard .org/June04_AfghanIraqSecurity.htm (accessed June 29, 2005; no longer posted).

———. 2004c. "Scores." From http://www.wglobalscorecard.org/scores.htm (accessed June 29, 2005; no longer posted).

Central Intelligence Agency. 1963. KUBARK *Counterintelligence Interrogation.* July. Available online at www.gwu.edu/~nsarchiv/NSAEBB/NSAEBB122/#kubark (accessed October 28, 2005).

———. *Human Resource Exploitation Training Manual.* 1983. Available online at www .gwu.edu/~nsarchiv/NSAEBB/NSAEBB122/#kubark (accessed October 28, 2005).

Chang, Nancy. 2002. *Silencing Political Dissent: How Post–September 11 Anti-Terrorism Measures Threaten Our Civil Liberties.* New York: Seven Stories Press.

Chavez, Linda. 2004. "Sexual Tension in the Military." May 5. Available online at www.townhall.com/opinion/columns/lindachavez/2004/05/05/11589.html (accessed June 4, 2005).

Cheney, Dick. 2005. "Vice President's Remarks at the Frontiers of Freedom Institute 2005 Ronald Reagan Gala." November 16. Available online at www.whitehouse .gov/news/releases/2005/11/20051116-10.html (accessed March 25, 2006).

Cheney, Lynne. 2001. "Women and the West." November 2. Available online at www .whitehouse.gov/mrscheney/news/20011102.html (accessed May 26, 2006).

Cloud, David. 2005a. "Psychologist Calls Private in Abu Ghraib Photographs 'Overly Compliant.'" *New York Times,* September 24.

———. 2005b. "Private Found Guilty in Abu Ghraib Abuse." *New York Times,* September 27.

———. 2006. "Here's Donny! In His Defense, a Show Is Born." *New York Times,* April 19, A1.

CNN. 2004a. "CNN Live at Daybreak." Transcript of program aired March 25. Available online at http://transcripts.cnn.com/TRANSCRIPTS/0403/25/ltm.01.html (accessed Nov. 1, 2006).

———. 2004b. "Abu Ghraib Was 'Animal House' at Night." August 25. Available online at www.cnn.com/2004/US/08/24/abughraib.report (accessed May 26, 2006).

Cohn, Carol. 1993. "Wars, Wimps, and Women: Talking Gender and Thinking War." Pp. 227–48 in *Gendering War Talk*, ed. Miriam Cooke and Angela Woollacott. Princeton: Princeton University Press.

Coleman, Isobel. 2006. "Women, Islam, and the New Iraq." *Foreign Affairs* 85, no. 1: 24–38.

Commission on Presidential Debates. 2004a. "The First Bush–Kerry Presidential Debate." September 30. Available online at www.debates.org/pages/trans2004a.html (accessed May 26, 2006).

———. 2004b. "The Cheney–Edwards Vice-Presidential Debate." October 5. Available online at www.debates.org/pages/trans2004b.html (accessed May 26, 2006).

Concerned Women for America. 2002. "Here Comes 'Sadism Rights': SM Group Targets CWA." April 18. Available online at www.cultureandfamily.org/articledisplay .asp?id=594&department=CFI&categoryid=cfreport (accessed May 26, 2006).

———. 2005. "CWA Calls for Miers' Withdrawal." October 26. Available online at www.cwfa.org/articles/9259/MEDIA/misc/index.htm (accessed April 20, 2006).

Coontz, Stephanie. 2000. *The Way We Never Were: American Families and the Nostalgia Trap*, 2d ed. New York: Basic Books.

Costello, Daniel. 2000. "Spanking Makes a Comeback: Tired of Spoiling the Child, Parents Stop Sparing the Rod; Dr. Dobson vs. Dr. Spock." *Wall Street Journal*, June 9. Available online at www.corpun.com/usd00006.htm (accessed June 15, 2005).

Crouse, Janice Shaw. 2006. "What Friedan Wrought." February 7. Available online at www.cwfa.org/articledisplay.asp?id=10088&department=BLI&categoryid=dot commentary (accessed April 21, 2006).

Cruz-Malavé, Arnaldo, and Martin Manalansan. 2002. *Queer Globalizations: Citizenship and the Afterlife of Colonialism*. New York: New York University Press.

Dahl, Robert. 1998. *On Democracy*. New Haven, Conn.: Yale University Press.

Daniels, Cynthia R., ed. 2000. *Lost Fathers: The Politics of Fatherlessness*. New York: St. Martin's Griffin.

Danner, Mark. 2004. *Torture and Truth*. New York: New York Review of Books.

Delphy, Christine. 1984. *Close to Home*. Amherst: University of Massachusetts Press.

Desai, Manisha. 2002. "Transnational Solidarity: Women's Agency, Structural Adjustment, and Globalization." Pp. 15–33 in *Women's Activism and Globalization: Linking Local Struggles and Transnational Politics*, ed. Nancy A. Naples and Manisha Desai. New York: Routledge.

Diamond, Sara. 1995. *Roads to Dominion: Right-Wing Movements and Political Power in the United States*. New York: Guilford Press.

Dionne, E. J. 2003. "Handing out Hardship: Is This the Bush Administration's Idea of Fiscal Discipline?" *Washington Post*, September 16, A19.

Dobson, James. 1992. *The New Dare to Discipline*. Wheaton, Ill.: Tyndale House Publishers.

————. 2000. *Bringing Up Boys: Practical Advice and Encouragement for Those Shaping the Next Generation of Men.* Wheaton, Ill.: Tyndale House Publishers.

Economic Policy Institute. 2005. "Productivity and Median and Average Compensation, 1973–2003." In *The State of Working America, 2004/2005.* March. Available online at www.epinet.org/content.cfm/datazone_dznational (accessed May 26, 2006).

Ehrenreich, Barbara. 2004a. "Feminism's Assumptions Upended." *Los Angeles Times,* June 4.

————. 2004b. "The New Macho: Feminism." *New York Times,* July 29, A19.

Eisenstein, Zillah. 2004a. "Sexual Humiliation, Gender Confusion and the Horrors at Abu Ghraib." June. Available online at www.peacewomen.org/news/Iraq/June04/abughraib.html (accessed June 4, 2005).

————. 2004b. "Is 'W' for Women?" Transcript of mock election debates, Cornell University, Ithaca, September 22. Reprinted on SMTP:moderator@portside.org.

Elshtain, Jean Bethke. 1987. *Women and War.* Chicago: University of Chicago Press.

————. 1991. "Sovereignty, Identity, Sacrifice." *Social Research* 58, no. 3 (Fall): 545–65.

Embser-Herbert, M. S. 2004. "When Women Abuse Power, Too." *Washington Post,* May 16.

Enda, Jodi. 2004. "Barbara Bush Tells Women What 'W' Stands for." August 31. Available online at www.womensenews.org/article.cfm/dyn/aid/1970 (accessed May 26, 2006).

Enloe, Cynthia. 2004a. *The Curious Feminist: Searching for Women in the New Age of Empire.* Berkeley: University of California Press.

————. 2004b. "Wielding Masculinity inside Abu Ghraib: Making Feminist Sense of an American Military Scandal." *Asian Journal of Women's Studies* 10, no. 3: 89–102.

Entman, Robert M. 1993. "Framing: Toward Clarification of a Fractured Paradigm." *Journal of Communication* 43, no. 4: 51–58.

————. 2003. "Cascading Activation: Contesting the White House's Frame after 9/11." *Political Communication* 20: 415–32.

Ezekiel, Judith. 2005. "Magritte Meets Maghreb: This Is Not a Veil." *Australian Feminist Studies* 20, no. 47: 1–17.

Faludi, Susan. 1994. "The Naked Citadel." *New Yorker,* September 5, 62–81.

Faramarzi, Scheherezade. 2004. "Former Iraqi Prisoner Says U.S. Jailers Humiliated Him." May 2. Available online at www.heraldnet.com/Stories/04/5/3/18561068.cfm (accessed May 26, 2006).

Featherstone, Liza. 2003. "Mighty in Pink." *The Nation,* March 3.

Ferguson, Michaele L. 2005a. "Home, Land, Security: Iraqi Feminists Respond to the Bush Administration." Paper presented at the Annual Meeting of the International Studies Association, Honolulu, March 1–5.

————. 2005b. "W Stands for Women: Feminism and Security Rhetoric in the Post-9/11 Bush Administration." *Politics and Gender* 1, no. 1 (March): 9–38.

Firestone, David. 2002. "Are You Safer Today Than a Year Ago?" *New York Times*, November 17.

Flanders, Laura. 2004a. *Bushwomen: Tales of a Cynical Species*. New York: Verso.

———. 2004b. "Introduction: Feigning Feminism, Fueling Backlash." Pp. xi–xxi in *The W Effect: Bush's War on Women*, ed. Laura Flanders. New York: Feminist Press at the City University of New York.

Flanders, Laura, ed. 2004. *The W Effect: Bush's War on Women*. New York: Feminist Press at the City University of New York.

Focus on the Family. 2006. "Our Guiding Principles." January 11. Available online at www.family.org/welcome/aboutfof/a0000078.cfm (accessed May 26, 2006).

Foucault, Michel. 1988. "Technologies of the Self." Pp. 19–49 in *Technologies of the Self: A Seminar with Michel Foucault*, ed. Luther Martin, Huck Guttman, and Patricia Hutton. Amherst: University of Massachusetts Press.

———. 1994. "*Omnes et Singulatim*: Toward a Critique of Political Reason." Pp. 298–325 in *The Essential Works of Foucault, Vol. 3: Power*, ed. James D. Faubion. New York: New Press.

———. 2003. *Abnormal: Lectures at the Collège de France, 1974–1975*. New York: Picador Press.

Frank, Sarah. 2004. "Afghan Women No Better Off: U.S. Accused of Not Fulfilling Promises." *Chicago Tribune*, September 23.

Frank, Thomas. 2004. "Failure Is Not an Option; It's Mandatory." *New York Times*, July 16, A21.

Gall, Carlotta. 2005. "Laura Bush Carries Pet Causes to Afghans." *New York Times*, March 31, A10.

Gallagher, Maggie. 2004. "Can Government Strengthen Marriage? Evidence from the Social Sciences." Available online at www.marriagedebate.com/pdf/Can%20Government%20Strengthen%20Marriage.pdf (accessed January 12, 2006).

———. 2005. "(How) Will Gay Marriage Weaken Marriage as a Social Institution: A Reply to Andrew Koppelman." *University of St. Thomas Law Journal* 2, no. 1: 33–70.

Geng, Veronica. 1976. "Requiem for the Women's Movement." *Harper's*, November.

Giddens, Anthony. 1998. *The Third Way*. Cambridge: Polity Press.

Giroux, Henry. 2004. "What Might Education Mean after Abu Ghraib?" *Comparative Studies of South Asia, Africa and the Middle East* 24, no. 1: 3–22.

Gledhill, Christine. 1992. "Between Melodrama and Realism: Anthony Asquith's *Underground* and King Vidor's *The Crowd*." Pp. 129–67 in *Classical Hollywood Narrative: The Paradigm Wars*, ed. Jane Gaines. Durham: Duke University Press.

Goldberg, Jonathan. 1992. *Sodometries: Renaissance Texts, Modern Sexualities*. Stanford, Calif.: Stanford University Press.

Goldstein, Joshua S. 2001. *War and Gender: How Gender Shapes the War System and Vice Versa*. Cambridge: Cambridge University Press.

Goldstein, Richard. 2003. "Stealth Misogyny." *Village Voice*, March 5–11. Available online at www.villagevoice.com/issues/0310/goldstein.php (accessed May 26, 2006).

Goodwin, Sarah Webster, and Elisabeth Bronfen. 1993. *Death and Representation.* Baltimore: Johns Hopkins University Press.

Gordon, Harvey. 2002. "The 'Suicide' Bomber: Is It a Psychiatric Phenomenon?" *Psychiatric Bulletin* 26: 285–87.

Grant, Rebecca, and Kathleen Newland, eds. 1991. *Gender and International Relations.* Bloomington: Indiana University Press.

Greenberg, Karen J., and Joshua L. Dratel, eds. 2005. *The Torture Papers: The Road to Abu Ghraib.* New York: Cambridge University Press.

Greven, Phillip. 1992. *Spare the Child: The Religious Roots of Punishment and the Psychological Impact of Physical Abuse.* New York: Vintage Books.

Gutterman, David. 2001. "Presidential Testimony: Listening to the Heart of George W. Bush." *Theory and Event* 5, no. 2. Available online at http://muse.jhu.edu/journals/theory_and_event/v005/5.2gutterman.html (accessed March 25, 2006).

———. 2005. *Prophetic Politics: Christian Social Movements and American Democracy.* Ithaca: Cornell University Press.

Harding, Luke. 2004. "The Other Prisoners." *The Guardian,* May 20.

Hardisty, Jean. 1999. *Mobilizing Resentment: Conservative Resurgence from the John Birch Society to the Promise Keepers.* Boston: Beacon Press.

Hardt, Michael, and Antonio Negri. 2000. *Empire.* Cambridge, Mass.: Harvard University Press.

———. 2004. *Multitude: War and Democracy in the Age of Empire.* New York: Penguin.

Hargrove, Thomas. 2006. "Gender Gap Returns as Most Women Turn against Bush." Scripps Howard News Service, March 22. Available online at www.newspolls.org/story.php?story_id=52 (accessed May 26, 2006).

Hawkesworth, Mary. 2004. "The Semiotics of Premature Burial: Feminism in a Postfeminist Age." *Signs* 29, no. 4: 961–86.

———. 2006. *Globalization and Feminist Activism.* Lanham, Md.: Rowman and Littlefield.

Herper, Matthew. 2004. "Sex on Demand: A Big Disappointment." *Forbes,* July 7. Available online at www.forbes.com/sciencesandmedicine/2004/07/21/cx_mh_0721viagra.html (accessed March 25, 2006).

Hess, Pamela. 2004. "Congress May Push for Larger Military." *Washington Times,* July 9. Available online at www.washtimes.com/upi-breaking/20040708-061323-1106r.htm (accessed May 26, 2006).

Higham, Scott, Josh White, and Christian Davenport. "A Prison on the Brink." *Washington Post,* May 9, 2004.

Hirschkind, Charles, and Saba Mahmood. 2002. "Feminism, the Taliban, and Politics of Counter-Insurgency." *Anthropological Quarterly* 75, no. 2: 339–54.

Hirschmann, Nancy J. 2002. *The Subject of Liberty: Toward a Feminist Theory of Freedom.* Princeton: Princeton University Press.

Hobbes, Thomas. 2004 (1668). *Leviathan*. Indianapolis: Hackett.

Hong, Cathy. 2004. "How Could Women Do That?" May 7. Available online at http://archive.salon.com/mwt/feature/2004/05/07/abuse_gender/index_np.html (accessed November 9, 2005).

Hooper, Charlotte. 2001. *Manly States: Masculinities, International Relations, and Gender Politics*. New York: Columbia University Press.

Htun, Mala. 2004. "Is Gender Like Ethnicity? The Political Representation of Identity Groups." *Perspectives on Politics* 2, no. 3: 439–58.

Hudson, Rex A. 1999. "The Sociology and Psychology of Terrorism: Who Becomes a Terrorist and Why?" Library of Congress, Federal Research Division, Washington, D.C., September.

Huffington, Arianna. 2004. "Shakespeare Turns a Spotlight on Bush and Iraq." June 2. Available online at http://dir.salon.com/story/opinion/huffington/2004/06/04/bush_and_shakespeare/index.html (accessed May 26, 2006).

Hughes, Karen, Peggy Conlon, and Leslie Lenkowsky. 2001. "President, Mrs. Bush Encourage Generosity." November 20. Available online at www.whitehouse.gov/news/releases/2001/11/20011120-2.html (accessed May 26, 2006).

Human Rights Watch. 2005. "Torture in Iraq." *New York Review of Books*, vol. 52, no. 17. Available online at www.nybooks.com/articles/18414 (accessed March 26, 2006).

Hutchens, Trudy. 1996. "Marriage: The State of the Union." From www.cwfa.org/library/family/1996-10_fv_marriage.s (accessed April 2, 2002; no longer posted).

Huyssens, Andreas. 1986. "Mass Culture as Woman: Modernism's Other." Pp. 188–207 in *Studies in Entertainment: Critical Approaches to Mass Culture*, ed. Tania Modelski. Bloomington: Indiana University Press.

InterParliamentary Union. 2005. "Women in National Parliaments." Available online at www.ipu.org/wmn-e/classif.htm (accessed May 26, 2006).

Iyengar, Shanto. 1991. *Is Anyone Responsible?* Chicago: University of Chicago Press.

Janabi, Ahmed. 2004. "Iraqi Women, Children in U.S. Custody." February 15. Available online at http://english.aljazeera.net/NR/exeres/7AF6D9CA-C897-4636-AFCA-44C93A66A9DA.htm (accessed May 26, 2006).

Jeffords, Susan. 1994. *Hard Bodies: Hollywood Masculinity in the Reagan Era*. New Brunswick, N.J.: Rutgers University Press.

Jehl, Douglas, and Eric Schmitt. 2004a. "Prison Interrogations in Iraq Seen as Yielding Little Data on Rebels." *New York Times*, May 27.

———. 2004b. "U.S. Rules on Prisoners Seen as a Back and Forth of Mixed Messages to GIs." *New York Times*, June 22.

Johnson, Kirk. 2004. "Guard Featured in Abuse Photos Says She Was Following Orders." *New York Times*, May 11.

Joint Chiefs of Staff. 2005. "Joint Doctrine for Detainee Operations." Joint Publication no. 3-63, March 23. Available online at http://hrw.org/campaigns/torture/Jointdoctrine/Jointdoctrine040705.pdf (accessed May 26, 2006).

Josephson, Jyl J., and Cynthia Burack. 1998. "The Political Ideology of the Neo-Traditional Family." *Journal of Political Ideologies* 3, no. 2: 213–31.

Kahneman, Daniel, and Amos Tversky. 1984. "Choices, Values, and Frames." *American Psychologist* 39: 341–50.

Kaldor, Mary. 1999. *New and Old Wars: Organized Violence in a Global Era*. Stanford, Calif.: Stanford University Press.

Kant, Immanuel. 1991 (1795). "Perpetual Peace: A Philosophical Sketch." Pp. 93–130 in *Political Writings*, ed. H. Reiss. New York: Cambridge University Press.

Kaufman-Osborn, Timothy. 1997. *Creatures of Prometheus: Gender and the Politics of Technology*. Lanham, Md.: Rowman and Littlefield.

————. 2005. "Gender Relations in an Age of Neoliberal Empire: Interrogating Gender Equality Models." Paper presented at the Annual Meeting of the Western Political Science Association, Oakland, Calif., March 19.

Keane, John. 2002. "Fear and Democracy." Pp. 226–44 in *Violence and Politics: Globalization's Paradox*, ed. Kentor Worcester, Sally Avery Birmansohn, and Mark Ungar. New York: Routledge.

Kelley, Jack. 2001. "The Secret World of Suicide Bombers." *USA Today*, June 26, 1A.

Kessler, Glenn. 2005. "Rice Visits Darfur Camp, Pressures Sudan." *Washington Post*, July 22. Available online at www.nwlc.org/pdf/AdminRecordOnWomen2004.pdf (accessed January 25, 2006).

Kingfisher, Catherine. 2002. *Western Welfare in Decline: Globalization and Women's Poverty* Philadelphia: University of Pennsylvania Press.

Kinsella, Helen. 2005. "Erotic Triangles in the Art of War." Workshop on the Art of Security: The Relation of Gender and Sex to Peace and Conflict at the Annual Meeting of the International Studies Association, Honolulu, March 1.

Kittay, Eva Feder. 1999. *Love's Labor: Essays on Women, Equality, and Dependency*. New York: Routledge.

Kline, Marlee. 1995. "Complicating the Ideology of Motherhood: Child Welfare Law and First Nation Women." Pp. 118–41 in *Mothers in Law: Feminist Theory and the Legal Regulation of Motherhood*, ed. Martha Fineman. New York: Columbia University Press.

Krugman, Paul. 2003. "Lessons in Civility." *New York Times*, October 10. Available online at www.nytimes.com/2003/10/10/opinion/10KRUG.html (accessed March 26, 2006).

Kurtz, Howard. 2005. "Bush Urges End to Contracts with Commentators." *Washington Post*, January 27, A4.

Kushner, Tony. 2003. "Only We Who Guard the Mystery Shall Be Unhappy. *The Nation*, March 6.

Lacey, Marc. 2004. "U.S. Suggests AIDS Fund Delay Grants." *New York Times*, November 17, A3.

Ladd-Taylor, Molly, and Lauri Umansky, eds. 1998. "'Bad' Mothers: The Politics of Blame in Twentieth-Century America*. New York: New York University Press.

LaFraniere, Sharon. 2005. "Women's Rights Laws and African Custom Clash." *New York Times*, December 30. Available online at www.nytimes.com/2005/12/30/inter national/africa/30africa.html?ex=1293598800&en=87f1d0f4c03a8554&ei=5090& partner=rssuserland&emc=rss (accessed May 26, 2006).

LaHaye, Beverly. 1993. *The Desires of a Woman's Heart: Encouragement for Women When Traditional Values Are Challenged*. Wheaten, Ill.: Tyndale Publishers.

LaHaye, Tim. 1996. *Understanding the Male Temperament*. Grand Rapids, Mich.: Fleming H. Revell.

Landy, Marcia. 1991. "Introduction." Pp. 13–30 in *Imitations of Life: A Reader on Film and Television Melodrama*, ed. Marcia Landy. Detroit: Wayne State University Press.

Lane, Robert. 1994. " 'When Blood Is Their Argument': Class, Character, and Historymaking in Shakespeare's and Branagh's *Henry V*." *English Literary History* 61, no. 1: 27–52.

Lawless, Jennifer. 2004. "Women, War, and Winning Elections: Gender Stereotyping in the Post–September 11th Era." *Political Research Quarterly* 57, no. 3: 479–90.

Lazreg, Marnia. 2001. "Decolonizing Feminism." Pp. 281–93 in *Feminism and Race*, ed. Kum-Kum Bhavnani. Oxford: Oxford University Press.

Lerner, Sharon. 2001. "Feminists Agonize over War in Afghanistan: What Women Want." *Village Voice*, October 31–November 6. Available online at www.villagevoice .com/news/0144,1erner,29544,1.html (accessed May 26, 2006).

Lester, David, Bijou Yang, and Mark Lindsay. 2004. "Suicide Bombers: Are Psychological Profiles Possible?" *Studies in Conflict and Terrorism* 27: 283–95.

Lewin, Adrienne Mand. 2005. "Covenant Marriage Offers Tighter Bonds." February 14. Available online at http://abcnews.go.com/US/Valentine/story?id=489389&page=1 (accessed July 27, 2005).

Linden, Robin Ruth, Darlene R. Pagano, Diana E. H. Russell, and Susan Leigh Star, eds. 1982. *Against Sadomasochism: A Radical Feminist Analysis*. San Francisco: Frog in the Well.

Longworth, R. C. 2002. "The Ball Is Rolling toward Iraq War." *Chicago Tribune*, December 22, sec. 2, 1, 6.

Lyotard, Jean-François. 1990. *Heidegger and "The Jews,"* trans. Andreas Michel and Mark S. Roberts. Minneapolis: University of Minnesota Press.

Machiavelli, Niccolo. 1992 (1515). *The Prince*, trans. and ed. Robert M. Adams. New York: W. W. Norton.

MacKinnon, Catharine. 1987. *Feminism Unmodified: Discourses on Life and Law*. Cambridge, Mass.: Harvard University Press,

———. 1989. *Towards a Feminist Theory of the State*. Cambridge, Mass.: Harvard University Press.

Mahmood, Saba. 2005. *Politics of Piety: The Islamic Revival and the Feminist Subject*. Princeton: Princeton University Press.

Mamdani, Mahmood. 2004. *Good Muslim, Bad Muslim: America, the Cold War, and the Roots of Terror*. New York: Pantheon Books.

Manning, Christel. 1999. *God Gave Us the Right: Conservative Catholic, Evangelical Protestant, and Orthodox Jewish Women Grapple with Feminism*. New Brunswick, N.J.: Rutgers University Press.

Mansbridge, Jane. 1986. *Why We Lost the ERA*. Chicago: University of Chicago Press.

Mattox, William Jr. "Gay Marriage Devalues Women." *USA Today*, August 21, 2001. Available online at www.allianceformarriage.org/reports/fma/usatoday.htm (accessed May 26, 2006).

May, Larry. 1998. *Masculinity and Morality*. Ithaca: Cornell University Press.

McClendon, McKee J., and David J. O'Brien. 1988. "Question-Order Effects on Subjective Well-Being." *Public Opinion Quarterly* 52: 351–64.

Milburn, Michael A., and Sheree D. Conrad. 1996. *The Politics of Denial*. Cambridge, Mass.: MIT Press.

Miller, Francesca. 1999. "Feminisms and Transnationalism." Pp. 225–36 in *Feminisms and Internationalism*, ed. Mrinalini Sinha, Donna Guy, and Angela Woollacott. Oxford: Blackwell.

Miskel, James F. 2004. "Violence as Strategy: The Palestinian Case." *Mediterranean Quarterly* 15, no. 2: 47–57.

Moghadam, Assaf. 2003. "Palestinian Suicide Terrorism in the Second Intifada: Motivations and Organizational Aspects." *Studies in Conflict and Terrorism* 26: 65–92.

Moghadam, Valentine. 2005. *Globalizing Women: Transnational Feminist Networks*. Baltimore: Johns Hopkins University Press.

Mohammed, Yanar. 2004. "U.S. Troops Have to Leave Now and We Will Take Care of Iraq." Interview by Amy Goodman, *Democracy Now*, September 13. Available online at www.democracynow.org/article.pl?sid=04/09/13/1428243 (accessed May 26, 2006).

Mohanty, Chandra Talpade. 1991. "Under Western Eyes: Feminist Scholarship and Colonial Discourse." Pp. 51–80 in *Third World Women and the Politics of Feminism*, ed. Chandra Talpade Mohanty, Ann Russo, and Lourdes Torres. Bloomington: Indiana University Press.

———. 2003. *Feminism without Borders: Decolonizing Theory, Practicing Solidarity*. Durham: Duke University Press.

Moi, Toril. 1999. *What Is a Woman?* Oxford: Oxford University Press.

Monroe, Kristen. 2004. *The Hand of Compassion: Portraits of Moral Choice during the Holocaust*. Princeton: Princeton University Press.

Moore, R. Laurence. 2003. *Touchdown Jesus: The Mixing of Sacred and Secular in American History*. Louisville, Ky.: Westminster John Knox Press.

Morin, Richard and Dan Balz. 2004. "Bush Support Strong after Convention." *Washington Post*, September 10. Available online at www.washingtonpost.com/wp-dyn/articles/A9060-2004Sep9.html (accessed April 26, 2006).

Mostaghimi, Arash. 2003. "The Erectile Olympics." *Motley Fool*, November 26. Available online at www.fool.com/news/commentary/2003/commentary031126am.htm (accessed March 25, 2006).

Moynihan, Daniel Patrick. 1965. *The Negro Family: The Case for National Action*. Washington, D.C.: U.S. Department of Labor.

MSNBC. 2005. "In Egypt, Laura Bush Urges Equality for Women: First Lady Wraps Up Controversial Five-Day Mideast Tour." May 24. Available online at www.msnbc.msn.com/id/7918891 (accessed January 25, 2006).

Murtha, John P. 2005. "War in Iraq." November 17. Available online at www.house.gov/apps/list/press/pa12_murtha/pr051117iraq.html (accessed March 25, 2006).

Narayan, Uma. 1997. *Dislocating Cultures: Identities, Traditions, and Third World Feminism*. New York: Routledge.

National Commission on Terrorist Attacks. 2004. *The 9/11 Commission Report: Final Report of the National Commission on Terrorist Attacks upon the United States*. New York: W. W. Norton.

National Security Council. 2002. "The National Security Strategy of the United States of America." September 17. Available online at www.whitehouse.gov/nsc/nssall.html (accessed May 26, 2006).

National Women's Law Center. 2004. "Slip-Sliding Away: The Erosion of Hard-Won Gains for Women under the Bush Administration and an Agenda for Moving Forward." April. Available online at www.nwlc.org/pdf/AdminRecordOnWomen2004.pdf (accessed January 25, 2006).

Nelson, Thomas E., Zoe M. Oxley, and Rosalee A. Clawson. 1997. "Toward a Psychology of Framing Effects." *Political Behavior* 19, no. 3: 221–46.

Neumayr, George. 2004. "Thelma and Louise in Iraq." *American Spectator*. Available online at www.spectator.org/dsp article.asp?art id=6522 (accessed May 5, 2005).

Newstrom, Scott. 2003. "'Step Aside, I'll Show Thee a President': George W as Henry V?" May 1. Available online at www.poppolitics.com/articles/2003–05–01-henryv.shtml (accessed May 26, 2006).

Niebuhr, Gustav. 1998. "Married Couples Should Be Led by Husband, Say Southern Baptists." *New York Times*, June 10.

Noonan, Peggy. 2004. "A Humiliation for America." *Wall Street Journal*, May 6. Available online at www.opinionjournal.com/columnists/pnoonan/?id=10005043 (accessed May 26, 2006).

Nozick, Robert. 1974. *Anarchy, State, and Utopia*. New York: Basic Books.

Nussbaum, Martha. 1996. "Compassion: The Basic Social Emotion." *Social Philosophy and Policy* 13 (Winter): 27–58.

———. 2001. *Upheavals of Thought: The Intelligence of Emotions*. New York: Cambridge University Press.

O'Connor, Karen. 2002. "For Better or for Worse? Women and Women's Rights in the Post-9/11 Climate." Pp. 171–91 in *American Government in a Changed World: The Effects of September 11, 2001*, ed. Dennis L. Dresang et al. New York: Longman.

Offen, Karen. 2000. *European Feminisms, 1700–1950*. Stanford, Calif.: Stanford University Press.

Ohnuki-Tierney, Emiko. 2002. *Kamikaze, Cherry Blossoms, and Nationalisms: The Militarization of Aesthetics in Japanese History*. Chicago: University of Chicago Press.

Okin, Susan Moller. 1989. *Justice, Gender, and the Family*. New York: Basic Books.

Olasky, Marvin. 2000. *Compassionate Conservatism: What It Is, What It Does, and How It Can Transform America*. New York: Free Press.

Oliver, Anne Marie, and Paul Steinberg. 2005. *The Road to Martyrs' Square: A Journey into the World of the Suicide Bomber*. New York: Oxford University Press.

Orford, Ann. 2005. "Workshop on the Art of Security: The Relation of Gender and Sex to Peace and Conflict." Annual Meeting of the International Studies Association, Honolulu, March 1.

Orwin, Clifford. 1997. "Rousseau and the Discovery of Political Compassion." Pp. 296–320 in *The Legacy of Rousseau*, ed. Clifford Orwin and Nathan Tarcov. Chicago: University of Chicago Press.

Owens, Mackubin Thomas. 2004. "George W. Bush as Henry V: The Guard Choice in Context." *National Review Online*. February 12. Available online at www.national review.com/owens/owens200402120830.asp (accessed May 26, 2006).

Pan, Zhongdang, and Gerald M. Kosicki. 1993. "Framing Analysis: An Approach to News Discourse." *Political Communication* 10: 55–75.

Pape, Robert. 2005. *Dying to Win: The Strategic Logic of Suicide Terrorism*. New York: Random House.

Parrenas, Rhacel Salazar. 2001a. *Servants of Globalization: Women Migration and Domestic Work*. Stanford, Calif.: Stanford University Press.

———. 2001b. "Transgressing the Nation-State: The Partial Citizenship and 'Imagined Community' of Migrant Filipina Domestic Workers." *Signs* 26, no. 4: 1129–54.

Pateman, Carole. 1988. *The Sexual Contract*. Stanford, Calif.: Stanford University Press.

Patterson, Molly, and Kristen Renwick Monroe. 1998. "Narrative in Political Science." *Annual Review of Political Science* 1, no. 1: 315–31.

Petchesky, Rosalind. 1997. "Spiraling Discourses of Reproductive and Sexual Rights: A Post-Beijing Assessment of International Feminist Politics." Pp. 569–88 in *Women Transforming Politics: An Alternative Reader*, ed. Cathy Cohen, Kathleen Jones, and Joan Tronto. New York: New York University Press.

———. 1998. "Introduction." Pp. 1–30 in *Negotiating Reproductive Rights: Women's Perspectives across Countries and Cultures*, ed. Rosalind Petchesky and Karen Judd. New York: Zed Books.

———. 2003. *Global Prescriptions: Gendering Health and Human Rights*. London: Zed Books.

Peterson, Susan Rae. 1977. "Coercion and Rape: The State as a Male Protection Racket." Pp. 360–71 in *Feminism and Philosophy*, ed. Mary Vetterling-Braggin, Frederick A. Elliston, and Jane English. Totowa, N.J.: Littlefield Adams.

Peterson, V. Spike, ed. 1992. *Gendered States: Feminist (Re)Visions of International Relations*

Theory, Gender and Political Theory: New Contexts. Boulder, Colo.: Lynne Rienner Publishers.

Peterson, V. Spike, and Anne Sisson Runyan. 1999. Global Gender Issues, 2d ed. Boulder, Colo.: Westview Press.

Phillips, Kevin. 2004. American Dynasty: Aristocracy, Fortune, and the Politics of Deceit in the House of Bush. New York: Viking Books.

Piper, Adrian M. S. 1991. "Impartiality, Compassion, and Modal Imagination." Ethics 101 (July): 726–57.

Piper, John, and Wayne Grudem. 1991. Recovering Biblical Manhood and Womanhood: A Response to Evangelical Feminism. Wheaton, Ill.: Crossway Books.

Pollitt, Katha. 2002. "Ashcroft [heart] Iran." The Nation, July 8.

Pope John Paul II. 1993. "Homily at Cherry Creek State Park." August 15. Available online at www.columbia.edu/cu/augustine/arch/jp2/denver17.html (accessed May 26, 2006).

———. 1995. Evangelium Vitae. March 25. Available online at www.vatican.va/holy_father/john_paul_ii/encyclicals/documents/hf_jp-ii_enc_25031995_evangelium-vitae_en.html (accessed May 26, 2006).

Post, Jerrold M. 1984. "Notes on a Psychodynamic Theory of Terrorist Behavior." Terrorism 7, no. 3: 241–56.

Powell, Colin L. 2002. "Remarks at Reception to Mark International Women's Day." March 7. Available online at www.state.gov/secretary/rm/2002/8691pf.htm (accessed May 26, 2006).

Promise Keepers. 1999. Seven Promises of a Promise Keeper. Nashville: Word Publishing.

———. 2006. "Seven Questions Women Ask about the Promise Keepers." Available online at www.promisekeepers.org/women (accessed January 11, 2006).

Prothero, Stephen. 2003. American Jesus: How the Son of God Became a National Icon. New York: Farrar, Straus and Giroux.

Puar, Jasbir K. 2004. "Abu Ghraib: Arguing against Exceptionalism." Feminist Studies 30, no. 2: 522–54.

Puar, Jasbir K., and Amit S. Rai. 2002. "Monster, Terrorist, Fag: The War on Terrorism and the Production of Docile Patriots." Social Text 20, no. 3: 117–48.

Putney, Clifford. 2001. Muscular Christianity: Manhood and Sports in Protestant America, 1880–1920. Cambridge, Mass.: Harvard University Press.

Reagan, Charles Wilson. 1980. Baptized in Blood: The Religion of the Lost Cause, 1868–1920. Athens: University of Georgia Press.

Reilly, Kristie. 2002. "Left Behind: An Interview with Revolutionary Afghan Women's Association's Shar Saba." In These Times, vol. 26, no. 11, 16–18.

Revolutionary Association of the Women of Afghanistan. 2002. "RAWA Statement on the Anniversary of the September 11 Tragedy." September 12. Available online at www.rawa.us/sep11-02.htm (accessed May 26, 2006).

Rice, Condoleezza. 2002. "Dr. Condoleezza Rice Discusses President's National

Security Strategy." October 1. Available online at www.whitehouse.gov/news/releases/2002/10/20021001-6.html (accessed May 26, 2006).

———. 2004. "Dr. Condoleezza Rice Previews the G-8 Summit on Monday." June 7. Available online at www.whitehouse.gov/news/releases/2004/06/20040607-2.html (accessed May 26, 2006).

Rich, Frank. 2003. "When You Got It, Flaunt It." *New York Times*, November 23, sec. 2, 1.

———. 2004. "It Was the Porn That Made Them Do It." *New York Times Magazine*, May 30.

Rodriguez, Robyn. 2002. "Migrant Heroes: Nationalism, Citizenship, and the Politics of Filipino Migrant Labor." *Citizenship Studies* 6, no. 3: 341–56.

Rosen, Ruth. 2002. "The Last Page." *Dissent* 49 (Spring).

Roth, Bennett. 2001. "Bush: Justice Will Be Done." *Houston Chronicle*, September 21.

Rousseau, Jean-Jacques. 1979. *Emile, or On Education*, ed. Allan Bloom. New York: Basic Books.

———. 1987. "Discourse on the Origin of Inequality." Pp. 25–110 in *Jean-Jacques Rousseau: The Basic Political Writings*, trans. Donald A. Cress. Indianapolis: Hackett.

Ruby, Charles L. 2002. "Are Terrorists Mentally Deranged?" *Analyses of Social Issues and Public Policy* 2, no. 1: 15–26.

Rupp, Leila. 1997. *Worlds of Women: The Making of an International Women's Movement*. Princeton: Princeton University Press.

Saar, Erik, and Viveca Novak. 2005. *Inside the Wire*. New York: Penguin.

Safire, William. 2001. "On Language: Compassion." *New York Times Magazine*, July 15.

Said, Edward. 1978. *Orientalism*. New York: Random House.

Samois. 1981. *Coming to Power*. Boston: Alyson Publications.

Santorum, Rick. 2002. "Aiding Africa: A Compassionate Policy Conservatives Should Support." *National Review Online*, August 7. Available online at www.nationalreview.com/comment/comment-santorum080702.asp (accessed May 26, 2006).

———. 2003. "The Necessity of Marriage." Heritage Lecture no. 804, Heritage Foundation, Washington, D.C., October 20.

Sassen, Saskia. 2002. "Global Cities and Survival Circuits." Pp. 254–74 in *Global Woman: Nannies, Maids, and Sex Workers in the New Economy*, ed. Barbara Ehrenreich and Arlie Russell Hochschild. New York: Metropolitan Books/Henry Holt.

Schatz, Thomas. 1991. "The Family Melodrama." Pp. 148–67 in *Imitations of Life: A Reader on Film and Television Melodrama*, ed. Marcia Landy. Detroit: Wayne State University Press.

———. 1998. "World War II and the Hollywood War Film." Pp. 18–128 in *Refiguring American Film Genres: Theory and History*, ed. Nick Browne. Berkeley: University of California Press.

Schlafly, Phyllis. 2004. "Feminist Dream Becomes Nightmare." May 17. Available online at www.townhall.com/columnists/phyllisschlafly/ps20040517.shtml (accessed May 18, 2005).

Schmidt, Randall M. 2005. *Investigation into FBI Allegations of Detainee Abuse at Guantá-namo Bay, Cuba Detention Facility*. April 1; amended June 9, 2005. Available online at http://balkin.blogspot.com/Schmidt%20Furlow%20rcport.pdf (accessed October 28, 2005).

Schmitt, Eric. 2006. "Iraq Abuse Trial Is Again Limited to Lower Ranks." *New York Times*, March 23.

Schneider, Howard. 2004. "In Breaking Taboos, Photos Add Insult to Injury." *Washington Post*, May 7.

Schuman, Howard, and Stanley Presser. 1982. *Questions and Answers in Attitude Surveys: Experiments on Question Form, Wording, and Context*. New York: Academic Press.

Segal, David R. and Mady Weschler Segal. 2004. "America's Military Population." *Population Bulletin* 59, no. 4.

Sevenhuijsen, Selma. 1998. *Citizenship and the Ethics of Care: Feminist Considerations on Justice, Morality, and Politics*. New York: Routledge.

Sewell Jr., William H. 1992. "A Theory of Structure: Duality, Agency, and Transforma-tion." *American Journal of Sociology* 98, no. 1: 1–29.

Shakespeare, William. 1914/2000. *Henry V. The Complete Works of William Shakespeare*. London: Oxford University Press.

Shklar, Judith. 1985. *Men and Citizens: A Study of Rousseau's Social Theory*. New York: Cam-bridge University Press.

Silverstein, Louise B., and Carl F. Auerbach. 1999. "Deconstructing the Essential Father." *American Psychologist* 54, no. 6: 397–407.

Simpson, Michael D. 2003. "ESEA Extends Federal Reach in Schools." *NEA Today*, February. Available online at www.nea.org/neatoday/0203/rights.html (accessed August 11, 2005).

Smith, Adam. 1984 (1759). *The Theory of Moral Sentiments*. Vol. 1 in Glasgow Edition of the Works and Correspondence of Adam Smith, ed. D. D. Raphael and A. L. Mac-fie. Indianapolis: Liberty Fund.

Smith, William. 2004. "World AIDS Day 2004: Playing Politics with Compassion." Center for American Progress website, December 1. Available online at http://www.americanprogress.org/site/pp.asp?c=biJRJ8oVF&b=259325 (accessed May 26, 2006).

Snyder, R. Claire. 1999. *Citizen-Soldiers and Manly Warriors*. Lanham, Md.: Rowman and Littlefield.

———. 2006. *Gay Marriage and Democracy: Equality for All*. Lanham, Md.: Rowman and Littlefield.

Southern Baptist Convention. 2000. "The Baptist Faith and Message." Available on-line at www.sbc.net/bfm/bfm2000.asp#xv (accessed May 26, 2006).

Spivak, Gayatri. 1985. "Can the Subaltern Speak? Speculations on Widow Sacrifice" *Wedge* 7–8 (Winter–Spring): 120–30.

Stacey, Judith. 1996. *In the Name of the Family: Rethinking Family Values in the Postmodern Age*. Boston: Beacon Press.

Steger, Manfred. 2002. *Globalism: The New Market Ideology*. Lanham, Md.: Rowman and Littlefield.

———. 2004. *Rethinking Globalism*. Lanham, Md.: Rowman and Littlefield.

Stiehm, Judith. 1982. "The Protected, the Protector, the Defender." *Women's Studies International Forum* 5, nos. 3–4: 367–76.

———. 2005. "Meditation on Two Photographs." Paper presented at the Annual Meeting of the Western Political Science Association, Oakland, Calif., March 19.

Stienstra, Deborah. 1994. *Women's Movements and International Organizations*. New York: St. Martin's Press.

Stout, David. 2001. "A Nation Challenged: The First Lady; Mrs. Bush Cites Women's Plight under Taliban." *New York Times*, November 18, sec. 1B, 4, 6.

Strauss, Murray, and Denise A. Donnelly. 2000. *Beating the Devil out of Them: Corporal Punishment in American Families*, 2d ed. New York: Transaction Books.

Suskind, Ron. 2004. "Without a Doubt." *New York Times Magazine*, October 17.

Tessier, Marie. 2002. "Bush Appointments Include Fewer Women." *Women's Enews*, February 11. Available online at www.womensenews.org/article.cfm/dyn/aid/812 (accessed January 25, 2006).

Thibault, David. 2004. "Abu Ghraib Abuse Is a Feminist's Dream, Says Military Expert." May 10. Available online at www.cnsnews.com/ViewNation.asp?Page=\Nation\archive\200405\NAT20040510b.html (accessed May 26, 2006).

Thomas, Evan. 2004. "Explaining Lynndie England: How Did a Wispy Tomboy Behave Like a Monster at Abu Ghraib?" May 15. Available online at http://msnbc.com/id/4987304 (accessed May 15, 2005).

Thompson, Bob. 2004. "The King and We: Henry V's War Cabinet." *Washington Post*, May 18, C1.

Tickner, J. Ann. 1992. *Gender in International Relations: Feminist Perspectives on Achieving Global Security*. New York: Columbia University Press.

———. 2001. *Gendering World Politics: Issues and Approaches in the Post–Cold War Era*. New York: Columbia University Press.

———. 2002. "Feminist Perspectives on 9/11." *International Studies Perspectives* 3, no. 4: 333–50.

Tronto, Joan. 1993. *Moral Boundaries: A Political Argument for an Ethic of Care*. New York: Routledge.

UNAIDS/World Health Organization. 2005. "AIDS Epidemic Update: December 2005." Report by the Joint United Nations Programme on HIV/AIDS and World Health Organization, December. Available online at www.unaids.org/epi/2005/doc/report_pdf.asp (accessed May 26, 2006).

United Nations. 2003. UN Resolution 58/142: Women and Political Participation. December 22.

UN Development Fund for Women (UNIFEM). 2006. "Gender Profile–Iraq–Women, War and Peace." Available online at www.womenwarpeace.org/iraq/iraq.htm (accessed May 26, 2006).

UN General Assembly. 2001. *Declaration of Commitment on* HIV/AIDS, *Global Crisis—Global Action.* June 27.

U.S. Bureau of the Census. 2003a. "Children's Living Arrangements and Characteristics: March 2002." *Current Population Reports,* no. P20–547, Washington, D.C., June. Available online at www.census.gov/population/www/socdemo/hh-fam/ cps2002 .html (accessed October 29, 2006).

———. 2003b. "Full-Time, Year-Round All Workers by Median Income and Sex, 1955–2003." *Current Population Survey, Annual Social and Economic Supplements, Table P36,* Washington, D.C.

———. 2003c. "Households by Type and Size: 1900–2002." *Statistical Abstract of the United States 2003,* no. HS-12, Washington, D.C.

———. 2003d. "Married Couple Family Groups, by Family Income, Labor Force Status of Both Spouses, and Race and Hispanic Origin of the Reference Person: March 2002." Available online at www.census.gov/population/socdemo/hh-fam/ cps2002/tabFG2-nhisp.pdf.

U.S. Department of the Army. 1987. "Intelligence Interrogation." In *Field Manual 34–52.* May 8. Available online at www.globalsecurity.org/intell/library/policy/army/ fm/fm34–52/index.html (accessed October 28, 2005).

———. 1992. "Intelligence Interrogation." In *Field Manual 34–52.* September 28. Available online at www.fas.org/irp/doddir/army/fm34–52.pdf (accessed October 28, 2005).

U.S. Department of Health and Human Services. 2001. "A Blueprint for New Beginnings: A Responsible Budget for America's Priorities." February 28. Available online at http://fatherhood.hhs.gov/index.shtml (accessed August 10, 2005).

U.S. Department of State, Office of International Women's Issues. 2004. "Office of International Women's Issues." Available online at www.state.gov/g/wi (accessed July 1, 2005).

U.S. Mission to the United Nations. 2004. "U.S. International Women's Initiatives Fact Sheet." May 8. Available online at www.un.int/usa/fact1 (accessed May 26, 2006).

Victor, Barbara. 2003. *Army of Roses: Inside the World of Palestinian Women Suicide Bombers.* Emmaus, Penn.: Rodale Press.

Waever, Ole, Barry Buzan, Morten Kelstrup, and Pierre Lemaitre. 1993. *Identity, Migration, and the New Security Agenda in Europe.* London: Pinter.

Waite, Linda J., and Maggie Gallagher. 2000. *The Case for Marriage.* New York: Broadway Books.

Waring, Marilyn. 1988. *If Women Counted: A New Feminist Economics.* San Francisco: Harper and Row.

Weber, Stu. 1995. *Locking Arms: God's Design for Masculine Friendship.* Sisters, Ore.: Multnomah Books.

Weisman, Steven R. 2005. "Saudi Women Have Message for U.S. Envoy." *New York*

Times, September 28. Available online at www.nytimes.com/2005/09/28/inter national/middleeast/28hughes.html?ex=1285560000&en=53e3bbcccd8fa7b4&ei =5088&partner=rssnyt&emc=rss (accessed May 26, 2006).

Weyrich, Paul. 2006. "A Moral Minority? An Open Letter to Conservatives." Free Congress Foundation website, March 25. Available online at www.freecongress.org/ misc/990216itr.asp (accessed May 26, 2006).

Wilco. 2002. "Ashes of American Flags." On *Yankee Hotel Foxtrot*. Nonesuch, B00005YXZH.

Wingrove, Elizabeth. 2000. *Rousseau's Republican Romance*. Princeton: Princeton University Press.

Wolfowitz, Paul D. 2004. "Women in the New Iraq." *Washington Post*, February 1, B7.

World Bank. 2002a. "Advancing Gender Equality: World Bank Action since Beijing." February 7. Available online at http://siteresources.worldbank.org/INTGENDER/ Resources/fullreport.pdf (accessed May 26, 2006).

———. 2002b. *Attacking Poverty: World Development Report 2000–01*. New York: Oxford University Press, 2002.

World Bank Gender and Development Group. 2003. "Gender Equality and the Millennium Development Goals." April 4. Available online at www.mdgender.net/ upload/monographs/WB_Gender_Equality_MDGs.pdf (accessed May 26, 2006).

World Health Organization. 2000. "Human Rights, Women and HIV/AIDS: Fact Sheet No. 247." June. Available online at www.who.int/mediacentre/factsheets/ fs247/en/index.html (accessed May 26, 2006).

Wuthnow, Robert. 1993. *Acts of Compassion: Caring for Others and Helping Ourselves*. Princeton: Princeton University Press.

Young, Iris Marion. 2003a. "Autonomy, Welfare Reform, and Meaningful Work." Pp. 40–60 in *The Subject of Care: Feminist Perspectives on Dependency*, ed. Eva Feder Kittay and Ellen K. Feder. Lanham, Md.: Rowman and Littlefield.

———. 2003b. "The Logic of Masculinist Protection: Reflections on the Current Security State." *Signs* 29, no. 1: 1–26.

Zeeland, Steven. 1995. *Sailors and Sexuality*. New York: Haworth.

Zerilli, Linda M. G. 2005. *Feminism and the Abyss of Freedom*. Chicago: University of Chicago Press.

Zernike, Kate. 2004. "Prison Guard Calls Abuse Routine and Sometimes Amusing." *New York Times*, May 16.

———. 2005. "Behind Failed Abu Ghraib Plea, A Tale of Breakups and Betrayal." *New York Times*, May 16.

Zernike, Kate, and David Rohde. 2004. "Forced Nudity Is Seen as a Pervasive Pattern, Not Isolated Incidents." *New York Times*, June 8.

Zivi, Karen. 2005. "Contesting Motherhood in the Age of AIDS: Maternal Ideology in the Debate over Mandatory HIV Testing." *Feminist Studies* 31 (Summer): 347–74.

Contributors

Andrew Feffer is associate professor of history and director of the Interdisciplinary Program in American Studies at Union College in Schenectady, New York. He is the author of *The Chicago Pragmatists and American Progressivism* (1993), as well as articles in nineteenth- and twentieth-century American intellectual and cultural history. His work has appeared in *Journal of the History of Ideas*, *Journal of Urban History*, and *Telos*. He is currently at work on a manuscript that explores contemporary film images of masculinity and democracy.

Michaele L. Ferguson is assistant professor in the Department of Political Science and junior faculty affiliate with the Woman and Gender Studies Program at the University of Colorado at Boulder. Her work in feminist and democratic theory has been published in *Politics & Gender* and *Hypatia*. She is currently finishing a book manuscript entitled *Sharing Democracy*.

David S. Gutterman is assistant professor of politics at Willamette University in Salem, Oregon, where he teaches courses on political theory, religion, and politics in the United States, and gender and politics. He has published work on the conversion narrative of George W. Bush, narrative theory, U.S. religious social movements, and gender and politics. He is the author of *Prophetic Politics: Christian Social Movements and American Democracy* (2005). He is currently working on a book project titled, *Narrating America: Political Discourse in the Bush Years*.

Mary Hawkesworth is professor of women's and gender studies at Rutgers University and editor of *Signs: Journal of Women in Culture and Society*. Her teaching and research interests include feminist theory, women and politics, contemporary political philosophy, philosophy of science, and social policy. Her most recent books are *Globalization and Feminist Activism* (2006) and *Feminist Inquiry: From Political Conviction to Meth-*

odological Innovation (2006). Her articles have appeared in leading journals, including *American Political Science Review, Political Theory, Signs, Hypatia, Women and Politics, Journal of Women's History, NWSA Journal, International Journal of Women's Studies,* and *Women's Studies International Forum.*

Timothy Kaufman-Osborn is the Baker Ferguson Professor of Politics and Leadership at Whitman College in Walla Walla, Washington. He is the author, most recently, of *From Noose to Needle: Capital Punishment and the Late Liberal State* (2002). He served two terms as president of the Western Political Science Association (2001–2003) and is currently president of the American Civil Liberties Union of Washington.

Lori Jo Marso is professor of political science and director of women's and gender studies at Union College. She is the author of *Feminist Thinkers and the Demands of Femininity* (2006) and *(Un)Manly Citizens: J. J. Rousseau's and Germaine de Staël's Subversive Women* (1999) and the coeditor (with Patricia Moynagh) of *Simone de Beauvoir's Political Thinking* (2006).

Danielle Regan graduated from Linfield College in 2005 and is currently pursuing her law degree.

R. Claire Snyder is associate professor of government and politics and a member of the Women's Studies Faculty at George Mason University, as well as a faculty fellow at the Women and Politics Institute at American University. She is the author of *Gay Marriage and Democracy: Equality for All* (2006) and *Citizen-Soldiers and Manly Warriors: Military Service and Gender in the Civic Republican Tradition* (1999).

Iris Marion Young is author of *Justice and the Politics of Difference* (1990), *Intersecting Voices: Dilemmas of Gender, Political Philosophy, and Policy* (1997), *Inclusion and Democracy* (2000), and *On Female Body Experience* (2005). She passed away in July 2006.

Karen Zivi is an assistant professor in the Jepson School of Leadership at the University of Richmond. Her work has appeared in *Feminist Studies, Politics and Gender,* and the *American Journal of Political Science.* Her research focuses on the theory and practice of rights in contemporary identity-based political movements. She is currently working on a book manuscript titled, *Making Rights Claims.*

Discourse on the Origins of Inequality, 47

Dissent, 130; death of feminism and occlusion of, 173; judicial and legislative branches and, 126–27; repression of, by security state, 121–25, 129; restriction of, under Bush presidency, 117, 126–27, 130. See also Feminization

Divorce: criticism of, by Christian Right, 19, 24; criticism of, by Neoconservatives, 29–30; marriage movement and, 31, 36–37; women and, 33, 36

Dobriansky, Paula J., 203–4, 207

Dobson, James, 20, 25, 28–29, 39 n.10

Dominance: conservative gender ideology and, 5, 10, 20; of Israel over Palestinians, 93; of males and militarism, 115, 161–62 n.12; of males in hetero-normative family: 10, 18, 20, 33, 36; of man over Earth in Christian Right ideology, 20; of men over women, 118, 120–21, 145–46; as protection racket, 130; in state of nature, 120

Domination and submission (D/s): at Abu Ghraib, 143–44; in Christian Right ideology, 20–22; coercive, 34; consensual, 18, 33–34; liberalism and, 35; marriage and, 33; masculinist protection and, 179; necessity of, to democracy, 40 n.14; reconciliation of, with democratic equality, 34–35, 37

Donnelly, Elaine, 143

Dostoyevsky, Fyodor, 224–25

Due process: endangered by logic of masculinist protection, 117, 132; limits on, after September 11, 2001, 127; USA PATRIOT Act and, 177

Eagle Forum, The, 144–45

Economic Policy Institute, 84 n.3

Edison Media Research, 75, 86 n.15

Ehrenreich, Barbara, 145–47, 158, 220 n.44

Eisenstein, Zillah, 158

Emasculation: basic training and, 155–56; at Guantánamo prison, 152; logic of, 149–51; techniques of, 152–53. See also Feminization; Masculinity

Embodiment as context for freedom, 230–31

Embser-Herbert, M. S., 143

Émile, 47–49

England, Lynndie, 12, 142–49, 153–54, 156–59, 160 nn.2–3; as gender-bending monster, 12, 143, 156–58; as gender decoy, 157–58; as unthinkable, 146. See also Abu Ghraib prisoner abuse

Enloe, Cynthia, 143, 154, 227–28, 233

Entman, Robert, 195, 216 n.14

Equality: compassion and, 44, 46–47, 49; democratic citizenship and, 139; dominance and submission and, 34, 38; non-assessment of worth and fault through, 44; in suffering, 47; U.S. and, 171–72. See also Democracy

Equal Rights Amendment (ERA), 24, 213

Erectile dysfunction, 11, 69–70, 72, 81–82, 101–2; Cialis and, 70, 85 n.7; Levitra and, 70; performance anxiety and, 10–11, 66–67, 70, 78, 85 n.7; Viagra and, 11, 70, 81–82, 85 nn.7–8; virility and, 69–71, 176. See also Masculinity

Evangelium Vitae, 110

Evans, Tony, 21

Executive power, 8, 126–27,

Existentialist ethics, 236; Simone de Beauvoir and, 6, 230–32, 236, 239

Ezekiel, Judith, 241

Faith-based initiatives, 217 n.22

Faith-based organizations, 42. See also Christian Right

Faludi, Susan, 156

Family, 3, 5; conservative, 3, 10, 17–19; conservative gender ideology and, 3–5, 7–10, 14, 17–19, 29, 79–80, 179; cultures of life and death and, 11, 90; dysfunctional, 17, 28; as foundation for democracy, 18, 30; hetero-normative, 3, 10–11, 18–19; homosexuality and, 25; justice in, 10, 32–35, 219 n.35; masculinist protection and, 118; nontraditional, 69; patriarchal, 18–19, 22–23, 25; production of healthy children in, 28–29; as "seedbed of virtue," 18, 30, 37–38; as source of terrorism, 92; women and, 203, 218 nn.28, 32. See also; Fatherless family; Fathers, fatherhood; Mothers; Patriarchy

Family Research Council, 19. See also Christian Right

Fatherhood Initiative, 32. See also Marriage

Fatherless family, 11, 17, 27, 30, 69; in Arab communities, 92; compassion and, 52; in Suddenly, 97; marriage movement and, 31; suicide bombers and, 92; violence against women and, 29

Fathers, fatherhood, 17, 69, 85 n.6; development of "normal" sexual identity in boys and, 25–26, 28; marriage movement and, 31; as masculine protectors, 121; obligations of, 24–25; Promise Keepers and, 21; security states as, 137; undermining of, by Israeli occupation, 93

Faulkner, Shannon, 156

Fay-Jones report, 147, 149, 151, 160 n.4, 161 nn.8, 11. See also Abu Ghraib prisoner abuse

Fear: of emasculation, 155; interrogation techniques and, 150; mobilization of, to support conservative gender ideology, 179; security state and, 121;

in state of nature, 120, 122; in United States after September 11, 2001, 125, 128. See also Rhetoric

Federal Marriage Amendment, 18, 39 n.1, 79

Feffer, Andrew, 5, 10–11

Femininity: military culture and, 144–45; peacefulness and, 116; in pseudo-democracy, 108; as sexual violability, 12; as submission, 20–21, 23; theories of, 118. See also Homosexuality; Inequality; Self-sacrifice; Submission

Feminism: Abu Ghraib scandal and, 143; Bush presidency and, 13, 200, 226; as call to action, 183; criticism of, 19, 24–25, 143; death of, 171–74, 187 n.3; masculinist protectors/protection and, 117–18, 136, 180; global, 164–66, 169–70, 172; as impossible ideal, 172; National, 241–42; neoliberalism and, 165–66, 169, 172; peace and security and, 117–18, 212; plural, 186 n.1; postfeminism and, 171–72; vision of future and, 166–67; Western, 117–18, 136

Feminist activism: in Afghanistan and Iraq, 234; campaign against the Taliban, 117, 134; in France among immigrants, 241–42; influence of, on Bush presidency, 192–93, 206–7, 211, 213–14; as solidarity, 240–42; unprecedented growth of, 169–70; via NGOs and state institutions, 170–71; on women and security, 193

Feminist activism, undercutting of: by pronouncements of feminism's death, 172–74; in United States, 209–11; by neoliberal feminization, 12–13; by war, 174, 180

Feminist Majority, 134, 192, 226. See also Feminist activism

Feminist responses to Bush presidency, 2, 6, 214 n.1; Abu Ghraib and, 145–

Feminist responses (*continued*)
47; of cynicism, 3, 134, 192, 214
nn.2–3; of praise, 192, 197; of skepticism, 192; strategies for resistance,
6, 13, 194, 212–14

Feminist rhetoric: co-optation of, 136;
use of, by Bush presidency, 3–4, 6,
13, 191–92, 211. *See also* Rhetoric

Feminization, 6, 12–13, 178; of Afghan
women, 176; of business opportunities, 168; of citizens, 167; delegitimization of feminist politics and,
12–13, 180; of democratic people by
security state, 6, 11, 116, 131, 137,
176–77; emasculation and, 149–51,
152–53, 155–56; globalization and,
12–13, 163, 169, 186–87 n.2; inequality and, 179; logic of, 168, 178,
180; marketization and, 168–69;
menialization of work and, 168; of
Iraq war critics, 76, 82–83; of Kerry,
85–86 n.14; of labor, 167–69; of men
at Abu Ghraib, 178; of migration,
167–69; of military recruits, 177;
neocolonialism and, 12; of non-Westerners, 135, 152; obedience and, 116,
121, 123–24, 129; of Palestinians, 93;
of poverty, 167–68, 172; of prisoners,
149–51; production of, by neoliberalism, 166–67; of racialized others,
152; as strategy of power, 168, 177–
78; subservience and, 168; of survival, 168; of United States by September 11 attacks, 175–76; of victims
of Taliban and Saddam Hussein, 210.
See also Masculinist Protection; Neoliberalism; Rhetoric; Subordination

Ferguson, Michaele, 4–5, 13, 89

Florence, Mary Sargent, 180

Focus on the Family, 20, 25; Dobson
and, 20, 25, 28–29, 39 n.10

Foucault, Michel, 121

Framing, 7, 13, 89, 142, 192–97, 203,
208, 213, 215 n.8, 215–16 n.13;

audience perceptions and, 195, 215
nn.9–10; cultural resonance and, 215
n.12; dialogicality and, 195, 215 n.11;
as important political activity, 212; of
security by Bush presidency, 194, 210;
transposition and, 195, 211–12. *See
also* Rhetoric

Frank, Thomas, 79

Frankenheimer, John, 101–2

Frederick, Sergeant Ivan, 160. *See also*
Abu Ghraib prisoner abuse

Free Assembly, right of, 117

Free Congress Foundation, 86 n.23

Freedom, 6, 13; as abstraction, 222, 225,
235; to choose practices of dominance and submission, 18, 34; cession of, for masculinist protection,
130, 132; colonialism and, 224; complexity of, in feminist politics, 221;
cultures of life and death and, 89, 90;
defense of, in War on Terror, 82–83,
208; delivery of, through violence
and war, 226; embedding of, within
a situation, 230–32, 234–35, 241; as
end in itself, 238; false opposition
of, to traditionalist fundamentalism,
225, 232–33; liberalism and, 13, 26,
28, 35, 45, 57, 58 n.4, 90; limitations
of, 222, 237; masculinist protection
and, 222, 242; as meaningful choice,
222, 242; plurality and, 236; realization of, as collective, 231, 242;
restriction of, after September 11,
2001, 117, 129–30; security state and,
125, 130; threat to, by fear, 128;. *See
also* Beauvoir, Simone de; Liberation;
Rhetoric

Freeing. *See* Liberation

Free market economy and women's
rights, 207. *See also* Neoliberalism

Friday Night Lights, 106–7, 112 n.18

Friedan, Betty, 19

Fundamentalist, Islamic, 227. *See also*
Taliban

Homosexuality (*continued*)
ishment of children and, 27; culture
of death and, 90; "ex-gay" movement
and, 25; masculinity and, 66–67;
military and, 91, 159; rejection of,
in pseudo-democracy, 108. *See also*
Feminization
Hoover Institution, 30. *See also* Neoconservatism
Huffington, Arianna, 112 n.16
Hughes, Karen, 2, 4, 218 n.26, 231,
237
*Human Resource Exploitation Training
Manual*, 150–51. *See also* Interrogation
techniques
Humanitarian intervention, 133, 137, 163
Hussein, Saddam, 164, 226; as barbaric,
199; conservative "femininity" demanded by, 228; mistreatment of
women by, 209–11, 221

Imagination, 48–49
Income, by gender, 68
Inequality: compassion and, 10, 43,
47–49; feminization and, 179; gender
and, 9–10, 18, 33, 121; globalization
and, 12–13, 163, 169, 186–87 n.2;
logic of masculinist protection and,
137; markets and, 13; patriarchal
family and, 18, 29, 38; women's, 18,
32–33. *See also* Feminization; Neoliberalism
Innocent victim: Afghan women as, 133;
Bush as, 83–84; children as, 52, 55,
59 n.11; Christian men as, 80, 83;
civilians of suicide bombings as,
88–89; United States as, 76
Insecurity: economic, 24; increased for
women by War on Terror, 6, 211, 219
n.38, 226; in state of nature, 120, 122
Instinct, 10, 46–47, 55, 201–2
Institute for American Values, 28. *See also*
Neoconservatism

Institute for Marriage and Public Policy,
30, 36–37; Marriage movement and,
30–32, 36–37
Intelligence manipulation and Iraq war,
78
International Criminal Tribunals for the
Former Yugoslavia, 193
International Monetary Fund, 165. *See
also* Neoliberalism
International relations, 116–17
International Reproductive Rights Research Action Group, 59 n.13
Interrogation techniques, 149–56, 160
n.6, 160–61 n.7, 161 nn.8–11, 161–62
n.12, 177. *See also* Basic training;
Emasculation; Masculinity
Intervention: humanitarian, 133, 137,
163; military, 199–200; paternalistic,
176. *See also* Colonialism; Masculinist
protection
Iran, 70
Iraq: casualties of war in, 180; children
in, 222–25; feminist activism in, 182,
228–29, 233–34; forced veiling of
women in, 229; gender quotas in,
181, 220 n.43, 240–41; insecurity in,
226, 228; justification for war in, 9,
78, 133, 178, 199, 221, 226; liberation of, 77; suicide bombers in, 95;
war against, 164; war in: 1, 13, 70,
84, 132, 223–24; weapons of mass
destruction and, 133; women's exclusion from constitution making in,
181; women's political inclusion in,
181; women's rights in, 2, 227–29. *See
also* Abu Ghraib prisoner abuse
Iraqi constitution and *sharia* law, 229,
240
Iraqi women, 1–2, 4, 204, 229; Abu
Ghraib and, 143; children and, 222–
25; difficulty of solidarity among,
234; gender quotas and, 181, 220
n.43, 240–41; in Iraqi Governing

Council, 181, 210; liberation of, 6, 13, 159, 209, 221, 226; rights of, 2, 227–29; veiling of, 229

Iraqi Women's League, 182

Islam: fundamentalism and, 224; as respectful of women, 201, 218n.26

Israel, 2, 93

John Paul II, 89–90, 93, 96, 101, 110 n.2. See also Culture of life

Josephson, Jyl, 29

Judgment of women's situations, 239–40, 243 n.4

Judicial review and USA PATRIOT Act, 126

Kant, Immanuel, 205; democratic peace and, 13, 163, 199, 205–6, 218 n.31

Kaufman-Osborn, Timothy, 6, 12, 168, 177–78

Keane, John, 128

Kerry, John, 75, 85–86 n.14, 86 n.15, 220 n.44; 2004 presidential election and, 8, 75, 85–86 n.14, 86 n.15, 179

Kinsella, Helen, 175

Kristol, Irving, 28, 30. See also Neoconservatism

Krugman, Paul, 73

KUBARK manual [Counterintelligence Interrogations], 150–51, 155, 177. See also Interrogation techniques

Kushner, Tony, 222–26, 230–31, 239

Lahaye, Beverly, 20, 22–23, 35; on feminist movement, 24

Lahaye, Tim, 17, 23, 35; Left Behind series and, 23, 39 n.6, 83

"La Lutta Continua," 186

Lane, Robert, 105

Language. See Rhetoric

Lawless, Jennifer, 179

Lawrence v. Texas, 36

Leacock, Phillip, 99, 111 n.11

Left Behind series, 23, 39 n.6, 83

Levitra, 70; Cialis and, 70, 85 n.7; erectile dysfunction and, 11, 69–70, 72, 81–82, 101–2; performance anxiety and, 10–11, 66–67, 70, 78, 85 n.7; Viagra and, 11, 70, 81–82, 85 nn.7–8; virility and, 69–71, 176

Liberal feminism, 24; Abu Ghraib scandal and, 145; criticism of, 19; George W. Bush and, 5, 7

Liberalism, 13; criticism of, 26, 28; dominance and submission and, 35; individualism and, 45, 57, 58 n.4, 90

Liberation: in Afghanistan and Iraq, 6, 13, 134, 221; from burqa, 226–27; civilian casualties and, 225; as form of colonialism, 224; insecurity and, 226; as justification for economic sanctions, 226; as justification for war, 133–34, 221, 226; unfreedom and, 226; of women, 6, 13, 134, 210, 221. See also Afghan women; Iraqi women

Lindsay, Hal, 22

"Lost Cause," 11, 79, 86 nn.19, 23; Civil War as, 79; masculinity as, 11, 81–82, 84, 102; War on Terror as, 82–84

Loyalty, 122; obedience and, 116, 121, 123–24, 129

Lyotard, Jean-François, 174

Machiavelli, Nicolo, 78

Mackenzie, G. Calvin, 1–2

Mahmood, Saba, 227, 234–35, 237–39, 243 n.4

Mamdani, Mahmood, 95

Mandeville, Bernard de, 55

Marketization, 163, 166–67; feminization and, 167; gendering of, 167. See also Neoliberalism

Marriage, 17, 120; children and, 29–30, 32; as covenant, 23, 36–37; decline in rates of, 69; heterosexual, 5, 17–18,

Marriage (*continued*)
23, 82; inequality within, 33; movement against, 30–32; patriarchal, 20–24, 25, 33; promotion of, by Bush presidency, 5, 32; same-sex 18, 29, 31–32. *See also* Conservative gender ideology; Family; Patriarchy

Marriage movement, 30–32, 36–37

Marso, Lori, 6, 13

Masculinist protection: colonialism and, 135, 222; democratic citizenship and, 138; freeing of Afghan and Iraqi women and, 222, 230; heads of household and, 118, 121; increased insecurity and, 131–32; logic of, 11–12, 117–25, 129, 132, 177, 210, 217 n.25, 218 n.27, 230; militarism and, 175; rhetoric of democratic peace and, 210. *See also* Feminization

Masculinist protector, 1, 3, 5–6, 8, 72, 81, 88, 115–19, 124, 129, 135; Christian Right ideology and, 20; civilization and, 135, 202, 210; contemporary U.S. state as, 128–29, 133, 177; democratic state as, 210; fathers as, 121; feminists as, 117–18, 133–35, 222, 230, 235; firefighters as, 132, 175; police as, 175; as self-sacrificing, 122, 124; soldiers as, 132, 175; state as, 121, 123, 124; violence against women and, 150–51. *See also* Bush, George W.; Innocent victim; Men; Women and children

Masculinity: armed, 156; challenges to, 67, 83–84; chivalry and, 118; courage and, 76; democracy and, 90, 109; development of, 11, 25–26, 28, 96–97; domination of: 20, 118–19; hyperbolic, 10; as impossible performance, 10, 63–64, 65–67, 70, 72, 74–75, 80–82, 84, 156; penal system and, 162 n.14; performance anxiety and, 10–11, 66–67, 70, 78, 85 n.7; post–September 11, 2001 elec-

toral success and, 179–80; pseudo-democracy and, 106, 109; respect and, 5; self-confidence and, 73–74; theories of, 118; violence and, 116. *See also* "Band of brothers"; Bush, George W.; "Lost Cause"; Men; Militarism; Militarized masculinity; Normative masculinity

Maternal ideology, 10, 43, 52–54, 58 n.7, 58–59 n.8; compassion and, 55–56. *See also* Mothers; Self-sacrifice

McCartney, Bill, 20; Promise Keepers and, 21

McQueen, Steve, 99, 111 n.10

Melodrama, 89–90, 95, 96, 109–10, 111 n.9

Men: as aggressors, 119, 143; bad, 11, 119, 129; good, 11, 119, 129; as patriotic soldiers, 11. *See also* Masculine protector; Masculinity; Self-sacrifice; Suicide bomber

Middle East, 231; culture of death and, 93; as eroticized Other, 178; pathology and, 90, 92; women's rights in, 2, 14 n.1

Middle East Partnership Initiative, 208

Mikolashek report, 147. *See also* Abu Ghraib prisoner abuse

Militarism: Bush foreign policy and, 6; corporal punishment of children and, 27; feminist activism and, 175; feminist support for war and, 135; logic of masculinist protection and, 175; male domination and, 115; military culture and, 12, 151; pseudo-democracy and, 104, 106; rhetoric of, in Promise Keepers, 21; torture and, 12, 71, 76, 177, 178. *See also* Basic Training; Discipline; Militarized masculinity

Militarized masculinity, 12, 64, 70–71, 76–77, 77 (fig. 4), 151, 157, 210; Abu Ghraib prisoner abuse and, 148, 154, 157; logic of, 142 military culture

Prisoners, 12, 71; torture of, 12, 71, 177. See also Abu Ghraib prisoner abuse; Feminization; Interrogation techniques

Progress and women's status, 182, 218–19 n.33, 219 n.35

Promise Keepers, 21. See also Christian Right

Prosperity and women's rights, 203–4, 206, 218–19 n.33, 219 n.35, 221; progress and women's status and, 182, 218–19 n.33, 219 n.35

Protection, 18, 109, 117, 120. See also Masculinist protector; Women and children

Protection racket: homeland security as, 130–31; male domination as, 129–30; security state as, 6, 117, 128, 130, 177. See also Authoritarianism; Masculinist protection

Protest, curtailment of, 127, 130, 167

Pseudo-democracy, 88, 90, 106, 112 n.19; in Henry V, 105–6; masculinity and, 109; military and 104, 106; rejection of feminine and homosexual by, 108–9

Puar, Jasbir K., 91, 94

Queer Eye for the Straight Guy, 66–67, 72

Quigley, Margaret, 20

Rai, Amit S., 91, 94

Rape as war crime, 193

Rawls, John, 34

Reagan, Ronald, 73–74, 87

Recovering Biblical Manhood and Womanhood, 20

Regan, Danielle, 5, 10–11

Religious Right. See Christian Right

Religious tolerance and women's rights, 203, 206–7

Rendition, 177

Reproductive freedom and health, 24, 59 n.13, 181, 192

Reproductive Health Advisory Committee (Food and Drug Administration), 7–8

Republican Party, 8, 78–79, 85–86 n.14, 87, 89; 2004 National Convention of, 85 n.10, 219–20 n.39; "Southern strategy" of, 78–79

Rescue, 175, 235, 242. See also Chivalry; Masculinist protection

Resolution 1325. See UN Security Council Resolution 1325

Respect, 5, 89; for authority, 38; civilization and, 217 n.23; within Christian Right marriage, 22; for husbands in Promise Keepers, 21; within just families, 33; for women, 89, 109, 203. See also Chivalrous Respect; Masculinist protection

Responsibility: of masculinist protectors, 118–19; of men and boys, 25, 28; to others in freedom, 239; pseudo-democracy and, 89; of women, 32

Revolutionary Association of the Women of Afghanistan (RAWA), 227, 232–33

Rhetoric, 183; of Bush, as cinematic, 87; of Bush's AIDS policy, 43; of Bush's conversion to Christianity, 86 n.23; distinguishing normal and pathological violence, 103; of death of feminism, 173–74; of democratic peace, 13, 196, 199–200, 203–10, 212–13; of fear and threat, 117, 131; of feminism and feminization, 136, 175, 196; of feminized security, 191–94, 198, 200; of freedom, 13, 224, 229; gap between reality and, 43, 185, 192, 226–29, 242 n.3; of "lost cause," 84; of militarism in Promise Keepers, 21; of national security, 191; as political action, 192–94, 197, 213; of rescue, 175, 242; of respect, 13, 196, 199–203; of rights, 44, 56, 60 n.14, 183; of security, 13, 192–

Silverstein, Louise B., 28
Simmons, Gene, 66
Simulacrum of masculinity. See Masculinity
Situation, 230, 231; Beauvoir and, 6, 230–32, 236, 239
Skeffington, Francis Sheehy, 180
Smeal, Eleanor, 134, 226
Smith, Adam, 46, 59 n.11
Snyder, R. Claire, 5, 8–11, 156–57
Solidarity: of citizens of a security state, 124; of civilized peoples against barbarism, 202; of feminists with oppressed women, 240; masculine, 91, 107–9; social, 42, 44–49, 50, 56, 57, 90; of Western and non-Western feminists, 222, 237; of women, 13, 235, 239, 242, 243 n.5. See also "Band of brothers"; Pseudo-democracy; Self-sacrifice
Southern Baptist Convention (1998), 23
"Southern strategy," 64, 78–79, 86 n.19
Sovereign, 121–23; Hobbes, and, 117, 119–24, 176. See also Authoritarianism; Security state
Spanking, 39 nn.8–9. See also Discipline
Spielberg, Steven, 103–4, 109, 112 n.20
Spivak, Gayatri, 176
State of emergency, 124, 131
State of nature, 119–20; Hobbes, and, 117, 119–24, 176
State of Working America, The, 84 n.3
"Stealth misogyny," 3, 192
Steger, Manfred, 186 n.2
Steihm, Judith, 118–19, 177
Structural adjustment policies, 166, 169, 172
Submission: of citizens to sovereign, 20, 122; as condition for agency, 235; of Earth to dominion of man, 20; of female in hetero-normative family, 10, 17–18, 22, 36; Lynndie England and, 157; women's desires for, 34. See also Authoritarianism; Dominance

and submission; Feminization; Patriarchy
Subordination: of citizens to security state, 116, 131–32; of people to U.S. hegemonic power, 137; of prisoners at Abu Ghraib, 158; of protected to masculine protector, 116, 119–21, 138; of women, 35
Suddenly, 96–98
Suffering, 44–45, 47–51, 55, 57; as equalizing, 47, 49; U.S. complicity in, 223. See also Compassion; Inequality
Suffering innocent, 80, 108. See also "Lost Cause"
Suffrage, women's, 200, 207
Suicide bombers, 11, 76, 88–92, 94–95; failed heterosexuality of, 91–92, 98, 109; female, 92, 94; similar to heroic masculine self-sacrifice, 95, 98, 100–101, 103, 105–6; studies of, 11, 90–95, 111 n.7; violence of, 93. See also Culture of death; Self-sacrifice
Supreme Court, U.S., 8, 36, 83
Surveillance: homeland security and, 130–31; logic of masculinist protection and, 119, 121; security state and, 122–23, 130; USA PATRIOT Act and, 126, 177
Survey by Scripps Howard and Ohio University, 76
Swift Boat Veterans for Truth, 85–86 n.14, 179. See also Bush-Cheney campaign

Taguba report, 147, 160 n.4. See also Abu Ghraib prisoner abuse
Taliban, 89, 133–35, 176, 191, 224, 227; as barbaric, 176, 199, 201–3; feminist campaigns against, 117, 134; mistreatment of women by, 201–3, 209–11, 221, 226
Teacher Protection Act, 39 n.9
Temporary Aid to Needy Families Program, 32

Women's rights (*continued*)
and, 207; health, 10, 53–54, 56–57;
human, 206; as justification for
Afghan war, 191; mothers and, 59
n.9; political, 2, 5, 167, 207; reproductive, 5, 43, 57, 59 n.9, 59 n.13,
59–60 n.14, 181; restriction of, by
Bush presidency, 4, 5; security and,
193, 200, 205; as sign of respect for
women, 201, 202–3; secularism and,
207; sexual, 41, 53–54, 57, 59 n.9;
social, 207; War on Terror and, 201.
See also Rhetoric

Word of God, 21. *See also* Christian Right

World Bank, 165, 167–68. *See also* Feminization; Neoliberalism

World Health Organization (WHO), 41, 56

World Summit for Social Development,
184

World War One, feminist activism during, 174, 180

World War Two, 104; feminist activism
during, 174

"W Stands for Women," 1, 3, 14, 89,
219–20 n.39

Wuthnow, Robert, 44

Young, Iris Marion, 5–6, 176, 218 n.27,
230

Zeeland, Steven, 162 n.16

Zerilli, Linda, 239, 243 n.5

Zivi, Karen, 5, 9–10, 58 n.7

Michaele Ferguson is assistant professor of political science at the University of Colorado, Boulder.

Lori Jo Marso is professor of political science and director of Women's and Gender Studies at Union College. She is the author of *Feminist Thinkers and the Demands of Femininity* (2006) and *(Un)Manly Citizens: J. J. Rousseau's and Germaine de Staël's Subversive Women* (1999).

Library of Congress Cataloging-in-Publication Data
W stands for women : how the George W. Bush presidency shaped a new politics of gender / edited by Michaele L. Ferguson and Lori Jo Marso.
p. cm.
Includes bibliographical references and index.
ISBN-13: 978-0-8223-4064-5 (cloth : alk. paper)
ISBN-13: 978-0-8223-4042-3 (pbk. : alk. paper)
1. Women—Government policy—United States. 2. Women's rights—United States. 3. Bush, George W. (George Walker), 1946– 4. United States—Politics and government—2001– 5. War on Terrorism, 2001—Social aspects. I. Ferguson, Michaele L. II. Marso, Lori Jo.
HQ1236.5.U6W2 2007
305.420973'090511—dc22   2007004081